KENTUCKY'S CIVIL WAR

1861-1865

Dan Dry

22nd Infantry battle flag

KENTUCKY'S CIVIL WAR

1861-1865

EDITED BY JERLENE ROSE

RESEARCH BY LISA MATTHEWS

BACK HOME IN KENTUCKY, INC.

Scott County Museum

Confederate Civil War veterans gathered for a reunion in 1917.
Seated left to right: John Crumbaugh, Thomas Allen, Will A. Gaines,
Dr. G.B. Brown, Walter Shropshire, and James F. Askew.
Back row: Mike Haggard, Thomas Ewing, Jeff Zeysing, and Elly Blackburn.

©2005 Back Home In Kentucky, Inc.
Publisher: Back Home In Kentucky, Inc.
295 Old Forge Mill Road
Clay City, Kentucky 40312
606.663.1011
Printed in China
Production Assistance: Harmony House Publishers - Louisville
Design: Karen Boone

Deluxe ISBN 0976923122
Library of Congress Number 2005927838

Soft bound ISBN 0976923106
Library of Congress Number 2005927835

Case bound ISBN 0976923114
Library of Congress Number 2005927836

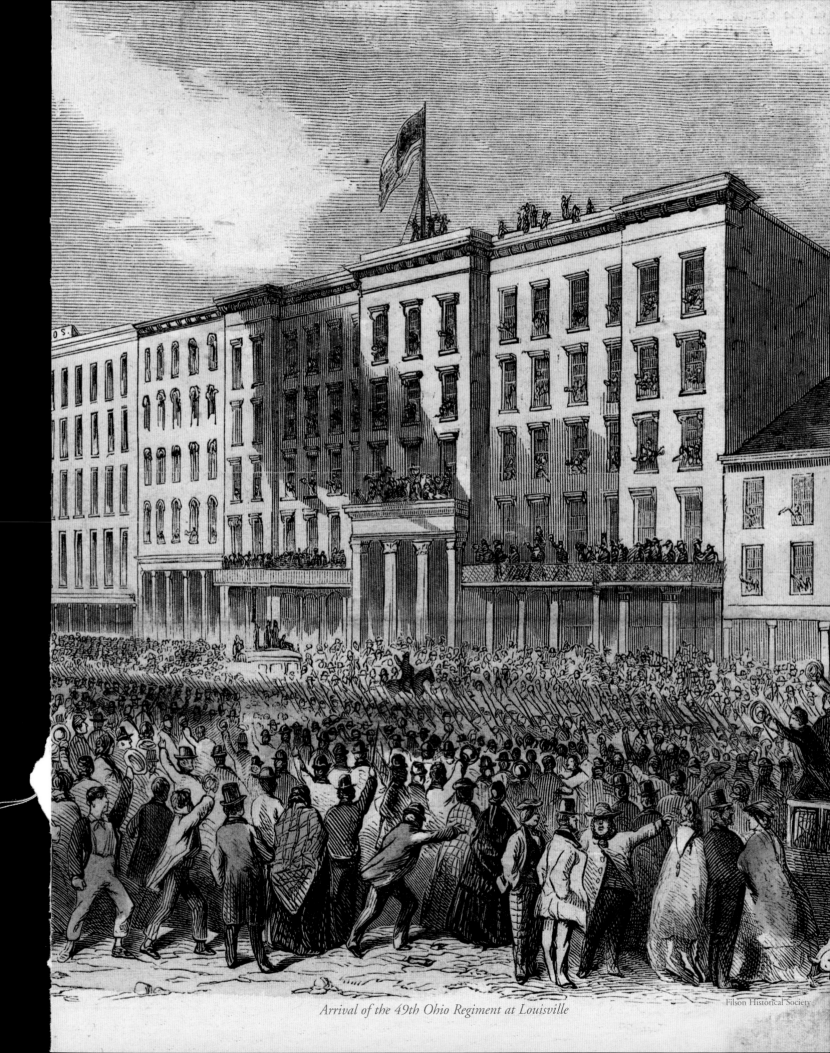

Arrival of the 49th Ohio Regiment at Louisville

CONTENTS

FOREWORD

By William E. Matthews

My great-great-grandfather, Keeling Carlton Gaines, and his three sons marched off to war in 1861 on behalf of the Confederate States of America. Of the four, only one son, John T. Gaines, came back. He served as a captain in Company K, 5th Regiment of the famed Orphan Brigade. Later, he would become superintendent of schools in Jefferson County, Kentucky. Keeling Carlton Gaines died in a Confederate camp in LaGrange, Georgia, in 1862.

As a young girl my mother, Zerelda Baxter Matthews, born in 1902 in Madison County, recalled hearing that one of Keeling's sons was taken prisoner at his family home near Bridgeport, Kentucky, by Union soldiers, also fellow Kentuckians. Although he was given leave to visit his family, he was incarcerated in a Union prison in Ohio and was never heard from again.

Stories about her ancestor's plight made my mother a Confederate sympathizer all her life. Her experience personally reflects the tragedy of a state where, more than any other state in the Union, loyalty to either North or South became and remained very personal. It split families, communities, churches and business relationships. The America of the Founding Fathers would never be the same. Post-war Kentucky, reeling from economic and personal losses, would

not begin to recover its pre-war social and economic status until the 20th century. Politically, the land that had nurtured Abraham Lincoln, Henry Clay and John T. Breckinridge is still struggling to reclaim a national presence.

Back Home in Kentucky, Inc. and Kentucky's foremost Civil War scholars have collaborated to bring you what we believe is the first full-color book about the Civil War in Kentucky. Here are accounts of 11 major battles and many minor skirmishes, stories about the personalities of Kentucky's military and political leaders on both sides of the conflict, and a full-color map giving the locations of the major battles, skirmishes, railroads, historic sites, troop movements and current sites of historical interest.

During the Civil War, more than 22,000 Kentuckians, fighting for both sides, died for a cause that they believed was just. It is said that history is written by the victors, but in the case of The War Between the States, scholarship has transcended boundaries in an effort to recount this important period in American history with utmost accuracy. We know that our readers will appreciate the diligent research and careful authorship of an outstanding group of scholars about a war which is still the most studied and written about conflict in our country's history.

ACKNOWLEDGEMENTS

Many individuals deserve a great deal of credit for this book. It all started in the summer of 2002 when the owners of Back Home In Kentucky, Inc., decided to publish an article in its magazine on the upcoming reenactment of the Battle of Perryville (October 1862) on the 140th anniversary of the battle.

Stuart Sanders, Battle of Perryville scholar and director of interpretation at the site, suggested we widen our scope and publish a separate magazine focusing on the 11 major Civil War battles in Kentucky, as defined by the U.S. National Park Service, in Washington, D.C.

We listened to Stuart and published what was to become a three-part magazine series depicting the Civil War in Kentucky. While that first issue included the 11 major battles and some skirmishes (Sacramento and Madisonville, among them) Volume II focused on, among many things, railroads, women, colored troops, the Cumberland Gap, Civil War bands, and the John Hunt Morgan raids. Volume III then looked at the Union and Confederate leaders of the war in Kentucky, including the victorious roles played by two future presidents, U.S. Grant in Western Kentucky and James Garfield in eastern Kentucky. We are indebted to Stuart Sanders for setting us off on the right track.

We are similarly indebted to Dr. James Klotter, Kentucky's State Historian, for without his encouragement and contributions, this book would not have been possible. We sat down one day with him at Georgetown College and made a list of those things that had to be included. He was most helpful in suggesting the names of individuals whose expertise he particularly valued. Hence, the scholarship and accuracy of the authors, whose brief biographies are contained on page 156, speak for themselves. We are proud that this book, unlike any other book ever published on the Civil War in Kentucky, brings together the writings of so many nationally renowned Civil War experts, notably Drs. Charles Roland, Lowell Harrison, and James Ramage, as well as Dr. Klotter. The enthusiasm and expertise of all of our authors were what made this book possible.

Special thanks go to Lisa Gaines Matthews, whose Confederate forebearer was one of those who did not survive the war, for her original, extensive, four-color map in the centerfold. No map of this kind has ever before been produced. She was assisted greatly by Tom Fugate, Kentucky's Civil War Sites Coordinator. Thanks also to Karen Simon at Progress Printing in Owensboro for her help in designing the map.

We are indebted to award-winning graphic designer Karen Boone for the creativity she brought to the book. We thank Charlene Smith, Photo Collections Assistant at the Kentucky Historical Society, and Becky Rice, who was so helpful at the Filson Historical Society.

Finally, two-time Pulitzer Prize winner Bill Strode worked unrelentingly, yet always cheerfully, to make sure that the book measures up to the standards which he has set for his Harmony House Publishing Company in Goshen, Kentucky.

Publishing this book was difficult and demanding not only because of the four-color throughout, but also because we were challenged to blend the text and graphics with the graphic displays (advertisements) from historic sites which also represented a first time achievement. As Bill kept saying, "I've never seen a book with ads in it." But ads there are, and we are indebted to those historically-minded organizations which wanted to be part of a pioneering work.

Finally, we wish to think all of you who will read this book. We hope it adds to your understanding of a war that claimed more lives than all of the other wars in our nation's history.

– *William E. Matthews*

Camp Boone Encampment, Louisville

THE ECHOES OF THE CIVIL WAR
IN KENTUCKY

By Dr. James C. Klotter

Confederates firing upon Fort Sumter

When the guns of war first boomed at Ft. Sumter in April 1861, Kentuckians could not hear those shots, but the effects of them would be long felt by all. The echoes of the distant thunder of that conflict would reverberate throughout the rest of the commonwealth's history, changing forever the way of life citizens had known before the war.

* * *

As the preparations for war unfolded, supporters of both the North and the South asked how Kentucky would go. Which side would it champion? For whom would its young men fight? Those key questions dominated discussions in 1861, for the commonwealth represented one of the most important states in the union. In the antebellum period, Kentucky boasted a sizeable population, plentiful agricultural wealth, a strong educational system (for the region), good transportation, excellent political leadership, and much more. It stood as a major prize for one side or the other – or both.

In population, for example, Kentucky had ranked sixth in size among the then-thirty states in 1840. A decade later its almost one million people placed it eighth among the thirty-two states, but with only 20,000 more people it would have been fifth. Kentucky's largest city, Louisville, had 43,000 citizens by the middle of the nineteenth century, which made it America's tenth biggest urban area, and the third largest city south of the Mason-Dixon line.

Much of the wealth of antebellum America came from agriculture. Given that, Kentucky was also a wealthy state by mid-century. A diversified crop system meant that the state ranked high nationally in a variety of areas. Kentucky was first in the production of hemp, second in tobacco and corn, and seventh in rye. While its wheat production had fallen drastically, as the new Midwestern fields had opened large-scale production, the commonwealth still stood eleventh in that area (down from fifth a decade earlier).

In the value of livestock, Kentucky ranked sixth overall, and second in the number of mules and hogs. Many considered its thoroughbreds unsurpassed in quality.

In education, the state also stood high, especially in the region. By the start of the Civil War, for example, it had one of the two best public school systems in the South. But its real strength came in higher education. Kentucky's preeminence there had caused Thomas Jefferson to complain that the lack of a good Virginia school meant "we must send our children for education to Kentucky or Cambridge [Harvard]." By the 1820s, Transylvania University represented the crown jewel of education in the South, and one of the best schools in the nation. Its undergraduate, law, and medical schools produced many leaders. In fact, when one-time attendee Jefferson Davis looked around him in Congress, almost one in ten of his fellow lawmakers were graduates of the school. By 1861, Transylvania had declined from those glory days, but other colleges, like Centre, Georgetown, and St. Joseph's, continued to add to the commonwealth's luster in that field.

Beyond education, Kentucky often was viewed as on the "cutting edge" in such areas as technology, science, and medicine. One of its inventors produced a steamboat before Fulton, one of its entrepreneurs built one of the early railroad systems in the nation, and one of its doctors performed the first operation for an ovarian tumor, for example. The names of architect Gideon Shryock, artist Matthew H. Jouett, and sculptor Joel T. Hart showed the achievement in those fields.

But Kentucky's greatest antebellum strength resulted from the national leaders it produced. While the state's sizeable electoral vote might mean much politically, its cadre of skilled leaders meant more. In fact, the importance of Kentucky on the national scene can be seen in the fact that in the ten presidential elections between 1824 and 1860, a

Kentuckian ran for president or vice president in seven of the ten races. And several times candidates not directly representing the state went on the ballot, and in each case they had a strong identification with Kentucky. Zachary Taylor, for instance, had lived most of his life in the commonwealth, though he did not do so at the time of his election. Native son Abraham Lincoln also resided elsewhere at the time of his race, but had kept close ties to Kentucky throughout his life. Others, however, ran and represented Kentucky – Henry Clay three times sought the presidency and John C. Breckinridge one, while Breckinridge and Richard M. Johnson won the vice presidency, and W. O. Butler lost his race for the office. Others, such as John J. Crittenden, also had a national impact on politics.

Yet, if antebellum Kentucky seemed so strong in many areas, its society had fundamental weaknesses. Opposition to immigrants in its borders emerged with a vengeance on "Bloody Monday" in 1855, when rioters killed over 20 people in Louisville. Women across Kentucky continued to toil in a legal limbo and second-class status. Their children died often and died young. And slaves – who made up one of every five Kentuckians – had almost no rights at all. Though legally listed as personal property – like a couch or a chair – slaves were, first and foremost, people – and all knew that. The cries from the whipping block, the screams of anguish from a slave mother seeing her children sold separately to a trader, the calls for humanity – all reminded Kentuckians of the curse in their midst.

* * *

As the bells tolled for war in 1861, then, Kentuckians listened and considered their options. Union and Confederate leaders watched as well, for Kentucky's choice could be crucial to the success of the side the state chose. In addition to the numbers of men, the agricultural wealth, the horseflesh, the leadership, and the other resources, the commonwealth also brought to the table a geography that could be a vital factor as well. At a time when no bridges crossed the Ohio River in Kentucky's borders, that body of water could provide a natural defense line, should Kentucky cast its lot with the South. Without that line, holding Kentucky would prove much more difficult for those who wore gray. But would citizens don that color, or the Union blue, or any at all?

Increasingly, the question was asked: "Who are you, Yankee or Rebel, Confederate or Union?" People's political, family, educational, and economic ties tore them both ways. The South now used the Kentucky-Virginia Resolutions of 1798 as a basis for secession, yet in 1850, the commonwealth had emblazoned on the Washington Monument the words: "Under the auspices of heaven and the precepts of Washington, Kentucky will be the last to give up the Union." But would it? As the conflict escalated, pro-southern

Kentucky Governor Beriah Magoffin replied to Lincoln's call for soldiers with the words, "I say emphatically, Kentucky will furnish no troops for the wicked purpose of subduing her sister southern states." But the increasingly pro-union legislature felt otherwise. So as state after state left the union, Kentucky remained – divided, confused, uncertain, but still in the union.

Officially, the state declared itself neutral in May 1861, and there were almost three nations – the United States, the Confederate States, and Kentucky. A lawyer looked back on that period and remarked, "My native state . . . solemnly voted to take neither side in the Civil War . . . and maintained her consistency . . . by taking both." He was right. At the time, an Adair County man recognized the difficulties of neutrality and noted of the General Assembly's action: "A number of the members seems to want Kentucky to be nutral [sic] and take no cides [sic] either with the North or South . . . . I myself think [that course] impossible for her to pursue." He was correct as well, for both sides sought to raise troops either in or near the state. Like two boxers, Davis and Lincoln both carefully maneuvered, trying to avoid making a mistake that would allow the other side to deliver a knockout blow to their cause in Kentucky. But, over time, the growing Union tide overwhelmed the pools of southern support. In September, the legislature reacted to a Confederate troop incursion and officially declared Kentucky a Union state. In the first phases of the fight for the soul of Kentucky, the Union had won.

Two months later, disgruntled sympathizers of the southern rebellion set up their own government, with its capital at Bowling Green, and elected their own governor. Kentucky soon became a star in both flags. Many quickly recognized, as did James Speed, that "So many of our giddy young men have gone into the Southern Army, that almost any man . . . knows that he has to fight a neighbor, a brother, a son or father." Men went off to war. Regiments formed for one side or the other. Families divided. For Kentucky, the Brother's War had begun in deadly earnest.

* * *

While the numbers can be counted various ways, as many as 100,000 Kentuckians fought for the Union, as many as 40,000 for the South. But the effect of the war on the state went far beyond just those numbers. Those away from the battlefield knew that many loved ones would never return. A woman watched the troops' departure and wrote, "I saw Brother pass by without being able even to shake hands & when he disappeared amid the dust, noise & confusion . . . I felt as if I would never see him again. I put my face down on the gate & cried with all my heart." A wife told a distant spouse what she felt as well: "Even as I write my eyes are blinded by tears and every breath I draw, every throb of my heart is a passionate prayer for your safety."

Camp Joe Holt across the Ohio River from Louisville

Those women had cause to worry and pray and hope, for before the conflict ended over four hundred battles and skirmishes occurred in the state. Even more took place outside the borders of the commonwealth. Military aspects of the war are well-know. Under Kentuckian Albert Sidney Johnston, the Confederates set up a defense line stretching from Cumberland Gap to Mill Springs to Bowling Green to Ft. Donelson in Tennessee, to "The Gilbraltor of the West," Columbus, Kentucky. Union victory at Mill Springs in January 1862, followed by the Confederate surrender of Ft. Donelson the next month, broke that line and most southern forces departed the state.

Six months later, however, a major Confederate invasion brought southern soldiers back into Kentucky. Those troops perhaps represented the Confederacy's greatest chance of ending the war, for at the same time Robert E. Lee headed an attack into Maryland as well. With foreign recognition possible should the two be victorious, southern hopes ran high. Success at Munfordville and Richmond and the inauguration of a Confederate governor in Frankfort fed those expectations. Then, almost by accident, the Union forces of Don Carlos Buell and the Confederate ones of Braxton Bragg met at Perryville in what some called the hardest day of battle during the entire war. But the level of military leadership that day did not match the courage of the common soldiers who bled and died. Neither side could claim a victory by nightfall, but Bragg's will failed him, and the Confederates retreated, never again to return in any sizeable numbers. Only the small-scale attacks of raiders like John Hunt Morgan or Nathan Bedford Forrest intruded into

the Union presence after October 1862. On the military front, the North had won as well, just as they had in the earlier fight for Kentucky's political support at the start of the conflict.

* * *

But in the crucial third struggle to win the hearts and minds of Kentuckians, the Union lost – and lost disastrously. While most commentators, then and later, have focused attention on the battlefield fights, perhaps equally important to Kentucky's future was what occurred on the homefront. Events there would change the story line of Kentucky in the Civil War.

In 1861, most Kentuckians had wanted union and slavery. They supported the Union fought for so long by Clay, Crittenden, and others. At the same time, they sought to keep slavery. Since the Lincoln administration had not yet made slavery's end a wartime goal, it seemed possible to have both. Numerous slaveholders thus fought for the Union.

But over the course of the war, two factors would cause Kentucky to change from its mostly pro-Union stance at the start of the war to one more favoring the southern viewpoint by conflict's end. One of those concerned slavery.

Lincoln's Emancipation Proclamation did not affect Kentucky as a loyal slave state. But it came as a stunning blow to Unionists who had tried to downplay the issue. Now it seemed only a matter of time before the peculiar institution in Kentucky would come under attack as well. As a member of the Union 22d Kentucky told his sister, "I enlisted to fight for the Union and the Constitution, but Lincoln puts a different construction on things and now has us Union men fighting for his Abolition Platform and thus making us . . . Negro thieves and devastators of private property." The still-loyal but angry legislature called the Proclamation, "unwise, unconstitutional, and void" – the very words a secessionist might use. Some Union officers resigned; one, Colonel Frank Wolford, called the president a tyrant and was arrested. So harsh was the lieutenant governor's criticism that the Union military commander of the state exiled him to the South for three months, until Lincoln pardoned him.

Soon after that, the Federal forces began enlisting slaves into the army, with many of them joining at Camp Nelson. In the end, Kentucky furnished over 23,000 black soldiers, the second highest number in the nation. In exchange for their services, they were declared free men, and, later, their spouses and children were freed as well. White Kentuckians bitterly opposed all those actions, and the state's highest court termed them unconstitutional. To a free citizenry which believed that without slavery, blacks would try to exterminate whites in a race war, putting guns in their hands seemed suicidal. Making them free seemed illegal to many. Suggesting they were equal to white soldiers seemed dangerous to others. Of course, the ex-slaves did not take revenge on their owners, but fear overrode reason, and white Kentuckians began to revolt against the Union, even as the war itself was being lost by the South.

The second factor in changing Kentucky's wartime sentiment concerned the actions taken by the Union forces in the commonwealth. Armies of occupation and military rule seldom prove popular, and wartime conditions in Kentucky – and the Union responses to them – would confirm that.

Some actions simply resulted from wartime. The Union arrested some southern sympathizers – including an aged ex-governor and numerous women – and that hurt the northern image. Unfriendly newspapers, perhaps giving important news to the enemy through their columns, were closed. That raised legitimate cries of censorship. But while those could be perhaps supported as legitimate responses, other actions seemed more arbitrary, or even criminal.

Southern sympathizers, or opponents of the administration, complained of military interference and intimidation at the polls. While the extent of that seems overstated, it certainly did occur. But, more than that, actions like the Great Hog Swindle added to the anger. In 1864, the military, needing pork to feed its soldiers, issued an order that required Kentucky farmers to sell their hogs to the army at a fixed price. As it turned out, that price fell below the market value of the pork. Angry Kentuckians claimed the policy cost them money, while businessmen complained of their

exclusion from the trade. The action was rescinded; the propaganda effects lived on.

A greater outcry came from the presence of guerrillas and outlaws in the state, and the army's actions – and inactions – on that issue. The Federal forces faced a major problem. As later would occur in Vietnam and Iraq, the military had no way of knowing who was friend or foe, ally or spy. In trying to deal with that, the Union made mistakes, terrible ones. With men away fighting, with no police force at the time in most places, few locals could defend themselves from the lawless attacks. One man told of the "thieves supposed to be bands of deserters from both armies. The country is in a most lawless state. Across the Cumberland murders and robberies are of daily occurrence." In rural Kentucky, such bands operated almost with impunity. For the last three years of the war, lawless violence left a legacy of ruin and anger that would be long remembered. Union efforts to control that proved limited; they had a war to fight, first and foremost.

But when the Federal forces tried to respond to the guerrilla-style attack on soldiers or Union sympathizers, their action produced even greater outrage. The infamous Order No. 59 decreed that for each Unionist killed by guerrillas, four captured prisoners would be executed. But who was a guerrilla and who was a legitimate Confederate soldier, separated from his command or just operating behind the lines? Numerous executions took place, and some innocent men died. Those memories and that bitterness continued after the firing ended.

* * *

The guns finally fell silent in 1865. One tired soldier simply wrote, "Good-bye shoulder straps." Another told how it went for him, a member of the famous Confederate Orphan Brigade, which had suffered so many losses in the war: "I took the train for Louisville [from Georgia] . . . and got off at Bardstown . . . got home around 10am the third of May, having been absent 3 years, 8 months, and 4 days."

What he, and others, saw on their return showed them the effects of the war on the commonwealth. The conflict left schools disrupted and once-proud Transylvania in ruins. Georgetown College saw its numbers of graduates fall from twenty-five in 1860 to zero three years later. Some elementary and secondary schools had not even met in wartime, for teachers had gone to fight.

Another effect of the Civil War concerned Kentucky's once-healthy economy. Real purchasing power had declined one-third; the tax rate had risen 70 percent; money for any southern loans had disappeared; all funds invested in slaves had vanished. The state had almost 90,000 fewer horses, over 170,000 fewer cattle, and half the number of mules it had half a decade earlier. Armies had stripped some places of all food and supplies, while guerrillas had burned homes and farms as well. While a few citizens, such as those in Louisville, had prospered during the war, most Kentuckians now faced a darker financial future.

Politically, the conflict left equally long-lasting results. The issue of the role of blacks, plus the memories of military rule, now made political allies of some men who had been military enemies only months before. As others have noted, the ex-Confederates – the vanquished – soon ruled the victors. The heroes became those who had waged the war against the Union, not those who had defeated the rebellion. The legend of "moon-light, magnolias, and mint-juleps" began to be the dominant vision for Kentucky, and postwar writers would create a different memory of the conflict. And, finally, because of events on the homefront, Kentucky's Democratic Party, a minority party in the commonwealth for most of its history, now became the dominant political force. The party of Lincoln, the "black Republicans," would have to wait a long time to break free of the wartime memories that shackled it.

But greater than all those results was what the war did to those involved. Perhaps as many as 30,000 died. (By comparison about 1,000 Kentuckians died in the Vietnam War.) Each of those deaths meant that the next generation would grow to maturity without some of its masterly leaders, ablest thinkers, strongest authors, finest artists, best businessmen, and foremost politicians. But even those who survived bore the scars of war, both hidden and obvious. Town after town had veterans who had lost a limb in battle. Many had ex-soldiers who lived their lives

staring out at a world they little understood. Some had returned with morphine addiction; others with addictions for action and violence.

The fighting had affected different people different ways. One person might return with new leadership skills, honed by acts of courage, with respect for his enemy. Another might come back with a reputation for merciless acts, and with a hate for the other side. For example, one soldier in 1864 wrote: "I love to kill them as good as you do to kill deer. I love to shoot them and see them jump." And in the areas where guerrilla warfare raged outside the rules of war, the fabric of compassion never fully mended, as the memories of past wrongs ruled even more supreme.

And, finally, in some ways the greatest effect of the war could be seen daily across Kentucky. Slavery had ended. The over 225,000 men, women, and children who had been in bondage in 1861 now were free. For them, the war marked a turning point in their life history. Now they faced a different fight, for equality.

So, as Kentucky turned to the postwar world, the state faced many obstacles and issues, many of them resulting from the conflict. But more than most places, the commonwealth had been a place divided, a state of the Brothers' War. As people walked the streets of their towns, they saw enemies as well as friends, unlike in most states of the nation. That would make it even harder for the state to remain true to its motto "United We Stand, Divided We Fall." The guns may have fallen silent after Appomattox, but the effects of the war roared on.

* * *

Louisville Wharf – inhabitants leaving the city, 1862

RELUCTANT UNIONISTS
KENTUCKY DURING THE CIVIL WAR

By Lisa Gaines Matthews

Union Troops storming Fort Donelson, Tennessee

Filson Historical Society

1861

When the American Civil War erupted in Charleston, South Carolina, on April 12, 1861, political leaders and legislators of Kentucky were in the midst of wrestling with the question of whether or not to hold a convention to decide on the state's course in the event of war. Unionists sought a compromise with the federal government while individuals, such as U.S. Senator and former Vice-president John C. Breckinridge, believed that the Union was a confederation of states and, as such, each state could choose its own path.

Immediately after the surrender of Fort Sumter, President Abraham Lincoln sent out a call for 75,000 men to suppress the rebellion. Kentucky was asked to furnish four regiments of militia (approximately 4,000 men) to the U.S. Army. Gov. Beriah Magoffin was quick to answer by telegram,

"I say, emphatically, Kentucky will furnish no troops for the wicked purpose of subduing her sister Southern states."

A position of neutrality was taking shape among the leaders of the Union Party and the States Rights Party. Kentuckians, in general, favored staying out of the conflict even though it was feared that despite their best efforts to avoid participation in the war, the state would be invaded from the north.

Gov. Magoffin called the legislature into session on May 6, 1861, and leaders of the Union Party and States Rights Party could not agree on calling a sovereignty convention. They did, however, agree upon armed neutrality. A resolution to that affect was proposed and passed the legislature by a vote of 69-26. The Senate followed suit by passing several resolutions favoring neutrality, 13-9.

Kentucky's position of armed neutrality was respected by both sides for several months. Neither the Union nor the Confederacy wanted to antagonize the state, as it was feared that a push from one side or the other might drive it into the opposing camp. Both sides recognized that Kentucky possessed substantial capital and valuable resources. At a time when the population of Kentucky ranked ninth in the nation (out of 34), the state was highly prized as a potential source of recruits.

It was Kentucky's geographic position which would end any possibility of avoiding war. Nestled between the northern states of Ohio, Indiana, and Illinois, and the southern states of Tennessee and Virginia, Kentucky could not avoid invasion. At a time when rivers provided the primary source of travel and transportation of goods it was significant that Kentucky possessed the highest number of navigable rivers in the country. The confluence of the Cumberland and Tennessee Rivers, near Paducah, was strategically significant. Railroads were in their infancy in 1861 but the Louisville & Nashville railroad line was of growing importance as a north-south transportation route.

By the first week of September, Union troops held positions on the northern bank of the Ohio River. Confederate Gen. Leonidas K. Polk feared that their entry into Kentucky was imminent and he ordered Gen. Gideon Pillow to leave Tennessee and take the river town of Columbus. This was accomplished on Sept. 4, a move that was quickly countered by Gen. Ulysses Grant when he marched his troops into Paducah on September 8.

Gov. Magoffin protested the "open violations of the neutral right of Kentucky," and Tennessee Governor Isham Harris complained of Gen. Polk's order to Confederate President Jefferson Davis. Davis replied, "The necessity justified the action." Kentucky's neutral stand was at an end.

By mid-September, troops for both armies were on the move into Kentucky. Gen. Grant remained in Paducah with his troops, who had also seized nearby Smithland. In Louisville, Kentuckian Gen. Robert Anderson established the headquarters of the state volunteers. Union training facilities, Camp Dick Robinson south of Lexington; Camp Kenton near Maysville; and Camp Andy Johnson, near Barbourville, opened in the fall.

For the Confederacy, Gen. Felix Zollicoffer advanced through the Cumberland Gap and established positions in eastern Kentucky. On September 18, Gen. Simon Bolivar Buckner, acting on orders from Department No. 2 Commander Gen. Albert Sidney Johnston, marched his troops into Bowling Green to begin building the fortifications necessary for the protection of the 400-mile east-west defensive line through the state. In October, Johnston established a headquarters in Bowling Green. The town was of strategic importance as a railroad hub and Johnston feared that if the Union advanced southward, it would do so along the L&N railroad line.

With Union and Confederate soldiers on Kentucky soil, early engagements were inevitable. The first engagement of the Civil War in Kentucky resulted when Gen. Zollicoffer dispatched a detachment of troops under the command of Col. Joel Battle to Barbourville to disperse the Union Home Guard at Camp Andy Johnson. On Sept. 19, the Confederates attacked and met little resistance. The camp was burned.

On Oct. 21, Gen. Zollicoffer and his 7,000 troops advanced northward along the Wilderness Road and encountered well-entrenched Union troops under the command of Gen. Albin Schoepf, near London, Ky. The Battle of Wildcat Mountain resulted in the first Union victory in Kentucky. Zollicoffer was forced to retreat. As the fall of 1861 progressed, skirmishes were recorded on Ivy Mountain (Nov. 8-9) in Floyd County, and at Rowlett's Station (Dec. 17) in Hart County. On December 28, there was a skirmish in Sacramento, near Madisonville. It was notable because Col. Nathan Bedford Forrest began the battle with a rifle shot as he led the Confederates to victory. The future General Forrest would become one of the most successful, if notorious, leaders of the Confederacy.

1862

In the winter of 1861-1862, Brig. Gen. Zollicoffer, who feared a Union attack on his position in eastern Kentucky, moved his troops westward to establish winter quarters at Mill Springs, near Somerset. Union troops, under the command of Gen. George Thomas (the future Rock of Chickamauga), were ordered to leave Lebanon and drive the Confederate troops across the Cumberland River. Prior to the impending battle, command of the Confederate troops was resumed by Maj. Gen. George Crittenden when he returned to the field.

Crittenden quickly realized that Zollicoffer had made a critical error in placing his army in front of the Cumberland River. On the morning of January 19, Crittenden decided his only recourse was a frontal assault. A dense fog caused tactical confusion, obscured the arrival of Gen. Shoepf's four brigades as reinforcement for Gen. Thomas, and resulted in the death of Gen. Zollicoffer when he accidentally rode behind Union lines.

The Battle of Mill Springs was a decisive Union victory. Crittenden's division of two brigades suffered nearly twice the casualties (522 to 262) as Gen. Thomas's troops. The battle followed closely on another Union success in eastern Kentucky. On Jan. 10, Union Col. (and future president)

James Garfield and 1,700 men successfully pushed a Confederate force under Gen. Humphrey Marshall out of Paintsville at the Battle of Middle Creek, near Prestonsburg.

In February, the Confederate cause suffered an even greater blow with the stunning losses of Fort Henry and Fort Donelson in Tennessee. With eastern Kentucky in Union control and Gen. Grant looming in the west, Albert Sidney Johnston had little choice but to withdraw from Bowling Green toward Nashville and then further south to Corinth, Mississippi. When Gen. Grant also moved south through Tennessee, the stage was set for the Battle of Shiloh (the planned Battle of Bowling Green) on April 6.

By the summer of 1862, the role of Kentucky in Union and Confederate strategy became clearer. The need for recruits and supplies had become acute. The Union needed to keep important supply lines open into the South and fortify the state against a Confederate invasion. In June, 1862, Union Gen. George W. Morgan implemented part of this plan by moving against Confederate forces in the Cumberland Gap, forcing their withdrawal.

On the Confederate side, military planners saw Kentucky as the place to draw the Union troops under Gen. Don Carlos Buell away from an advance on Chattanooga, Tennessee.

General Braxton Bragg

On July 4, Confederate Col. John Hunt Morgan undertook the first of four daring raids into Kentucky from his home-base in Knoxville, Tennessee. In just three weeks, Morgan and his men captured 17 towns, among which were Glasgow, Lebanon, Lawrenceburg, Versailles, and Georgetown. They captured and paroled 1,200 Union soldiers, confiscated and destroyed munitions and supplies, and recruited 300 men. By July 17, they were in Cynthiana. During the first Battle of Cynthiana, near Licking Creek, Morgan's men clashed with 350 Union troops (rather than the 450 Home Guard troops they'd expected) and after three unsuccessful assaults on the well-entrenched Federals, Morgan and his men smashed through the Union line and took control of the town.

By August, Morgan was back in Tennessee. He notified his superiors that if Kentucky were occupied by a Confederate army, 25,000 Kentuckians would join the Southern cause. On July 31, Confederate Gen. Braxton Bragg and Gen. Edmund Kirby Smith met in Chattanooga to plan a two-pronged advance into Kentucky. Kirby Smith would enter the state through the Cumberland Mountains, by-passing the Federals in the Cumberland Gap. Bragg would take a more central route northward, toward Louisville. Eventually the two armies would join into one.

Smith began to move his troops on August 13 and by August

18 the Confederates captured Barbourville and 50 Union supply wagons headed for the Gap. Still needing supplies and determined to maintain an independent course, Kirby Smith communicated that he needed to press on toward Lexington.

By August 29, his army of 18,000 was outside Richmond. Learning that Union reinforcements were on their way from Cincinnati, he ordered an attack. Three engagements comprised the Battle of Richmond and by the afternoon of August 30, the Federals were falling back toward Lexington. At this time Union Gen. William "Bull" Nelson confronted his retreating army and shouted "If they can't hit me, they can't hit anybody!" Nelson was struck almost immediately in the thigh and the Confederate rout was on.

The Battle of Richmond was one of the most complete Confederate victories of the entire Civil War. Over 80% of the 6,500 Union troops became casualties, while Smith's army lost a mere 700 men. The Confederate army under Kirby Smith went on to capture Lexington and Frankfort in September. The Union line retreated to the Ohio River where the inhabitants of Louisville, Newport, Covington, and Cincinnati began to prepare for the reality of a Southern invasion.

On August 28, Gen. Bragg's army of 22,000 men marched northward from Chattanooga and entered Kentucky. By the time he reached Glasgow, Bragg learned that General Buell had left Tennessee and was heading toward Bowling Green. The Confederate plan had worked. It was at this point Bragg inexplicably marched his army to Munfordville. He had learned that the Union garrison responsible for guarding the Green River railroad bridge refused to surrender. Once Bragg and his army arrived, Union Col. John Wilder realized his position was hopeless and he surrendered.

This Battle of Munfordville may tally in the Confederate win column, but it cost Gen. Bragg valuable time and allowed Gen. Buell the chance to get his army to Louisville for much needed supplies and reinforcements. Bragg's army continued on to Bardstown, where he expected to join the force under Kirby Smith. Both generals were uneasily aware that any effort to rally Kentuckians to the Southern cause was not going to be successful. Kentuckians were wary of a cause that had not yet proven itself overwhelmingly on the battlefield. Wagonloads of weapons, which the Confederates had hoped to supply their new recruits, remained, for the most part, unloaded.

On October 2, Gen. Bragg met with Gen. Kirby Smith and Confederate Governor-elect Richard Hawes in Lexington. It was decided that Bragg and Hawes would proceed to

Frankfort where Hawes would be installed as the Confederate governor of Kentucky. Since the Confederate Congress in Virginia had passed a conscription law in April 1862, Bragg would then be able to draft the reluctant Kentuckians into his army.

On October 1, Gen. Buell's Army of the Ohio left Louisville. Buell sent 20,000 men toward Frankfort as a diversion and the remaining 58,000 men advanced in three columns toward Bragg's command in Bardstown. Bragg believed that the main Union force was headed toward Frankfort and he ordered Gen. Leonidas Polk to sweep the "lesser" force, marching on Bardstown, from the field.

On the afternoon of October 4, Richard Hawes was duly sworn in as the Confederate governor of Kentucky. While giving assurances to a packed House of Representatives and a crowd of on-lookers that he "was there to stay," the ceremony was abruptly halted by Union cannon-fire from the bluffs overlooking the Capitol. The Confederates were forced to flee and after burning the bridges over the Kentucky River, they fled Frankfort forever.

Gen. Bragg planned to join with Gen. Kirby Smith's army near Harrodsburg but then discovered that the main Union army was in Perryville. Both armies desperately needed water and Doctor's Creek had already attracted the attention of an advance unit of Arkansas troops. In the early hours of October 8, Union troops were ordered to secure the water and the surrounding area. The Battle of Perryville had begun.

General Don Carlos Buell

The main battle would be delayed for several hours due to miscommunication and indecisiveness on the part of Confederate Gen. Leonidas K. Polk. An irate Gen. Bragg rode into Perryville at 10 a.m. after discovering his order to attack had not been carried out. He quickly realigned the troops and ordered a frontal assault. At 2 p.m. Confederate troops, under Gen. Benjamin F. Cheatum, smashed into the left flank of the Union I Corps, commanded by Gen. Alexander McCook. Despite heavy artillery fire, the Confederates rolled the Union troops back nearly a mile. To the south, the Confederate left attacked the Federal right and after initially pushing the Unions troops back, the advance was checked. After five hours of furious fighting, night fell and the battle ended. Union casualties amounted to 845 killed, 2,851 wounded, 515 missing. The Confederates counted 510 dead, 2,635 wounded, 251 missing.

After the Battle of Perryville, Gen. Bragg discovered that his army of 18,000 had battled three divisions of Gen. Buell's Army of the Ohio, nearly 55,000 men. Fearing that Buell might attack again on Oct. 9, Bragg retreated during the night to Harrodsburg where his army finally united with the

army of Edmund Kirby Smith. Buell followed on October 10 and, for the second time in two days, a Northern army faced a Southern counterpart. The scene for a Battle of Harrodsburg was set, but neither general would order the attack. As it turned out, larger circumstances would intervene that would cause the Confederate army to retreat into Tennessee.

News arrived from the west that a Confederate assault on Corinth, Mississippi, had been thwarted and in the eastern theater, Gen. Robert E. Lee's Army of the Virginia had suffered a crippling defeat at Antietam, Maryland, forcing a reluctant Lee to retreat into Virginia. President Jefferson Davis feared that if Bragg's army in Kentucky was defeated, the door to Chattanooga would be wide open for a Union invasion. Bragg and Smith agreed that their best course was to return to Tennessee. Smith proceeded through the Cumberland Gap, which had been evacuated by Gen. George W. Morgan when his supply lines had been cut, and Bragg headed south toward Middle Tennessee. A Confederate officer wrote, "Kentucky . . .is hopelessly lost." When the two armies left Kentucky soil, the course of the Civil War would be decided elsewhere.

During the remainder of the Civil War there would never again be a major invasion into Kentucky. Union troops remained stationed in the state until after the war and their presence prompted several Confederate forays or raids to disrupt supply and communication lines. One of the most famous of these raids was John Hunt Morgan's "Christmas Raid," which began on the night of Dec. 23. Morgan and his regiment crossed into Kentucky near Tompkinsville and moved toward Elizabethtown through Cave City. In the next week and a half, Morgan's raiders would capture Elizabethtown; destroy the trestles at Muldraugh's Hill and wrecked the railroad line from Upton nearly to Shepherdsville. They also took 2,000 prisoners and captured much-needed weapons, clothes and horses. Total losses for Morgan, 2 killed, 24 wounded, and 64 missing.

1863

January 1, 1863 marked a milestone in U.S. history when President Abraham Lincoln announced the Emancipation Proclamation Act. This act freed all slaves in the Confederacy, gave the United States a renewed sense of purpose for the war, kept European powers from siding with the South, and sparked an influx of black soldiers into Union training camps.

In June, Camp Nelson, located just south of Nicholasville and named for Gen. William "Bull" Nelson, was established. The administration of this training and refugee camp was shared by the Army and the American Missionary

Association. Former slaves arrived with their families and at times Camp Nelson housed as many as 3,000 individuals. John G. Fee, an ordained minister and co-founder of Berea College, began a school for these future Union soldiers and their families.

By June, Gen. Braxton Bragg's army was under pressure in Chattanooga. Once again John Hunt Morgan was asked to lead a raid into Kentucky, as far north as the Ohio River. On July 2, Morgan and 2,460 men crossed the Cumberland River near Burkesville and began the "Great Raid." Morgan and his army soon reached the Green River, near Campbellsville, and on July 4, the Confederates confronted 200 well-entrenched men of the 25th Michigan Infantry. The hastily assembled timber fortification could only be assaulted from the front and, eight times during the Battle of Tebbs Bend, Morgan's men tried and failed to dislodge the determined Michiganders. After 30 minutes, Morgan's casualties numbered 24 experienced officers and 50 "good" men. A future Kentucky governor, Maj. James B. McCreary, wrote, "Many of our best men were killed or wounded. The beginning of this raid is ominous."

Morgan moved northward to Lebanon where, after seven hours of fighting, an out-numbered Union force of 450 was defeated. It was a hollow victory for Morgan, however, since his 19-year-old brother, Tom, was killed. After putting the town of Lebanon to the torch, Morgan proceeded through Bardstown. Within days, he reached the Ohio River at Brandenburg and, contrary to orders from Bragg, Morgan and his raiders captured two steamboats, the *J.T. McCombs* and the *Alice Dean*, and crossed into Indiana.

Morgan moved swiftly through Indiana into Ohio, resupplying his men and leaving railroad tracks torn and depots burning in his wake. A Union force under Gen. Edward Hobson was in pursuit and on July 19, near Buffington Ford, Ohio, Morgan and his 1,700 men suffered heavy casualties (120 killed or wounded, 700 captured). Morgan and 400 men would escape that day only to be surrounded and captured near New Lisbon, Ohio, a week later. Morgan was sent to Columbus to the Ohio Penitentiary, but few could discount this amazing Confederate raid which had covered nearly 1,100 miles and disrupted Union supply lines for weeks.

1864

By March, 1864, the Union army was actively recruiting black soldiers and Camp Nelson became the premier recruiting and training center for black troops. By the end of 1864, more than 25,000 black soldiers had enlisted for the Union in Kentucky, second only to Louisiana. Refugees continued to arrive at the camp until the 13th Amendment to the Constitution freed all slaves. In 1866 a portion of Camp Nelson was designated a National Cemetery.

Although John Hunt Morgan remained incarcerated until his escape in November, 1863, other Confederate raiders ranged through Kentucky, seeking horses and supplies and attempting to disrupt Union supply and communication lines.

In March, Gen. Nathan Bedford Forrest took Union City, Tennessee, and headed toward Paducah in search of horses. On March 25, Forrest led a force of nearly 3,000 men against the 650 Union defenders of Paducah. The Confederates were unsuccessful in their assault on Fort Anderson and the horses they desperately needed were nowhere to be found. Soon after the Battle of Paducah, a Union newspaper reported that the 140 horses that Forrest sought had been hidden from him. This story prompted Kentucky-born Confederate Gen. Abraham Buford to enter the city, drive off the Union garrison and secure the horses for the Southern army.

After his escape, Morgan established a base-camp in Abingdon, Va. His troops lacked shoes, weapons and horses and these deficiencies again prompted him to reenter Kentucky. He reached Mt. Sterling on June 8, where his men captured 300 prisoners. Union forces regrouped and soon Morgan and his raiders were pressed toward Lexington. Reaching that city, Morgan's men burned Union supplies, captured horses and destroyed railroad bridges. Military discipline suffered and looting occurred.

Morgan reached Georgetown and then rode on toward Cynthiana where Union troops were fortified within local homes. Morgan's men lacked artillery and resorted to burning out the enemy. During this second Battle of Cynthiana, 500 Union men were captured, but the victory was short-lived as reinforcements streamed toward Cynthiana from Cincinnati. By June 12, Morgan's camp was overrun, 250 Confederate men were killed or captured, and he was forced to retreat back to Abingdon. On Sept. 4, a Union force caught up with Morgan, near Greeneville, Tennessee. After a brief skirmish, one of the great icons of the Southern cause was shot and killed.

In October, the military commander of the district of Kentucky, Gen. Stephen Burbridge, issued what appeared to be an innocent order regarding the future purchases of hogs from Kentucky farmers by the federal government. During the war, hog prices had risen steadily, driven by dwindling supply and speculation by market investors. Union Maj. Henry Symonds convinced Gen. Burbridge that the federal government could save money buy buying hogs directly from the farmers, thus circumventing agents for the meat packing industry. In what became known as "The Great Hog Swindle," newspapers were quick to report that this Union "scheme" was illegal and resulted in favoritism and fraud. Many farmers were prevented from transporting their livestock across the Ohio River causing them to refuse to sell to the government. The firestorm of criticism resulted in the revocation of "all orders affecting the hog trade in Kentucky" on November 27. Gen. Burbridge was removed as military commander and farmers resumed selling their stock to the meat packers. The incident had a longer term effect on Kentucky's political landscape as voters swung even further away from Washington and the Republican Party. In the presidential election of 1864, Kentuckians overwhelmingly voted for Democrat George McClellan, 64,301 votes to Lincoln's 27,787. Kentucky was joined by New Jersey and Delaware in casting its eleven electoral votes for McClellan. Lincoln won an Electoral College landslide, 212 to 21.

1865

By 1865, Americans were tired of war. Southern homes had fallen into disrepair, farms were neglected and Kentuckians were suffering the effects of an insidious type of violence. Acts of guerrilla warfare plagued the state throughout the war. Guerrillas or bushwhackers professed loyalty to whatever side suited as the main motives were personal gain and misplaced desire for revenge. By 1864, Maysville, Owingsville, Clinton and Owensboro were attacked.

In January, 1865, William C. Quantrill entered Kentucky to begin a five-month reign of terror. In February, he joined forces with the most notorious pro-Confederate guerrilla, Marcellus Jerome Clarke (Sue Mundy), and for several weeks they swept through the state. Clarke had served under John Hunt Morgan and had returned to Kentucky after Morgan's death. By March, federal troops were in pursuit of Clarke and his men. Union Maj. Cyrus Wilson surrounded the band in a barn in Meade County and negotiated a surrender. On March 12, Clarke was taken into custody by Union forces, was found guilty of murder by a military commission in Louisville, and was executed by hanging on March 15. In May, William Quantrill was shot in the back by the pro-Union guerrillas under Edwin Terrell in Spencer County. He died in June as a result of his injury.

By the time of Quantrill's death, the American Civil War had ended. On April 9, Gen. Robert E. Lee surrendered the Army of Northern Virginia at Appomattox, Va., and on April 26, the Army of Tennessee under Gen. Joseph Johnston laid down its arms.

It is indisputable that Kentucky played an integral role in the panorama of the American Civil War. Of the Border States, Kentucky was the most significant, because of its population, wealth, river systems and railroads. The bonds of family and community loyalty were tested and in many cases broken forever. Nearly 100,000 Kentuckians fought on the side of the Union, while approximately 35,000 Kentuckians fought for the South. Whether soldier or civilian, few families survived unscathed by death, injury, or financial hardship.

Kentucky had held a prominent place in the national economy and political scene prior to the Civil War. With the end of slavery, Kentuckians suffered a tremendous economic loss in property value and agricultural productivity. Labor shortages lasted for years after the war and crop production dropped dramatically while prices of finished goods rose. Industrialization in the state was in its infancy and Kentucky was slow to see manufacturing as an answer to its economic woes.

One Confederate soldier wrote, after his experience at the Battle of Perryville, "Oh, wretched war!" While he referred to one battle, these apt words effectively summarize Kentucky's post-Civil War history.

* * *

Bowling Green, Kentucky

BERIAH MAGOFFIN, 1815-1885

By Dr. Lowell Harrison

Governor Beriah Magoffin

After the fall of Fort Sumter, President Lincoln called for 75,000 90-day volunteers to put down the rebellion. Secretary of War Simon Cameron notified Kentucky Governor Beriah Magoffin that his state was to supply four regiments for immediate service.

Magoffin replied immediately: "In answer, I say, emphatically, Kentucky will furnish no troops for the wicked purpose of subduing her sister Southern States."

Few governors had the problems that confronted Magoffin during the Civil War. While Kentucky remained in the Union, there was considerable support within the commonwealth for the Confederate cause.

Beriah Magoffin was born in Harrodsburg on April 18, 1815. His father, after whom he was named, had come to America from Ireland; his mother, Jane McAfee Magoffin, was a member of one of Kentucky's most distinguished pioneer families.

Beriah graduated from Centre College in 1835 and from the Transylvania University law school in 1838. He practiced law briefly in Jackson, Mississippi, but soon returned to Kentucky. On April 21, 1840, he married Anna Nelson Shelby, a granddaughter of Isaac Shelby. Ten of their children survived infancy.

A staunch Democrat, Magoffin was a delegate to that party's national conventions in 1848, 1856, and 1860, and he was a presidential elector in 1856. Elected to the state Senate in 1850, he refused nomination to the national House of Representatives in 1851. The candidate for lieutenant governor on the Democratic ticket with Beverly L. Clarke in 1855, he lost to the successful American Party slate headed by Charles S. Morehead. Four years later, Magoffin won the governorship over Joshua Bell. His administration would be dominated by the sectional conflict and the Civil War.

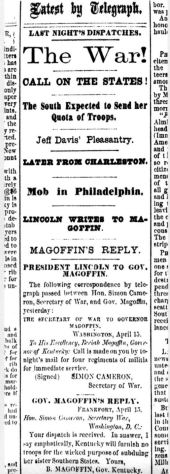

During his 1859 campaign, Magoffin had supported the Supreme Court's Dred Scott decision, had called for a strict fugitive slave law, and had demanded repeal of the Missouri Compromise. Anxious to avert a sectional division, he supported the John J. Crittenden Compromise, but he also presented ideas of his own to the governors of slave states. He believed that their united demand for the protection of the institution of slavery, the return of fugitive slaves to their owners, and a division of the national territories at the 37th parallel between slave and free would force the North to agree to such concessions. As he wrote an Alabama representative in December 1860: "You seek a remedy in secession from the Union. We wish the united action of the slave states, assembled in convention with the Union."

After compromise efforts, including his own, failed to avert the developing crisis, Magoffin called a special session of the General Assembly to convene on January 17, 1861. He had concluded that Kentucky could not — should not — remain in the Union without the guarantees of protection against antislavery forces. He recommended the selection of delegates to a state sovereignty convention that would determine Kentucky's future. He believed that only such a special convention, not the state legislature, would have the power to make such a fateful decision. By this time, Governor Magoffin wanted Kentucky to join the growing number of states that had seceded from the Union unless major concessions were made to hold Kentucky in the Union.

In the excitement of early 1861, such a convention might have voted to have Kentucky join the secession movement and the impending formation of the Confederate States of America. State Unionists had to play for time until they had a majority that would oppose secession. They refused to call for the convention that Magoffin proposed, and President Lincoln accepted for the present the unusual status of neutrality that Kentucky declared on May 20, 1861. Lincoln depended heavily upon the efforts of state Unionists to hold Kentucky in the Union, and he won his gamble. In a June 20, 1861, special election for members of the national House of Representatives, Unionist candidates won nine of the 10 seats; they lost only the Jackson

Governor Magoffin's Neutrality means holding the cock of the walk (Uncle Sam) while the Confederate cat (Jefferson Davis) kills off his chickens.

Purchase district. And after the August 5, 1861, election for members of the General Assembly, Unionists had veto-proof majorities of 76-24 in the House and 27-11 in the Senate.

In early September, 1861, when both Union and Confederate armies entered the state, the legislature ordered only the Confederates to withdraw. Kentuckians could — and did — often clash with the Lincoln administration, but a majority of Kentuckians had decided to remain in the Union.

A provisional Confederate Government that was formed at a Russellville convention on November 18-20, 1861, was admitted into the Confederate States of America on December 10. That government may have expected Magoffin to join it, but he condemned it as being "self-constituted" and "without authority from the people." In an open letter to the *Louisville Journal*, Magoffin denounced the actions of the Russellville group.

Despite such disclaimers, Governor Magoffin was viewed with deep suspicion by Unionists who could not understand the distinction that he had made, and a tight rein was imposed on his powers. In his proclamation of July 28, 1861, that called for a special session of the legislature, he complained that "I am without a soldier or a dollar to protect the lives, property, and liberties of the people, or to enforce its laws." His requests were usually ignored, and his vetoes were quickly over-ridden. Magoffin finally realized that his status was intolerable and that the best solution was his resignation.

Lt. Governor Linn Boyd had died on December 17, 1859, and Senator John F. Fisk, Speaker of the Senate, would become governor if Magoffin vacated his office. Fisk was not acceptable to the governor. In delicate negotiations with Adjutant General William A. Dudley, Magoffin outlined the conditions that he could accept. "Could I be assured that my successor would be a conservative, just man, of high position

and character; and that his policy would be conciliatory and impartial toward all law-abiding citizens, however they may differ in opinion; and that the constitutional rights of our people would be regarded, and the subordination of the military to the civil power be insisted on and maintained to the utmost extent our disturbed condition will admit — I would not hesitate an instant in putting off the cares of office..."

Details were worked out, and the result was one of the most interesting chapters in Kentucky's colorful political history. In a few carefully choreographed days in mid-August: John F. Fisk resigned as Speaker of the Senate, James F. Robinson was elected Speaker of the Senate, Beriah Magoffin resigned as governor. James F. Robinson took the oath of office and became governor, John F. Fisk was re-elected Speaker of the Senate.

His honor satisfied, Magoffin retired to his farm and resumed his legal practice. Astute real estate investments in the Chicago area made him wealthy.

He served a term (1867-1869) in the Kentucky House, and he retained a keen interest in state politics. Magoffin urged Kentuckians to accept the results of the war, to ratify the 13th amendment to the federal constitution, and to grant civil rights to the freed blacks. Often misunderstood by his contemporaries and some modern historians, Beriah Magoffin died at his home on February 28, 1885.

* * *

COLUMBUS-BELMONT
'THE GIBRALTAR OF THE WEST'
By Kentucky Department of Parks

Battle of Belmont, Missouri, opposite Columbus, Kentucky

A 32-pounder cannon, a piece of a giant chain with 20-pound links and a huge anchor that once blocked the passage of Union gunboats on the Mississippi, and a network of earthen trenches were part of an impregnable Confederate stronghold known as "The Gibraltar of the West."

These artifacts are preserved at Columbus-Belmont State Park. Columbus, Kentucky, is off the beaten path. Neither side was the victor in this Battle of Belmont, which took place November 7, 1861, and cost the country more than 1,000 lives.

No matter what the reason, control of Columbus was critically important during the Civil War and many strategies were planned by both sides to control the position. In addition, the Battle of Belmont was instrumental in the rise to power of one General Ulysses S. Grant, who led Union forces on that day.

The Columbus Fortifications

In September 1861, Confederate General Leonidas Polk, who was also the Bishop of Louisiana, moved his forces from Tennessee to occupy the heights at Columbus, Kentucky, and established a camp at Belmont on the Missouri side of the river. Throughout the autumn and winter, as many as 19,000 Confederate troops labored incessantly to make the position at Columbus impregnable. A floating battery was positioned on the Mississippi, including river steamers which were converted to gunboats; more than 140 heavy guns were positioned on the bluffs; and a huge chain, firmly anchored on the Columbus shore and resting on rafts, was stretched across the river. In addition, numerous trenches were dug at Columbus to further fortify what would be called Fort DeRussey.

According to William G. Stevenson, who served in the Confederate army at the Columbus fortifications, the lifestyle at Fort DeRussey was one of "hard work and harder drill. ...at one time we worked 12 hours out of every 36 so every other work turn came at night. Generals Polk, Pillow, Cheathum, and McGown were present day and night encouraging the men with words of cheer. General Pillow at one time dismounted and worked in the trenches himself to quiet some dissatisfaction which had risen."

"Torpedoes and other obstructions were placed in the river; but all this kind of work was done secretly by the engineer corps, and the soldiers knew but little of their number and location. Some of these torpedoes were made of cast iron at Memphis and Nashville, and would hold from 100 to 200 pounds of powder as a charge. Others were made of boiler plate, of different shapes and sizes. They were to be suspended near the surface of the water by chains and buoys, and discharged by wires stretched near the surface, which a boat would strike in passing over them."

In a letter written early in January 1862, General Polk said of the works at Columbus: "We are still quiet here. I am employed in making more and more difficult the task to take this place... I have now, mounted and in position, all round my works, 140 cannons of various calibers, and they look not a little formidable. Besides this, I am paving the bottom of the river with submarine batteries, to say nothing of a tremendous heavy chain across the river. I am planting mines out in the roads also."

Union General Henry Halleck, in a letter to General McClellan stated: "Columbus cannot be taken without an immense siege-train and a terrible loss of life. I have thoroughly studied its defenses – they are very strong; but can be paralyzed, and forced to surrender."

"Pillow's Folly" – The Giant Chain

To ensure that no enemy vessels sneaked past the fortifications at Columbus, the Confederates strung the big chain – said to have been more than a mile long – across the river, securing it on the Columbus end with a huge anchor.

A poster that has hung in the park museum for many years provides some of the only details known about the anchor. According to the poster, the anchor was taken from the Washington Naval Yard and brought up the Mississippi from Mobile Harbor in Alabama by Southern sympathizers when the war broke out. It was floated across the river on log pontoons, then was tied to two large sycamores on the Missouri shore. A capstan allowed it to be raised or lowered.

Estimates of the anchor's weight range from four to six tons. Its hooks measure nine feet from point to point. Each link of the chain is 11 inches long and six inches across. The anchor's weight and the swift Mississippi current eventually caused the chain to break. About 65 feet of the chain and the anchor are displayed at the park.

In one historical account, the chain was referred to as "Pillow's Folly," an apparent reference to General Gideon Pillow of Tennessee, commander of the Confederate troops along the Mississippi and logically the author of the chain idea.

"Lady Polk"

During the Battle of Belmont, Fort DeRussey, situated high on the Columbus bluffs, raked Grant's lines with merciless fire from its 140 cannons. One of the guns, known as the "Lady Polk" in honor of the wife of General Polk, was the

Torpedoes with their weights and anchors on the Levee

largest breech-loading cannon in use at the time. It was an 8-ton, rifled Dahlgren gun, capable of firing 128-pound, cone-shaped projectiles. The projectiles prepared for this gun had copper saucers attached to the bottom with flanges fashioned to fit the rifles. The flanges were too large and had to be filed to lift the gun.

During the Battle of Belmont, the heat from firing the gun expanded the barrel and after the battle it was left loaded with unfired projectiles. Two days later when the Lady Polk was fired again, it exploded, broke into pieces, killing 18 men and wounding 20.

The Strategies of Grant and Polk

The Battle of Belmont was significant in the Civil War because it marked the opening of the campaign in the West, as well as the opening of the Mississippi River to Union supplies.

On September 1, 1861, Brigadier General U.S. Grant, in command of the Union District of Southeast Missouri, seized Cairo, Illinois, on the Mississippi and Paducah, Kentucky, on the Ohio. Grant was preparing to occupy the heights of Columbus, Kentucky, when General Leonidas Polk moved up from Tennessee with a considerable force and seized the strategic position for the Confederates, establishing his impregnable fortress at Columbus and a camp at Belmont on the Missouri shore across the Mississippi River.

Following the occupation of Columbus, which became the most heavily fortified area in North America, the Confederates extended their line of defense in the West to Fort Henry on the Tennessee River, Fort Donelson on the Cumberland River, and on to Bowling Green.

Early that November, Grant was advised that General Polk was sending reinforcements from Columbus to General Sterling Price in Missouri and it was of vital importance that this movement be stopped. On the morning of November 7, 1861, Polk sent 2,500 men, under the command of General Gideon Pillow, across the Mississippi. They took up positions just beyond the camp at Belmont in Missouri. Grant landed a force of 3,100 men on the Missouri shore. Grant's forces were escorted by the two gunboats *Tyler* and *Lexington*.

When Polk learned of the Federal approach, he thought it was a feint to disguise an attack on Columbus itself. When he sent General Pillow across the river he was playing along, but kept his main line of forces in Columbus. Little did he know, Grant had no intention of attacking the well-fortified camp on the Columbus side.

Grant, meanwhile, made an aggressive decision: he would attack Belmont at dawn. By 8:30am, his men were ashore three miles above Belmont. In the lead was a company of the 22nd Illinois under Captain John Seaton, who specialized in skirmish-line tactics. Seaton made this speech to his men: "Many of us have seen the sun rise for the last time. I do not know what the crucial test may cause, but – if I should show the white feather, shoot me dead in my tracks and my family will feel that I died for my country." A few moments later, muskets rattled and the battle was on. The fierce fighting began at about 10:30am; the battle would not end until sunset.

"They opposed us step by step," Seaton wrote, but his men forced Confederates "from tree to tree." Grant was at the front rallying his troops. His mount was shot; he took an aide's horse and galloped forward.

Polk, meanwhile, sent General McGown with a force of infantry and artillery up the east bank of the river to reinforce his troops. Grant bore down upon the Confederate position, and the Rebels stubbornly resisted. Gradually, the Union forces drove the Confederates to the riverbank and captured the camp, setting fire to it while celebrating their supposed victory.

Across the river in Columbus, General Polk was surprised to find no attack developing on his main position. He ordered heavy cannon fire on the Federals in Belmont and sent several regiments to land between them and their boats.

General Benjamin Cheathum, landing Confederate reinforcements, attacked Grant's column on the flank as it withdrew from Belmont. The Federals' celebration turned suddenly to panic. Some of the officers thought surrender was the only answer. Grant's reply was: "We must cut our way out as we cut our way in."

Losses were heavy for the Union forces as they retreated to their transports waiting at the bend of the river. During the course of the second battle, the *Lexington* and *Tyler* made three unsuccessful attempts to silence the batteries at Columbus which were raking the retreating Union lines. Eventually, Union forces succeeded in reaching their transports, covered by protective fire.

The Federals had been driven away and the Confederates counted Belmont their victory, as did the Union. In fact, neither side had won or lost, but the Battle of Belmont resulted in the loss of 1,000 lives. According to Polk's report on the battle, his casualties numbered 641 and he estimated the Union loss at 400 to 500. He also noted that General Grant was "reportedly killed."

The Aftermath

This first major battle of the Western Campaign did enhance Federal morale, even though it ended all serious efforts to take Columbus by direct assault. It was also a milestone in the career of Ulysses S. Grant. In a period when generals on both sides felt ill-prepared to meet the enemy, and Lincoln was growing desperate for action, Grant showed himself willing to fight. The battle and its aftermath proved Grant's strategical genius as well.

The Union troops proceeded to capture the weaker positions nearby at Fort Henry on the Tennessee River and Fort Donelson on the Cumberland River. The capture of these positions, in February of 1862, not only opened the way to central Tennessee, but also outflanked Columbus. General Polk favored standing a siege in the elaborate earthworks so laboriously constructed at Fort DeRussey, but was overruled and Columbus was evacuated. Columbus was occupied by Union forces on March 3, 1862, resulting in the reopening of the Mississippi and the severing of the Confederacy.

Columbus and the Flood of '27

In the years following the Civil War, Columbus enjoyed a steady growth in population and income, further spurred by the Mobile and Ohio Railroad, originating from Mobile in 1852. It had a population of 2,600 in 1870 and 3,100 in 1880. In 1871, the St. Louis and Iron Mountain Railroad was built to Belmont and a ferry made it possible for connection and transport to the South.

Meanwhile, Columbus had changed from a thriving riverboat town to a factory town. The commercially advantageous site on the river, however, was subject to flooding. In 1927, the greatest flood in Mississippi River history swept away the protection levee and the town was virtually destroyed. Only 13 of the town's buildings were left untouched, while 43 were swept down the river and the rest were seriously damaged.

F. Marion Rust, in charge of flood relief after the disaster, conceived the idea of moving the shattered town from its site along the river to the top of the high bluffs away from the raging waters of the Mississippi. Both through Rust's efforts and the active support of Secretary of Commerce Herbert Hoover, this idea was implemented with an appropriation of over $90,000 from the Red Cross. It was thought to be the first time in history that an entire town was moved to a new location.

Rust also became deeply interested in the well-preserved remains of the old Confederate fortifications at Columbus and led the effort for development of Columbus-Belmont Battlefield Memorial Park. This area became part of the state park system February 10, 1934.

* * *

Columbus-Belmont State Park

GRANT'S OCCUPATION OF PADUCAH

By Dr. James A. Ramage

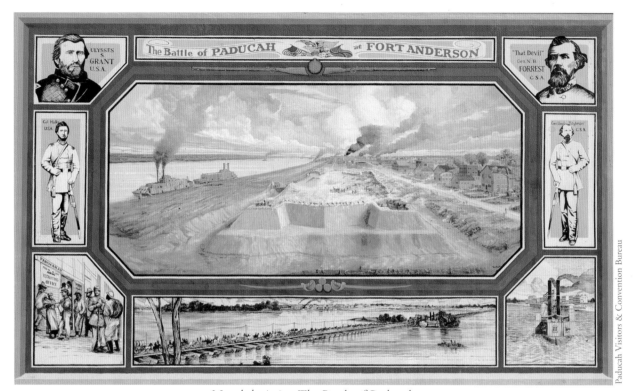

Mural depicting The Battle of Paducah

"The Yankees are coming!" was the shocking news in Paducah at 8:30 that Friday morning. It was September 6, 1861, and this was a total surprise because the people were expecting the arrival of Confederates. In an atmosphere of excitement and anticipation they had decorated their homes and public buildings with Confederate flags.

Reports were that since Confederate forces had occupied Columbus three days ago and violated Kentucky's neutral status, Confederate General Gideon Pillow and his army were marching from Columbus through Mayfield on the way to Paducah. Many citizens planned to gather on the sidewalks to welcome them.

Instead, they took down the flags, and men, women and children walked to the riverfront to see the Union men. Every informed person realized that Paducah was a highly strategic town. One only had to go down to the river and watch the Tennessee flowing into the Ohio to know that troops would occupy the town sooner or later. The Tennessee River and the Cumberland River, a few miles east, went deep into Confederate territory and were vital to the military control of the region.

Paducah was a thriving river town, and people were accustomed to seeing several steamboats at the landing at once. This morning there were three tall-stack steamboats, and in the river on guard, two wooden gunboats, each with two tall stacks sending up plumes of black coal smoke. Cannons, protruding from openings in the thick planking, reminded onlookers that gunboats were the noisiest and most powerful machines in the war, and the Union Navy had many of them. The gangplanks of the steamers were thrown out and soldiers with dark blue uniforms and rifles were marching ashore and forming in columns on the landing. There were 1,200 of them, and they had four pieces of artillery pulled by horses. They had come to stay, and Federals would occupy Paducah the rest of the war.

Everyone wanted a look at the commander of these men, and it was obvious which one he was. Brigadier General Ulysses S. Grant was a small man with a large beard who dressed like a private and paid no attention to spit and polish. His father, Jesse Root Grant of Covington, Kentucky, said that if you went looking for him in his army he would be the very last one you would suspect of being the commander. But this morning he moved with self-confidence and authority, and in his dark eyes there was the twinkle of a man who knew he was in the right place at the right time and accomplishing a great thing for his country.

He ordered the soldiers to move through the streets and set up a defensive perimeter around the town with stations on the Blandville Road, Mayfield Road, and toward Island Creek on the left. As they marched past crowds of civilians gathered at the landing and along the sidewalks on Broadway, women yelled, "Hurrah for Jeff Davis!" The troops were the 9th and 12th Illinois Infantry Regiments, and they expected taunting from the secessionists of this pro-southern region; they said they admired the women for their spunk. When things settled down, and they had time to write home, they wrote that Paducah had the most beautiful women they had ever seen.

Grant's men took control of the telegraph office, railroad depot, marine hospital, George Oehlschlaeger's bake shop, and Fred Hummel's gun shop. Not a shot was fired, and Grant had indeed achieved a major, bloodless victory for the Union.

The previous morning he had been 45 miles away, in his office in Cairo on the second floor of a former bank building. From his desk he could look out the window and see the fleet of gunboats tied up at the wharf boat in the Mississippi River. He could see the Kentucky shore, and he may have been reflecting on reports that the Confederate army, under General Leonidas Polk, had occupied Columbus two days before, on September 3. Columbus was about 20 miles south of Cairo, and artillery on its high bluffs could control the river. It was called the "Gibraltar of the Mississippi," and Grant hated to see it occupied by the Confederates. Then all of a sudden, in walked Union scout, Captain Charles de Arnaud, with word that Polk had sent Pillow and 4,000 men marching overland from Columbus to capture Paducah. With the enemy already occupying Columbus, Grant could not afford to lose Paducah and the Tennessee and Cumberland Rivers.

He immediately ordered boatmen to load coal and fire up, and he selected two regiments and directed them to prepare to board. He telegraphed his superior officer, General John C. Fremont, in St. Louis, reporting that unless he received orders otherwise, he was going to Paducah. Late in the afternoon he had received no reply, and he sent a second message: "I am getting ready to go to Paducah. Will start at 6 1/2 o'clock." He moved the flotilla into the river; when there was still no answer, before midnight, he moved on his own authority.

General Ulysses S. Grant

Grant's public reputation and his evaluation in history textbooks is that he did not understand politics and when he got involved he usually stumbled. Such is far from the truth. Grant was one of the most politically astute persons of his day, and he demonstrated it in the occupation of Paducah. Before he cut himself off from the telegraph at Cairo, he sent a message to the Speaker of the Kentucky House of Representatives notifying him that the Confederates had occupied Columbus. This perceptive, delicate action shielded Grant from any accusation that he was guilty of violating Kentucky neutrality – the Confederates had already violated it, and his message showed that he knew this.

And no one in the Union was more careful to avoid needlessly insulting the people of the Confederacy. Throughout his Civil War career he kept in mind that Southerners would have to be welcomed back into the Union and reconciliation would be easier if offenses were kept at a minimum. In Paducah, he behaved with humility and did nothing arrogant or offensive. He issued a printed proclamation to the citizens that began: "I have come among you, not as an enemy, but as your friend and fellow-citizen, not to injure or annoy you, but to respect the rights, and to defend and enforce the rights of all loyal citizens."

There was deep meaning behind the words of Grant's proclamation for it contrasted greatly with Fremont's famous proclamation in St. Louis one week earlier. Fremont stirred up a storm by declaring martial law and confiscating the property of all secessionists in his department, and emancipating all of their slaves. Lincoln had not yet decided to free the slaves, and to calm Kentucky and other slave border states still in the Union, he revoked Fremont's declaration.

Grant's Paducah proclamation did not get ahead of Lincoln, and not only did it ease the minds of Paducah citizens, it caused no controversy in the nation. About one year later, Grant's wife Julia was visiting in Georgetown, Ohio, where Grant grew up, and the people welcomed her as the wife of "Unconditional Surrender" Grant, the hero who captured Fort Donelson. In her Personal Memoirs, she told how one evening at a party, about 12 men called her into an adjoining room and said they were friends and they wanted to confirm that Grant stood by his "Paducah platform."

At first, Julia did not know what they meant, and she felt that she was in deep water. But they told her they were referring to his proclamation to the people of Paducah – they said they approved. Now she understood, and sensing that their approval was based mostly on Grant's not freeing

Battle of Paducah Reenactment

the Paducah slaves, she answered that Ulysses felt great sympathy for Southerners and wanted to make restoration of the Union as peaceful as possible. The men were pleased with her answer. Later, when Lincoln announced emancipation as a war aim, no one in the Union army supported emancipation more than Grant, and no one was more in favor of the use of African-American soldiers. Lincoln was referring to Grant when he said that some of the Union army's commanders considered the use of black troops the heaviest blow given to the Confederacy.

Before departing Paducah that afternoon, Grant ordered the general left in charge to make certain that the troops did not harm inoffensive citizens. The men were not to enter private dwellings or search any homes without the commander's permission. They were to abstain from plundering and avoid insulting individuals. When he arrived back in Cairo, he had a message from Fremont giving him permission to take Paducah if he thought he was strong enough. A few days later, when Fremont learned about Grant's message to the Kentucky legislature, he reprimanded Grant, and ordered him to leave all such matters in the future to him as department commander. Fremont should have commended him for sending an appropriate message at the right time.

Grant believed for the rest of his life that his occupation of Paducah prevented a Confederate force of nearly 4,000 men from marching into Paducah that day. Actually there was no such Confederate movement. At the time, Polk was satisfied with Columbus, and he made no move to seize Paducah.

Grant's forces soon occupied Smithland at the mouth of the Cumberland River, and when he went on the offensive on the Tennessee and Cumberland, his army flanked Columbus on the Mississippi, and the Confederate army withdrew from

it without a fight. For Grant and the Union, the occupation of Paducah was a win-win maneuver. Polk, in seizing what seemed the greater prize of Columbus, violated Kentucky neutrality first, paving the way for Grant to take Paducah inoffensively. And as it happened, Paducah was more significant.

* * *

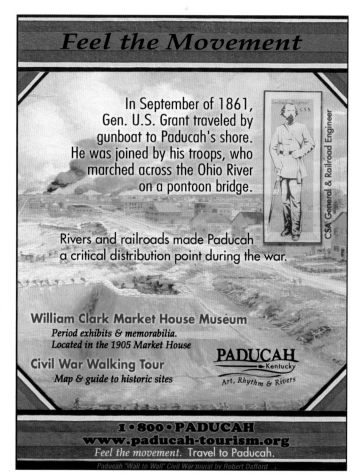

BARBOURVILLE

KENTUCKY'S FIRST CASUALTIES

By Charles Reed Mitchell

Battle of Barbourville Reenactment

On September 19, 1861, the first armed skirmish in Kentucky between the Union and Confederacy took place in Barbourville, 34 miles north of Confederate fortifications at Cumberland Gap. Earlier the same month in western Kentucky, Confederates had occupied strategic locations at Hickman and attempted to blockade the Mississippi River at Columbus, but the Knox County scene was the first encounter in which the heat of battle resulted in fatalities.

In August when the Union established a recruiting camp called Camp Dick Robinson in central Kentucky, the Confederate government declared Kentucky's neutrality violated. Southern commanders made plans to enter the state through Cumberland Gap and up the fabled Wilderness Road. Thought to be a vital invasion road by both sides, the Wilderness Road and its gateway, Cumberland Gap, suffered

four shifts of military occupation during the first two years of the war. As late as 1864 Ulysses S. Grant was examining the road as a possible invasion route.

Many East Tennesseans were crossing the mountain into Kentucky to join the Union. The occupation of Cumberland Gap and the swift movement of Confederate forces into eastern Tennessee made a Union recruiting station within that state's borders impossible. In early August, Samuel P. Carter and his brother James selected Barbourville as an alternative camp site to assemble eastern Tennesseans for service in the Union army.

Confederate Gen. Albert Sidney Johnston considered the Wilderness Road a direct route to strike at the heart of Kentucky's Bluegrass region and ordered Brig. Gen. Felix

By then Camp Andy Johnson had been quickly evacuated and most recruits sent north to Camp Dick Robinson. The Barbourville Home Guard gathered a force, from 150 to 300 men, to challenge the Confederate troops at Barbourville (or Tanyard) Bridge, which crossed a deep ravine a few yards south of present day Daniel Boone Drive and Cumberland Avenue. The Home Guard removed the bridge floorboards and watched the road.

An advance cavalry troop approached in the pre-dawn hours and exchanged gunshots with the Home Guard before retreating. Most of the Union volunteers also fled, leaving only some 20 or 30 Home Guard, under the command of either Dr. R.T. Tuggle or Capt. Isaac J. Black, to face the Confederate cavalry and army in the next day's morning fog.

Kirk Zollicoffer to cross the border into Kentucky and remove Kentucky's southernmost Union recruiting station. The Barbourville station was named "Camp Andy Johnson" for the Tennessee Senator who was the voice of the loyal Tennesseans in the U.S. Senate. Andrew Johnson was probably the most important loyal Tennessean working for Lincoln in that state during the early years of the war and would be his vice president in his second term.

Word had spread quickly in Barbourville after Gen. Zollicoffer began moving Confederate forces into Kentucky on September 9, 1861. The Confederates quickly established an advance post at Camp Buckner, near present-day Pineville. From there, some 18 miles from Barbourville, a detachment of 800 men commanded by Col. Joel A. Battle was ordered to remove the Union camp on September 19.

At dawn the few remaining Union soldiers fired at approaching Confederate cavalry and repulsed them twice before the Confederates realized that they could cross the gully above the bridge on the eastern side of town and sweep around behind the Home Guard. Observing the cavalry's movement and being greatly outnumbered, the Unionists fled up Little Richland Creek toward Cannon, had another encounter with Confederates there, then made their way to Camp Dick Robinson, where they were greeted as heroes, even in defeat.

Zollicoffer was pleased to write his commander, Gen. A.S. Johnston, to report the Confederate victory. He reported that during the 20-hour campaign 18 Federalists had been killed and two captured, an unknown number wounded, and that, "The enemy fled precipitously." He stated that he

had lost only two men; three wounded. (Local historians mention only two deaths at the battle of Barbourville Bridge, one on each side.)

The town was thoroughly ravaged by the invading Confederates, who captured the county tax records, hampering tax collection and court sessions for the first two years of the war.

Sgt. Eastham Tarrant of the 1st Kentucky Cavalry (better known as Frank Wolford's Wild Riders) was stationed at Camp Dick Robinson when the Barbourville Home Guard reached camp after the September 19 skirmish and had high compliments for those few who held their ground: "This was one of the most gallant fights, considering their isolated situation and the numbers against them, that took place during the war."

Zollicoffer's troops passed through Knox County on September 25 to engage Home Guards at Laurel Bridge near London and to take the Goose Creek Salt Works in Manchester. On October 19, 1861, Zollicoffer's troops again passed through Barbourville enroute to engage Union troops at Camp Wildcat under the command of Clay Countian Col. Theophilus Garrard on October 21.

* * *

Replica of Barbourville bridge

BATTLE OF CAMP WILDCAT
DISEASE AND FEVER CLAIMED MANY LIVES

By Steve Kickert, U.S. Forest Service

Tom Fugate

Camp Wildcat Reenactment, Laurel County

The Civil War lasted barely a month for Private Lewis McFerren of the Union Army. He died on the morning of October 21, 1861, less than 20 minutes into his first battle. He was one of 15 men listed as killed in the fight at Camp Wildcat, the first engagement of regular troops in Kentucky. Camp Wildcat was not one of the great battles of the Civil War; yet, for the inexperienced soldiers who faced the fire for the first time, it might as well have been Gettysburg.

The road to battle

In the summer of 1861, Kentucky was officially neutral, but both the North and South were recruiting soldiers from the state. The South was concerned that Union troops being recruited would invade east Tennessee. The North worried that Confederate troops would move into Kentucky in an effort to control the Bluegrass region, thereby gaining access to the Ohio River. The main artery of travel in eastern Kentucky was the Wilderness Road and control of this artery also meant control of the mountaineers whose sentiments were pro-Union.

In July of 1861, General Felix Zollicoffer assumed command of Confederate troops in Bristol, Tennessee. His task was to

General Felix Zollicoffer

organize regiments plagued by confusion and to prevent a Union invasion of east Tennessee. That same month in Kentucky, Colonel Theophilus Garrard, grandson of the former governor, was given command of a Union regiment that existed only on paper. He set up a recruiting station near his home town of Manchester and by the end of August he had enlisted nearly 1,000 men.

On September 9, Zollicoffer ordered his troops to move into Kentucky through the Cumberland Gap. Within 10 days, his 5,400 men took possession of the Cumberland Ford at Pineville, Kentucky, and defeated a group of home guard volunteers from the town of Barbourville.

On September 23 distressing news for Union forces reached Camp Dick Robinson near Lancaster, Kentucky, where Colonel Garrard was just beginning to assemble his regiment. Advanced units of Zollicoffer's forces had already reached the Laurel River outside London.

Garrard's poorly outfitted soldiers were rushed forward to the Wilderness Road and were ordered to guard a ford across

38

the Rockcastle River in the rugged Rockcastle Hills. The 1st Kentucky Cavalry, which was sent ahead of them, was also less than battle ready. Training had consisted of little more than instructions on how to shoot a musket. Garrard's troops established camp on a ridge three miles above the south side of the Rockcastle River at a fork in the road. It was named Camp Wildcat. On September 29, Garrard reported that the Laurel County Home Guard had been routed at Laurel River and were straggling into his camp. His report included evidence of the inadequate training of the new recruits.

"One of Wolford's men fired upon another of his own men, wounding Bailey in the arm and killing one horse and wounding another. The private who shot himself at camp ... died yesterday." The next day Garrard sent an urgent request asking for uniforms, blankets, and coats for his 975 men.

Colonel Theophilus Garrard

While Garrard was preparing Camp Wildcat, Confederate troops continued their push northward. Travel was slowed by a lack of forage and the poor conditions of the road. Later, in his report on the battle, General Zollicoffer wrote, "The country is so poor we had exhausted the forage on the road for 15 miles back in 24 hours." Still, by October 17 his entire force had reached the Laurel River.

Union troops came from Camp Dick Robinson, which was approximately 40 miles from Camp Wildcat. Confederate troops traveled nearly 60 miles from Cumberland Gap.

Reinforcements race to Wildcat

As Zollicoffer's troops advanced, Garrard's requests for aid became more desperate: "...if I do not receive more troops (I intend) to abandon this place...I have no idea of having my men butchered up here where they have a force of six to one...I would like to hear from you immediately."

On October 19, with time running out, Brig. Gen. Albin Schoepf was ordered to take command of Camp Wildcat. Coming with him were reinforcements Garrard had so urgently requested. Troops from the 33rd Indiana Infantry, 17th, 14th and 38th Ohio Infantries, and Battery B of the Ohio Light Artillery were ordered to move to the camp as quickly as possible. The 1st and 2nd East Tennessee (USA) were also enroute. In order to reach Wildcat before the Confederates, they had to negotiate roads so deep with mud that it reached the axles on their wagons.

Zollicoffer's force passed London on October 20, and advanced rapidly toward Garrard's undermanned position. Fortunately for Garrard, Union reinforcements began arriving late that morning. By nightfall, Camp Wildcat had a new commander and more than triple the number of troops that were present when the day began.

Tests of courage

"...it was their first battle. All their faces wore a serious expression. There was a shade of dread on all countenances, while some showed cool determination, others were excited and tremulous," wrote Eastham Tarrant, 1st Kentucky Cavalry.

Early on the morning of October 21, Confederate troops began making their way up wooded slopes toward a knob held by the 33rd Indiana Infantry. It later became known as "Hoosier Knob." The attack began about nine o'clock. It was not long until the woods were filled with the smell of gun powder and the cries of charging soldiers. Fire from both sides was intense. Ten minutes after the first rounds were exchanged, Union Colonel John Coburn, commander of the 33rd Indiana, received a glimpse of how many soldiers his men were facing. Coburn wrote, "They were in large numbers, and were over half-an-hour in passing by an open space in the woods."

As the fighting raged, the 1st Kentucky Cavalry came up to assist the Union troops. The men dismounted, but wavered and almost panicked before being rallied. Later, the 14th and 17th Ohio Infantry moved up and joined the battle. After an hour-and-a-half of fierce firing at close range, Confederate Colonel Tazwell Newman, who was leading the 17th Tennessee Infantry, ordered four of his companies to charge the Union position. They rushed up the hill with bayonets flashing. The Colonel described what happened next: "After fortification was reached and many of my men had got within the works...not receiving any support, and being nearly destitute of cartridges, I ordered my command to fall back."

A second offense was mounted in the afternoon. According to one account, Confederate forces, supported by artillery, made an attempt to move up the Wilderness Road toward Camp Wildcat but were repelled. A correspondent for the Cincinnati Gazette wrote, "Zolicoffer's attack was unsuccessful, simply because it came 24 hours too late."

Union forces spent that night fortifying their entrenchments for an attack that never came. Late in the night the sound of beating drums and moving Confederate wagons rose from the valley floor. When the sun rose, the valley was empty. Zollicoffer wrote, "Having reconnoitered in force under heavy fire for several hours from heights on the right, left, and front, I became satisfied that it could not be carried otherwise than by immense exposure...I deemed it proper the next day to fall back." The battle of Camp Wildcat was over.

Disease kills more than bullets

The inexperience of both Union and Confederate soldiers and the cover provided by the heavily wooded terrain helped keep the number of casualties low. General Schoepf reported four Union soldiers killed, 18 wounded. Zollicoffer reported 11 killed, 42 wounded or missing.

The aftermath of the battle proved more deadly than the assault itself. Measles and fever took a heavy toll. Twelve of 21 Union prisoners taken by General Zollicoffer died within six months. The 33rd Indiana alone lost 50 men to sickness and hundreds of others were reported ill within the few weeks of the battle. Like Private McFerren, their battles were over. For the rest of the country, the war lasted four more years.

Army units at Camp Wildcat

Union: 33rd Indiana Infantry, 1st Kentucky Calvary, 3rd (7th) Kentucky Volunteer Infantry, 17th Ohio Infantry, 14th Ohio Infantry, 38th Ohio Infantry, 1st Ohio Light Artillery, Battery B, 1st East Tennessee Infantry, 2nd East Tennessee Infantry, Kentucky Home Guard.

Confederate: 15th Mississippi Infantry, 11th Tennessee Infantry, 17th Tennessee Infantry, 29th Tennessee Infantry, 2nd Tennessee Cavalry, Tennessee Artillery Corps, Battery #1.

Wildcat Mountain today

Though the armies have long since disappeared, many of their trenches remain as reminders of what happened on that October day. If you stand quietly behind the trenches, you may feel your heart begin to pound just like the soldiers' hearts pounded in 1861.

The noise of the war has long since been replaced with the sounds of rustling leaves and singing birds. Still more than a hundred autumns have failed to bury the evidence of the violence that took place on that day in 1861. Entrenchments, gouged out with soldiers' bayonets and sweaty hands, still encircle the top of Hoosier Knob. A well maintained trail, lined with interpretive signs and towering cliffs, leads visitors from the parking area, up the steep slopes, to the site of some of the most intense fighting.

* * *

Camp Wildcat

Ohio Historical Society

40

Fort Duffield Played Prominent Role in Stopping Confederates from Taking Kentucky

By Mary Jo Harrod

Fort Duffield Reenactment, 2004

Though no major battle was ever fought in West Point, Kentucky, the area played a vital role in preventing the Confederate Army from claiming the state during the Civil War. Commenting on the importance of keeping Kentucky in the Union, President Abraham Lincoln said, "I think to lose Kentucky is nearly the same as to lose the whole game."

Rivers were the favored method of transportation for the area in the 1800s. Situated where the then navigable Salt River flowed into the Ohio River, West Point was known as a major boat town long before 1861. Supplies, after being unloaded from the steamboats, were transported to the south by wagons along the Louisville and Nashville Turnpike and the backroads. Union General William Tecumseh Sherman realized that protecting this turnpike – now his only supply route to his front-line troops – was critical.

In 1861, Sherman ordered Captain Nathanial Michler, a talented young topographical engineer, to travel to the historic town of West Point, Kentucky, to draw up the plans and oversee the construction of a fortification that is now known as Fort Duffield. Located on Muldraugh Hill (also known as Pearman Hill and Fort Hill), 300 feet above West Point, the 1,000-foot-long fort would also serve as General Sherman's headquarters.

Though the whereabouts of Captain Michler's plans or "blueprints" of Fort Duffield are unknown, they most certainly did exist. A walking tour brochure for Fort Duffield explains, "Civil War fortifications were precisely designed. Every angle, every mound of earth, and every slope you see in Fort Duffield had a specific purpose. The ten angles of the fort were designed to allow infantry or artillery to sweep every inch of ground in front of the fort. There were no 'dead spaces' where an attacking foe could take refuge." Captain Victor DeLand, Commander of Company C, 9th Michigan Infantry, stated in a letter that "every gun in the Fort will sweep the turnpikes and rivers with shot and shell for three miles."

Several thousand Union soldiers from the 37th Indiana, 9th Michigan Infantry and eventually the 1st Wisconsin, 1st Ohio, 18th Ohio Infantry, and 16th and 28th Kentucky regiments, using shovels and picks, created an intimidating military installation. With embankments and trenches on three sides and a sheer 300-foot cliff on the fourth side, Fort Duffield was not an easy target for the opposing army. Soldiers reported having to walk two miles away for firewood because the area around the fort was treeless and afforded no hiding places for an approaching army. Two large timbered gates hugged the cliff to provide maximum protection for the soldiers in the fort. The fort was so secure that when a request was made for locks to put on the gates, the quartermaster sent two toy locks as a joke.

Though Fort Duffield experienced no major military attacks, disease was a tremendous problem during the construction of the fort. The commander, Colonel William Duffield of the 9th Michigan regiment, wrote to his commanding officer, Adjutant General Robertson, in Michigan:

"November 14, 1861: Agreeable to your request I write of our whereabouts and condition. The measles have made bad havoc with us and this has been aggravated by the severe labor we have been compelled to perform in building roads and construction field works upon Muldraughs Hill. Our hospital contains over 300 men and I have taken possession of three houses [in West Point] for the hospital. The patients increase on our hands and I fear we will have to go through this before it stops." (*The Saga of Fort Duffield: Kentucky's Civil War Treasure,* by Richard A. Briggs, 1999, p. 29)

Pneumonia and typhoid were also a problem as long as the soldiers had to camp below the hill in the damp, muddy river flats. Built atop the westernmost point of the Allegheny Mountains, the completed fort became home to 1,000 Union soldiers by Christmas of 1861.

Soon after the soldiers moved into the elevated fortress, their health improved dramatically. One officer wrote that his "new camp was a paradise, with its pure air and water." By January 1, 1862, the soldiers in the fort were living in newly constructed cabins, which offered more protection from the winter weather.

The Union Army's supply line was now secure. Eventually, the war moved south and soldiers from Fort Duffield were sent to other areas. When the Civil War ended in 1865, Fort Duffield, having served its purpose, was abandoned, including the hilltop cemetery containing the 61 graves of soldiers who had succumbed to disease.

Around the time of World War I, Camp Knox was established in West Point, and included the old Civil War fort site. Camp Knox later became Fort Knox, a Federal military installation. Then in 1978, the land on Muldraugh Hill, where so many troops had been stationed to protect the Union Army's vital supply route, was deeded to the town of West Point by Fort Knox for use as a park.

With the town of West Point having a significant historical background of its own, accepting the donation of the overgrown Fort Duffield site was a natural thing to do. Since that time, volunteers have donated their time and money to restore and maintain the fort, with grassy slopes replacing dense thickets, construction of the type of cabins that were built during the Civil War, and an amphitheater for living

history demonstrations, and reenactments at various times of the year. Currently, volunteers are using money obtained from a grant to construct a pavilion at the base of the hill.

Today the fort is Kentucky's largest and best-preserved earthen fortress. Schoolchildren, tourists, and historians, alike, visit the fort and learn of the important role it played in the outcome of the American Civil War. Visitors marvel at the brilliant design of Fort Duffield, the breathtaking beauty of the panoramic river views, and the tranquility of the Memorial Hill Cemetery. Fort Duffield is on the National Register of Historic Places and the Civil War Trust's Civil War Discovery Trail.

The Annual Civil War Days is held annually during Memorial Day Weekend in May. The Living History Program is held on Labor Day Weekend.

* * *

Fort Duffield guides

Ivy Mountain

Confederate Recruiters Forced to Withdraw

By Lisa Gaines Matthews

Brig. Gen. William T. Sherman, Union commander

During the summer of 1861, Union and Confederate recruiters opened training camps in Kentucky, despite the state's position of neutrality. Camp Beauregard (CSA) was established in western Kentucky; Camp Dick Robinson (US) was located south of Lexington; Camp Andy Johnson (US) inducted recruits near Barbourville; and Camp Wildcat was established near London.

Eastern Kentucky was a fertile recruiting ground for the Confederacy as many residents traced their lineage from ancestors in Virginia. Near West Liberty, Confederate sympathizer Capt. Jack May was instrumental in forming a recruiting camp for the Morgan County Guards. Union positions had already been established in Louisa and Catlettsburg, the northern reach of the Big Sandy River basin. May decided that the mountainous region around Prestonsburg would offer greater security to his men and the Confederate recruiting effort so the Guards moved to land owned by his cousin, William James May, just north of Prestonsburg. By the end of September, thousands of Confederate recruits streamed through Prestonsburg, on their way to southwestern Virginia.

In October, 1861, Captain May learned that the Union was amassing troops in Maysville. The Morgan County Guards returned to West Liberty and were mustered into the Confederate army as Company A of the 5th Kentucky Infantry, under the command of Col. John S. Williams. Union Gen. William T. Sherman, military commander of the Department of the Cumberland in Louisville, ordered Gen. William Nelson, in Maysville, to proceed south and drive the Confederates out of the Big Sandy region. A skirmish ensued at West Liberty on October 23 and the 5th Kentucky Infantry was forced to pull back to Prestonsburg.

The Confederates were well aware that the Union mission was to remove them from eastern Kentucky. Ammunition was low which forced a further Confederate evacuation to Pikeville. Williams realized that retreat to Virginia was essential and dispatched 1,000 men of the 5th Kentucky Infantry and two cavalry units to create enough of a diversion to allow the retreat. Capt. May chose a position at Ivy Narrows, along the road between Prestonsburg and Pikeville. The road narrowed at a bend in the Big Sandy River and the steep banks of Ivy Mountain further confined any troop movement to single file. The Confederates concealed themselves behind hastily constructed breastworks and in a cornfield on the other side of the river. The plan was to ambush the Union troops as they made their way through the narrowing road toward Pikeville.

Gen. Nelson had captured Prestonsburg without a fight on November 5. He was considering a two-pronged attack on Pikeville when Union scouts reported that they had discovered the Confederate position at Ivy Mountain. On November 8, Nelson positioned two of his six cannon on the bank of the big Sandy and began to bombard the Confederate positions. A Union regiment was ordered to ascend Ivy Mountain and take a position above the Confederates. Another Union regiment was ordered to commit to a full frontal assault.

At 1:30pm rifle shots were exchanged and the Battle of Ivy Mountain was fully engaged. The Confederates held their position for about an hour until a third regiment of Union troops joined the fray. Confederate casualties were 263 killed or wounded, while Union losses only amounted to 30 men. Gen. Nelson decided not to pursue the enemy through Pound Gap on their way to Abingdon, Virginia and, after occupying Pikeville for a week, the Union force withdrew.

The Battle of Ivy Mountain was the first Union victory in eastern Kentucky. The Battle of Middle Creek on January 10, 1862, would solidify Union control of the region but the earlier battle near Pikeville demonstrated to Confederate planners that the Union was willing to commit troops to thwart Confederate recruiting efforts and would move swiftly against any attempt to establish a Confederate presence in eastern Kentucky.

Col. John S. Williams (CSA)

CAPTAIN JACK MAY
AN EASTERN KENTUCKY FAVORITE SON

By Lisa Gaines Matthews

Captain Jack May

At the turn of the 19th century, settlers eager for inexpensive western land surged into Kentucky. John and Sarah May, previously of western North Carolina and eastern Tennessee, arrived on the banks of Shelby Creek in eastern Kentucky in 1800. Their son, Samuel, was seventeen years old at the time of this move. After helping his father establish a farm, Samuel purchased three Prestonsburg town lots in 1807. In 1808, he married Catherine Evans. The marriage produced fourteen children, of which Andrew Jackson May, was the fourth son and twelfth child.

Andrew Jackson May was born on January 28, 1829. He was educated at Prestonsburg Academy. Prestonsburg grew rapidly in the 1830s. In 1837 the first steamboat docked in Prestonsburg and in 1841, Richard Deering started the first coal mine in the region. In 1849, Samuel May built the first steam-powered saw mill and grist mill on his land. During the 1840s, the Mount Sterling-Pound Gap road was begun. This road linked farmers of the Bluegrass region to the markets of southwest Virginia. Today, this road is U.S. 460, Ky. 114 and Ky. 80, which links Mount Sterling, West Liberty, Salyersville, Prestonsburg and Pikeville to Elkhorn City.

In 1849, Jack followed his father to California, two of many men bitten by the gold bug during the Gold Rush. Samuel May died in February, 1851, and Jack returned to Prestonsburg. After reading for the law, Jack was licensed to practice in 1854. He married Matilda Davidson in 1855 and set up a law office in West Liberty, Kentucky.

By September 1861, the Civil War reached Kentucky when Confederates established base camps in Columbus, Bowling Green and Prestonsburg. Union troops were stationed in Paducah, Louisville, Cincinnati, Maysville and Louisa. Many eastern Kentucky men, who traced their roots to Virginia, were sympathetic to the Southern cause. It is unclear from the record why Jack counted himself a secessionist, but his grandfather, John, had been born in Martinsburg, Virginia.

In September, Jack closed his law office and began organizing the Morgan County Guards in West Liberty. It was soon decided to move the Guards to Prestonsburg. On October 2, 1861, Captain Jack May wrote a letter to Confederate president, Jefferson Davis. In this letter he states, "Our legislature has betrayed us." He announced that 1,000 men were already in Prestonsburg and promised a contingent of 5,000 "in two weeks."

Captain May and the Morgan County Guards were assimilated into the Confederate Kentucky 10th Infantry. On October 23, a Union army under Gen. William "Bull" Nelson left Maysville to drive the Confederates out of eastern Kentucky. Prestonsburg was captured on November 4 and The Battle of Ivy Mountain, between Prestonsburg and Pikeville, took place on November 5-6. The Confederates were forced to retreat into Virginia but Union sympathizers in the region were alarmed when the Gen. Nelson and his army returned to Maysville.

After the Battle of Ivy Mountain, Captain May was awarded a number of field promotions. As a colonel, he organized the 10th Kentucky Cavalry in late 1862. He continued to serve the Confederate army until 1864, when he resigned his commission due to illness. After the Civil War, he resumed his law career in Tazewell, Virginia, and he died in 1903.

* * *

Ivy Mountain Monument Dedication

BATTLE OF ROWLETT'S STATION

By Bryan Bush

Battle of Green River

In mid September 1861, Confederate General Albert Sidney Johnston, commander of the Western Department No. 2, ordered Confederate forces to take Bowling Green, Kentucky. On October 28, Johnston moved his headquarters from Nashville, Tennessee, to Bowling Green. Johnston's Confederate line stretched from Columbus, Kentucky, to Somerset, Kentucky, and the Federals did not take long to test it.

In November 1861, Union General Ulysses S. Grant attacked Belmont, Kentucky. The Federal forces were not able to take Columbus. During that same month, Union General Don Carlos Buell began to concentrate his forces in the direction of Bowling Green, and Union General George Thomas was moving towards Somerset.

General Benjamin Terry

In early December 1861, Johnston ordered Confederate General Benjamin Terry and the 8th Texas Cavalry to help support General Thomas Hindman's brigade. The command consisted of 300 cavalry, four pieces of artillery, and two regiments of Arkansas Infantry. Johnston heard rumors that the Federals were planning to repair the Green River bridge at Munfordville, Kentucky, so that they might be able to cross over the river to reach Bowling Green. General Hindman, along with the Texas Rangers, moved out for the Green River, reaching Woodsonville.

General Thomas Hindman

When Hindman reached the stream he found the Unionists on the north bank of the Green River. Hindman deployed some infantry skirmishers, who engaged the enemy at long range, but with little effect. Hindman decided to ride to the front, where he left Col. Terry in charge with instructions to decoy the Union men up the hill and away from support to a point where the Confederate infantry and artillery could be used to better advantage. The Unionists allowed themselves to be decoyed. Terry sent Capt. Stephen C. Ferrell, commander of Company D, with 75 men against their left. Terry led the rest against the right. Ferrell and his men, yelling, each man riding as fast as his horse could carry him, charged the skirmishers of the 32nd Indiana Volunteers. The Texans got within 20 yards and opened fire with their rifles and revolvers.

As the story goes, while Terry was watching Ferrell, another Federal party was hiding in a blackjack thicket, and opened fire on Terry's men. Terry yelled out, "Charge, my brave boys, charge!" and taking the lead, Terry dashed toward the thicket. The Unionists broke and ran. But after a few moments, Terry noticed a small group of Unionists in some bushes a short distance away and he called, "Yonder is a nest of birds." Terry and five men charged the men in the bush. Terry shot two of them with his pistol. One man remained, who raised his pistol, and fired point blank into Terry's face. The bullet came out at the back of his head. Capt. Evans of the Texas Rangers was reported to have shot the last Unionist.

Meanwhile, Ferrell continued to lead his force into an open field against the body of Union soldiers, who rallied behind a makeshift breastwork made from straw stacks and fences. They were pouring musket fire into the Rangers' ranks. A disorderly charge of undrilled men was sent into one of the best drilled regiments, the 32nd Indiana Infantry. Col. August Willich reported that

Colonel August Willich

the fight now became the "most earnest and bloody part of the struggle. With lightening speed, under infernal yelling, great numbers of Texas Rangers rushed upon our whole force. They advanced to 15 or 20 yards of our lines, some of them even between them and opened fire with rifles and revolvers. Our skirmishers took the thing very coolly, and permitted them to approach very close, then they opened a destructive fire on them. They were repulsed with severe loss, but only after Lt. Sachs, who left his covered position with one platoon, was surrounded by about 50 Rangers, several of them demanding of him three times to give up his sword and let his men lay down their arms. He firmly refused and defended himself till he fell with three of his men, before the attack was repulsed.

"Lt. Col. Von Trebra now led on another advance of the center and left flank, when he drew down upon his forces a second attack of the Rangers in large numbers, charging into the very ranks, some dashing through to the rear. In the fight participated three field officers, one staff and 16 officers of the line, 23 sergeants and 375 men. Our loss is one officer and 10 men dead, 22 wounded and five missing." Ranger losses were four killed and eight wounded.

In mid January of 1862 Private August Bloedner of the 32nd Indiana placed a memorial for his comrades killed in action at the Battle of Rowlett's Station, at Fort Willich, in Munfordville, Kentucky. On June 6, 1867, 14 bodies, along with the monument, were moved to Cave Hill Cemetery in Louisville, Kentucky, where it remains to this day.

Captain John Walker, of the Eighth Texas, and those who were able to travel, escorted Col. Terry's body to Nashville, Tennessee, to the State Capitol where funeral services were held. The Legislature, Masonic fraternity and the military paid Terry their final respects.

Terry's body was put on a train and taken to Texas. When his body arrived in Houston a large military escort and a regimental band joined the Masons of Holland Lodge #1 and formed a procession that occupied 12 blocks. They accompanied Terry's body to the Tap and Harrisburg Depot and then to his plantation in Sugar Land. In 1880, Terry's body was moved to Houston.

* * *

Confederate destruction of the Bacon Creek Bridge, Hart County

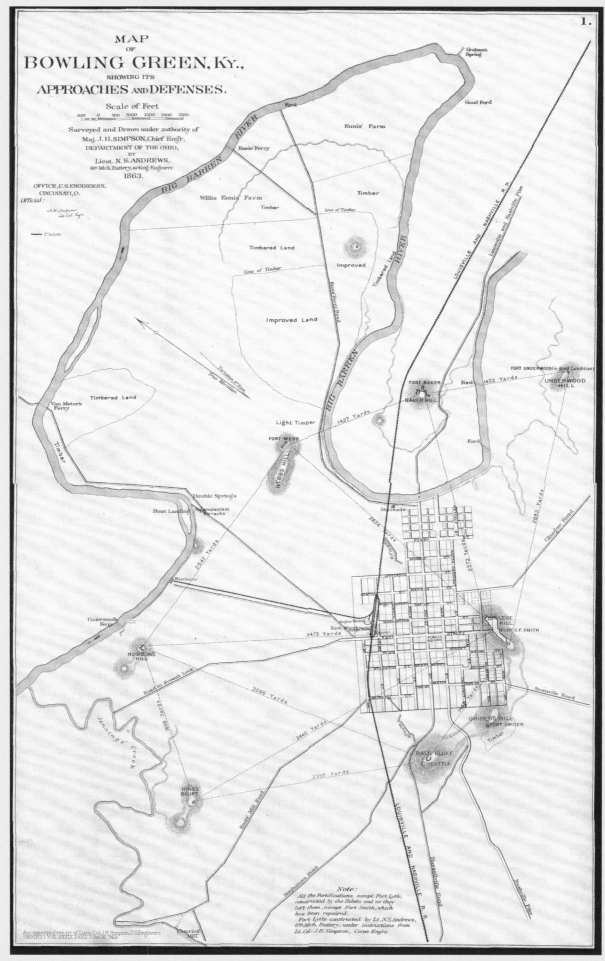

MAP
OF
BOWLING GREEN, KY.,
SHOWING ITS
APPROACHES AND DEFENSES.

Scale of Feet.

Surveyed and Drawn under authority of
Maj. J. H. SIMPSON, Chief Engr.
DEPARTMENT OF THE OHIO,
BY
Lieut. N. S. ANDREWS,
6th Mich. Battery, acting Engineer.
1863.

OFFICE, U.S. ENGINEERS,
CINCINNATI, O.
Official:

Note:
All the Fortifications, except Fort Lytle,
constructed by the Rebels and as they
left them, except Fort Smith, which
has been repaired.
Fort Lytle constructed by Lt. N.S. Andrews,
6th Mich. Battery, under instructions from
Lt. Col. J. H. Simpson, Corps Engrs.

1.

Defenses around the Confederate Capital
The Civil War in Bowling Green, Kentucky

By Dr. L. Michael Trapasso

Bowling Green, Kentucky – Rebel damage

When hostilities began in April, 1861, both Union and Confederate combatants viewed the neutral and border state of Kentucky as an important prize. Both sides prepared for entry into the State almost simultaneously, with the same motivation. By mid-September, both armies had entered and secured strongholds in various regions of the Commonwealth.

Federal forces easily occupied Louisville, Kentucky; Cincinnati, Ohio; Evansville, Indiana; and other cities sympathetic to the Union cause. On 6 September 1861, Union General Ulysses S. Grant took Paducah, Kentucky. Once there, Grant continued to recruit and train his army and joined forces with U.S. Naval Flag Officer Andrew Foote, who was assembling a flotilla for assaults along major river routes.

Prior to this time, Kentucky-born, West Point-trained, Confederate General Albert Sidney Johnston was placed in command of the "Confederate Department Number 2." This region was comprised of a line extending from the Appalachians in the East, to the Indian Territory to the West. A Confederate army of about 40,000 men was stationed at strategic points along this line in southern Kentucky. The

major locations were Pikeville in the east, Bowling Green in central Kentucky, and Columbus in the west.

Under Johnston's command, fellow Kentuckian and West Point graduate, General Simon Bolivar Buckner entered the city of Bowling Green on 17 September 1861, with some 4,000 to 5,000 troops. Buckner's troops immediately overwhelmed the civilian population of about 2,500, and began building fortified positions on all the available high ground surrounding the city. In addition, he built earthwork defenses at major roads, railway crossings and river fords.

The presence of such a force certainly affected local political sentiment. Safely behind fortified Confederate lines, a "Sovereignty Convention" was held in Russellville, Kentucky, on 20 November 1861. There, Bowling Green was designated as the capital of the newly-declared "free and independent State of Kentucky." A gentleman farmer by the name of George Johnson was elected as the governor and soon took up residence in the new capital city.

In addition to its role as capital and military stronghold, Bowling Green was a vital link in Kentucky's central corridor. The L & N Railroad was one of the few north-south rail lines at the time. Running almost parallel to the tracks, the

Louisville and Nashville Pikes represented the major north-south road system. This added to the other five roads radiating out from Bowling Green to surrounding communities. Both modes of transportation criss-crossed Bowling Green, which was a port city on the (then navigable) Big Barren River. In Albert Sidney Johnston's opinion, the deciding battle for Kentucky would take place in Bowling Green.

As these fortifications took shape, Bowling Green earned the sobriquet "The Gibraltar of the West." During the Civil War, there were several sites which earned the nickname "Gibraltar," and Bowling Green was among the first. A Union officer who inspected the forts after the Confederate evacuation, found it difficult to believe the Southerners could have completed such a vast works during their short occupation. "The labor has been immense; their troops cannot be well drilled, their time has been chiefly spent in hard work with axe and spade," he reported.

Beginning in January 1862, Eastern Kentucky began to fall under the control of the Federal army. On 10 January, Union Colonel James Garfield (later President of the United States) defeated Confederate General Humphrey Marshall at Middle Creek, near Prestonsburg.

On 19 January, the army of Union Generals A. Schoepf and George Thomas soundly defeated Generals George Crittenden and Felix Zollicoffer's Confederates at Mill Springs, Kentucky. Gen. Zollicoffer was killed and his army routed in this battle, also known as "Logan's Crossroads" or "Fishing Creek."

In early to mid-February 1862, the combined army and navy operations by Grant and Flag-officer A.H. Foote won Union victories at Forts Henry (6 February), and Donelson (14-16 February), in Tennessee. These actions effectively placed the Tennessee and Cumberland Rivers, respectively, into Union hands.

With the Federals in control of these rivers to the south, in addition to their strong presence to the west, north, and east, Bowling Green and the rest of Kentucky became untenable. Evacuation was imminent. So in essence, the Confederate State of Kentucky collapsed around the well-fortified capital city.

The Battle of Bowling Green
On 13 February 1862, Union Major General Don Carlos Buell, in command of the Army of the Ohio in Louisville, ordered Brigadier General Ormsby Mitchel to advance upon Bowling Green. Mitchel's forces were positioned some 40 miles to the north on the Green River. Moving south on the Louisville Pike, Mitchel's advance column drove back a half-dozen or so cavalry pickets (Terry's Texas Rangers).

Confederate Generals Hardee and Hindman sent a message to Mitchel stating, "Give us six hours, and we shall give you Bowling Green." To which Mitchel responded, "I will not give you six minutes," and immediately began to unlimber his artillery at Fort Baker. This abandoned fort was the only one located north of the Big Barren River. The Confederates had already burned the bridges and the train trestle over the river. Under Union artillery fire, they burned the train station, warehouses, and military supplies in Bowling Green before retreating to Nashville, Tennessee.

On approaching the city, one Union infantryman commented to his comrades, "That big black plume of smoke out there is Bowling Green!" (No less than 37 fires had to be extinguished by the incoming Federals.) The bombardment continued until a few citizens were seen on the opposite

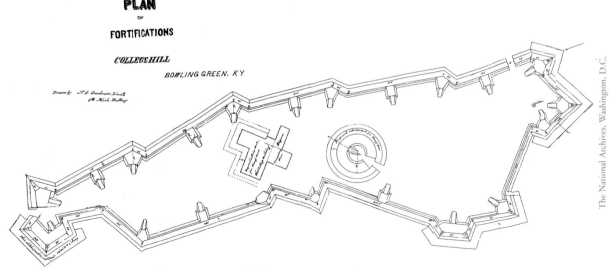

Fort C.F. Smith was constructed of limestone-covered earthen walls, atop College Hill, and was the largest of Bowling Green's eight forts.

riverbank announcing the Confederates were gone. From that point until the end of the war, the Union Army controlled Kentucky, Bowling Green, and the fortifications left behind by the Confederate Army.

Though no real battle for Bowling Green ever took place, these sites are still considered "hallowed ground." Disease, the primary killer during the war, ravaged the city. Epidemic illnesses such as typhoid, measles, dysentery, scurvy, pneumonia, and influenza claimed one-tenth of the Confederate forces, and thousands of lives during the war, in the seemingly impregnable "Gibraltar of the West."

Bowling Green During the War

Throughout the war, Bowling Green maintained its role as a vital transportation hub. The L & N Railroad once again ran from Louisville through to Nashville. Likewise the Louisville and Nashville Pikes continued to allow road traffic to flow as did boat traffic on the Big Barren River.

At any given time however, there were only a few thousand troops garrisoned at Bowling Green. The remainder of the Union forces in the area were utilized to protect the major roads and railways, and pursue of marauding bands of Confederate raiders and independent guerrilla forces.

Architectural plans from the National Archives in Washington, D.C., indicate many barracks were constructed during the war. Bowling Green was an important recruitment center for both white and colored troops. An inordinate amount of stables and corrals suggests the gathering and training of large numbers of horses and mules. Bowling Green was also the location of many hospitals, indicating that it was a major convalescent center for the Union Army. Certain building layouts also locate bakeries where hard tack was baked for the Union Army.

It is quite ironic that, though heavily fortified, the city of Bowling Green never sustained a serious attack by either side. In essence it was a city preparing for a battle that never came. It is believed, however, that these fortifications may have acted as a strong deterrent to attack. During the Confederate invasion of Kentucky in late summer of 1862, culminating with the Battle of Perryville, neither Generals Braxton Bragg nor Edmund Kirby Smith took a route through Bowling Green. Throughout his many raids General John Hunt Morgan also stayed clear of Bowling Green's guns. Untouched for the duration of the war, the city remained a vital transportation hub, and a center of activity for the Union Army.

* * *

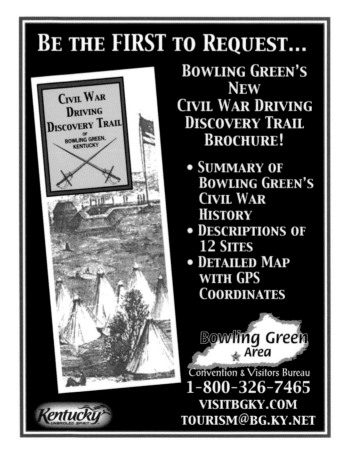

HARPER'S WEEKLY.

A JOURNAL OF CIVILIZATION.

Vol. VII.—No. 358.]   NEW YORK, SATURDAY, NOVEMBER 7, 1863.   [SINGLE COPIES SIX CENTS.
[$3.00 PER YEAR IN ADVANCE.

Entered according to Act of Congress, in the Year 1863, by Harper & Brothers, in the Clerk's Office of the District Court for the Southern District of New York.

THE ARMY OF THE CUMBERLAND—A TROOP TRAIN PASSING THROUGH THE BIG CUT ON THE LOUISVILLE AND NASHVILLE RAILROAD.—[SEE PAGE 711.]

Kentucky's Railroad Network, 1861

By Charles H. Bogart

The War Between the States was the first war to see railroads used as a component of the overall strategy of warfare. Railroads were the arteries of supply that fed the armies and allowed them to fight their campaigns. The length and scope of the fighting during the period 1861 to 1865 would have been impossible without the

The Frankfort, Kentucky LF&L depot, circa 1860

railroads. Thus one major factor in understanding the strategy of both sides during the war is to understand what railroads were available for use in a particular theater of campaign. Numerous maps, both contemporary and modern, have been published showing the rail net of the United States in 1861. Most of these maps contain small to major errors. The following will be an accounting of the 14 railroads operating in or into Kentucky in 1861.

First it must be pointed out that in 1861 railroads were built to whatever gauge the promoters thought was best for their railroad. The general rule was to build your railroad to a gauge different than a competitor so those goods had to be transloaded between railroads. Track gauge is measured in distance between the inside of the track's two rails. Rail gauge in 1861 ran the gauntlet from 3' 6" to 6'. The most common gauge was 4' 8.5" and this gauge was generally found North of the Ohio River. South of the Ohio, the preferred gauge was 5'. Today, the standard gauge is 4' 8.5". Gauge wider than standard gauge is called "broad gauge" and smaller, "narrow gauge."

Extending southward from Covington to Nicholasville was the Kentucky Central Railroad Association's 5-foot gauge track. This line was referred to as the Kentucky Central Railroad, a title that was but a marketing ploy. The Kentucky Central (KC) consisted of three separate lines selling rail service under a common banner. Extending south from Covington to Paris was the Covington & Lexington (C&L). This connected to the railroads terminating in Cincinnati via wagons that crossed the Ohio on ferryboats. At Paris the C&L joined with the Maysville and Lexington for the run to Lexington. At Lexington the rails of the the Lexington & Danville (L&D) extended the line to Nicholasville.

South of Nicholasville the L&D had been in the process of bridging the Kentucky River at Wilmore when the company ran out of money in 1860. In 1863 the Union investigated extending the KC to Somerset and on to Knoxville, Tennessee. Cost and time to build the line ruled out its construction. Today, the track from Covington to Paris is operated by CSX, formerly Louisville & Nashville railroad (L&N). The track between Paris and Lexington was abandoned by the L&N in 1951. The rails between Lexington and Nicholasville were acquired by the Cincinnati Southern Railway and are now part of the Norfolk Southern Railway system.

Tying Lexington to Louisville were two railroads. The track between Lexington and Frankfort had been laid by the Lexington & Ohio Railroad (L&O). The L&O was the second oldest railroad west of the Appalachian Mountains. Construction had started on the line in 1832. Its original terminus was on a hill above Frankfort at what is now Kentucky State University. In 1848 the L&O went into receivership and was reorganized as the Lexington & Frankfort Railroad (Le&F). A new right-of-way was constructed from Jett into downtown Frankfort using Vaughn Branch to reach the Kentucky River. A tunnel was then dug under the State Arsenal to provide direct access into Frankfort.

In 1850 the Louisville & Frankfort (Lo&F) reached Frankfort from Louisville. It entered into Frankfort by crossing the Kentucky River on a suspension bridge that had to be rebuilt in 1855 with piers to support the weight of an engine. Both the LEX&F and the LOU&F were built to 4' 8.5" gauge and provided through service under the marketing facade of the Lexington, Frankfort & Louisville railroad. (LF&L). In 1863 Union authorities ordered the LF&L to convert its track to 5'-gauge. Its tracks were then tied to the KC in Lexington and the L&N in Louisville. This allowed trains to run through from Covington to Louisville and then on to Nashville. This line is now operated by R.J. Corman Railroad.

Running south of Louisville was what was to become the most important railroad in the western theater of operations, the Louisville & Nashville Railroad (L&N). Construction on this line started in 1850 with the goal of tying the two cities together. This 5-foot gauge track work was finished to Nashville in 1860 but there was no rail connection to Indiana. Two branch lines extended eastward from the L&N mainline. The Bardstown & Louisville Railroad (B&L) was leased by the L&N during the was to connect it to Bardstown. From Lebanon Junction, the L&N Lebanon branch ran to Lebanon. This line was originally a planned route to the Atlantic seaboard but never got beyond eastern Kentucky. The L&N mainline is now operated by CSX. The Bardstown line is currently the property of R.J. Corman Railroad, and the Lebanon Branch, which terminates in Lebanon, is now owned by the Kentucky Railroad Museum.

Extending westward from Memphis Junction, south of Bowling Green, was the L&N Memphis line. It ended at Guthrie on the Kentucky-Tennessee line. Due to a quirk in Tennessee law, the line from Guthrie to Memphis was operated by the Memphis, Clarksville & Louisville Railroad. This rail line, while it offered easy rail service from the north to Memphis, soon fell into disfavor due to its exposure to Confederate attacks. During the months leading up to the firing on Fort Sumter and for a few months thereafter, both the L&N mainline and the Memphis Branch were used to move large quantities of goods south from northern markets. The Memphis Branch is now owned by R.J. Corman Railroad and has been abandoned west of Clarksville, Tennessee.

Joining the Memphis Branch at Guthrie was the Edgefield and Kentucky Railroad. This line was projected to reach Henderson, but had stalled a few miles north of Guthrie in 1861. The line was to be completed to Henderson in 1871 by the Evansville, Henderson & Nashville Railroad. This line was then bought by the L&N and today is part of CSX.

Western Kentucky had three railroads crossing its territory. Heading south from Paducah toward Fulton was the New Orleans & Ohio Railroad. By 1861, it had proceeded a few miles south of Mayfield. Here it stalled until after the war when it was finished to Fulton. It later became part of the Illinois Central Railroad and today is operated by the Paducah & Louisville Railroad. The line has been cut back from Fulton to Mayfield.

Running South out of Columbus for its terminal at New Orleans was Mobile & Ohio Railroad (M&O). This 5-foot gauge road connected itself to Cairo, Illinois, with a ferry that transported the railcars. Completed in 1861, this line, like the L&N, moved heavy volumes of goods south in the month before and after the firing on Ft. Sumter. Expected to play a major role in the northern advance down the Mississippi River, the railroad turned out to be a minor player in the logistical war. It was too exposed to attacks by Confederate raiders, and the necessary Union manpower to defend it was not available. Instead, the paralleling Mississippi River carried all the goods that the M&O was expected to carry. The M&O later became part of the Illinois Central Railroad and was abandoned in the 1980s.

Based at Hickman was the Nashville & Northwest Railroad (N&N). Its purpose was to extend the reach of the port of Hickman into Central Tennessee. Built to 5-foot gauge it played a minor, but important part in the war. The N&N, like the M&O, moved considerable northern goods inland, into Tennessee, from steamboats landing at Hickman during the months before the Confederates seized Columbus, Kentucky. The N&N fell into Union hands and helped supply troops in western Tennessee when the Tennessee and Cumberland Rivers were not navigable due to low water. After the war the line became part of the Nashville, Chattanooga & St. Louis Railroad and was abandoned in 1951.

Two other railroads served Kentucky. Both were of little importance to the overall strategic use of railroads in Kentucky. The Breckinridge Railroad in Breckinridge County ran from the Ohio River, 8.5 miles to a coal mine. The mine shut down during the war and no traffic moved over the road. This line was abandoned for good in 1893. The Lexington and Big Sandy (L&BS) ran from Ashland to Coalton where a coal mine was located. The L&BS was of considerable importance in supplying coal to the iron furnaces and auxiliary industries in the Ashland/Ironton area during the war. In the 1880s the line was extended to Lexington and became part of the Chesapeake & Ohio Railway. During the 1980s the line was controlled by CSX which abandoned the line west of Coalton.

It needs to be mentioned that the L&N Glasgow Branch which runs from Glasgow Junction to Glasgow, Kentucky, was once owned by the L&N. It was projected to be built in 1861, but was not constructed until 1867. It is now part of the CSX.

Kentucky's Civil War railroad network was thus not as extensive as the other states, yet the Union's march from the Ohio River to Nashville, Chattanooga, Atlanta and Savannah could not have happened without the rail supply line based in Louisville, Kentucky. Lincoln' statement, "I hope to have God on my side but I must have Kentucky," sums up the importance of Kentucky's rail system to the Union.

* * *

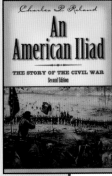
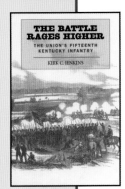

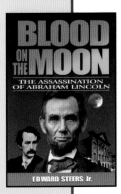

VICTORY AT MIDDLE CREEK

By Lisa Gaines Matthews

Col. James Garfield

Kentuckians do not usually associate Ohio native and 20th President of the United States James Garfield with the history of the Commonwealth. In the early stages of the Civil War in Kentucky, however, Col. Garfield played a pivotal role in Union success by leading the 18th Brigade of the Army of the Ohio against the Army of Southwestern Virginia under Brig. Gen. Humphrey Marshall at the Battle of Middle Creek, near Prestonsburg.

Marshall had been ordered back into Kentucky to continue the recruitment of troops, which had been abandoned by Col. John Williams after the Battle of Ivy Mountain. Eastern Kentucky not only offered the prospect of filling the rank and file, but was also the site of the strategically important Cumberland Gap, a main transportation route for the region.

James Abram Garfield was born on November 19, 1831 in Cuyahoga County, Ohio. His father, Abram, died in 1834, leaving a wife and five children to fend for themselves in a frontier setting. James balanced work with learning to read and, at the age of 16, went to Cleveland to pursue a career as a sailor. He was unsuccessful in being hired by a commercial sailing company but did secure work leading the horses that pulled boats along the canal between Cleveland and Pittsburgh. His career ended abruptly when he became ill with malaria and he returned home to recuperate.

Garfield dreamed of becoming a teacher. Upon recovery, he enrolled in Geauga Seminary in Chester, Ohio, and went on to complete his courses at Western Reserve Eclectic Institute. His studies prepared him for the college level and he entered Williams College in Massachusetts in 1854. He graduated in 1856 and returned to Ohio to teach at the Eclectic Institute. Within a year he was named the president of that school.

By the time of his return to Ohio, Garfield had aligned himself with the Republican Party. Founded in 1854, this party opposed the spread of slavery into the western territories and stood for preserving the Union at any cost. The bitter debate between proponents of a strong Union vs. states rights had raged since the Compromise of 1820. Garfield abhorred slavery, attended meetings held by avowed abolitionists and

above all believed in the United States. As a Republican candidate, he won a seat in the Ohio Senate in 1859.

When the war of words became a military reality in 1861, James A. Garfield was appointed Colonel of the 42nd Ohio Volunteer Infantry by Gov. William Dennison. The regiment was organized and trained at Camp Chase, near Columbus, Ohio, between September and November, 1861. Garfield had no military experience but drilled his men using borrowed military textbooks. By mid-December the 42nd was attached to the 18th Brigade of the Army of the Ohio. The 18th had been ordered to Louisa, Ky., via Catlettsburg by Gen. Don Carlos Buell for the purpose of driving Gen. Humphrey Marshall and his army from eastern Kentucky.

The 40th Ohio Infantry Regiment had already left Lexington for Prestonsburg in order to prevent a Confederate retreat. At Louisa, the 42nd Ohio Infantry, and the 14th and 22nd Kentucky Infantries met up with the 1st Ohio, 1st Kentucky and 2nd West Virginia Cavalry regiments. On January 7, 1862, the 2nd West Virginia skirmished with Confederate cavalry as the brigade moved southward on Marshall's headquarters in Paintsville.

Brig. Gen. Humphrey Marshall

With the Union approaching, Marshall abandoned Paintsville and established defensive positions around the forks of Middle Creek, near Prestonsburg. The forks of the creek were well suited for defense as troops could be situated along the hills overlooking the creek and facing the approaching Union force. Difficult marching conditions and cold weather impeded the 18th but by January 9, 1862, 1,700 Union troops prepared to attack the 2,000 well-placed but hungry and ill-equipped Confederates.

Before dawn on January 10, Garfield's men marched to the mouth of Middle Creek. The Confederates were arranged in a battle line to the west and south of the creek. Marshall had placed the 29th Virginia Infantry and the 5th Kentucky Infantry on his right wing overlooking the creek. Capt. William C. Jeffress' artillery battery held the center and the 54th Virginia Infantry was positioned, in reserve, on a hill behind the artillery.

As Jeffress would soon discover, the effort of hauling four artillery pieces, weighing either 884 or 1,227 pounds each, from Virginia into Kentucky would prove frustratingly futile. The guns and ammunition were vintage 1841 and damp storage conditions took their toll on the gunpowder in the shells. Early in the battle, the cannons were fired and briefly checked Garfield's skirmish line. However, once the Union commander realized that the shells were poorly aimed and did not detonate, his troops were urged on with the confidence that there was no danger from explosion or shrapnel. Garfield sent the 40th and 42nd Ohio Infantry units across the creek to engage the 29th Virginia. Once this aspect of the battle began, he sent the 14th and 22nd Kentucky Infantry units against the 5th Kentucky Infantry, under Col. John S. Williams.

The Confederates doggedly maintained their positions throughout the afternoon but as the sun set they began to retreat up the hill at their backs. Marshall feared that his demoralized men might desert so he ordered his heavier weapons burned and withdrew his army along the left fork of Middle Creek to the Joseph Gearhart farm, where food and fodder awaited. By January 24th the Army of Southwestern Virginia had returned to Virginia. Garfield did not pursue the retreating Confederates but maintained his position on the battlefield to deal with burying the dead of both sides. He returned to Prestonsburg and established a temporary headquarters. As a result of his victory, Garfield was rewarded with a promotion to Brigadier General.

The Battle of Middle Creek illustrated to Union commanders the importance of the Big Sandy River Valley in countering any future Confederate threat. The Confederate side realized the difficulty of maintaining a relatively long supply line in the mountains of eastern Kentucky and the area became a "no-man's land" for the remainder of the war.

After Middle Creek, Garfield was ordered to join Gen. Don Carlos Buell in Nashville, Tennessee. The 18th Brigade was sent back to Louisville, so Garfield assumed command of the 20th Brigade. This Union unit saw action at Shiloh in April, 1862, and participated in the pursuit of the Confederates to Corinth, Mississippi. Garfield then became ill with dysentery and withdrew from his command to return to Hiram, Ohio, to recover. In October, 1862 Garfield won a seat in the U.S. House of Representatives. Since his term would not begin until December, 1863, a healthy Brig. Gen. James Garfield returned to the army and reported to Washington, D.C., where he acted as the judge in the courtmartial of Maj. Gen. Fitz-John Porter, who was accused of disobeying orders and misconduct during the Second Battle of Bull Run. The courtmartial found Porter guilty and Garfield then joined Gen. William Rosecrans and the Army of the Cumberland in Tennessee. Garfield would act as Rosecran's Chief of Staff.

The Army of the Cumberland had been engaged in pursuit of the Army of Tennessee, under Gen. Braxton Bragg. By September, 1863, the two armies met at the battle of Chickamauga in north Georgia. On the second day of the battle, Confederate troops, under John Bell Hood, penetrated a poorly managed Union line. Rosecrans panicked and fled the field, returning to Chattanooga. James Garfield accompanied his commander to safety but then decided to return to the battlefield. The Union line had been reestablished by Gen. George Thomas with the aid of an attack of the Lightning Brigade under Col. John Wilder. Garfield stayed with Thomas for the remainder of the battle and was promoted to Major General for this action.

Garfield Drives Marshall from Eastern Kentucky

In December, 1863, Garfield resigned his commission in order to take his seat in Congress. During his 17 years in Congress, he helped revamp the Census Bureau and was involved in the establishment of the National Department of Education. He supported the gold standard for currency and served as the chairman of the Banking and Currency Commission.

In the summer of 1880, the Republican Party was embroiled in a deadlock between supporters of Ohio Senator John Sherman, Maine Senator James Blaine and former President Ulysses Grant. Garfield became the compromise candidate during the fractious convention and in November he narrowly defeated the Democratic candidate, Winfield S. Hancock. Early in his presidency, the reform-minded Garfield would be sharply criticised for his nominees to key Cabinet and Federal postings. He had begun his attack on the patronage system but it would be short lived. On July 2, 1881, President Garfield was shot twice by Charles Guiteau, a mentally unstable attorney who had petitioned Secretary of State James Blaine for a consular posting. He died from the resulting infection on September 19.

Throughout his life, James Garfield distinguished himself as a man of conviction, honor, and bravery. From the ranks of frontier poverty, he taught himself to read, pursued an education, and at the age of 26 became the president of a college. An early Republican, his staunch anti-slavery and pro-Union stances made him a natural choice for a leadership role in the Union army. He acquitted himself well at Middle Creek by boldly taking the charge to Marshall's slightly superior force. His return to the Battle of Chickamauga further established his reputation as a man of integrity and action. Though he would not live long enough to enact substantial reform to the American political system during his presidency, his legacy can be linked to the reforms of the Progressive Movement which began in 1895.

* * *

BATTLE OF MILL SPRINGS
GEN. ZOLLICOFFER SLAIN, UNION IS VICTORIOUS

By Mill Springs Battlefield Association

Battle of Mill Springs – Carrying the body of General Zollicoffer from the field of battle to Somerset

After marching for six hours through a cold rain that turned the road into a sea of mud, the vanguard of the Confederate forces arrived near Logan's Crossroads about 6:30am on January 18, 1862. At the foot of a ridge a mile and a half from Logan's Crossroads, the advance Confederate cavalry met a strong picket force of Thomas's 1st Kentucky Cavalry and 10th Indiana Infantry regiments. Far from being surprised, the Federals were on watch, and this picket force stubbornly resisted the Confederate advance up the hill. At the top of the hill (where Fairview Cemetery is today) the Union pickets were reinforced by the rest of the 10th Indiana, and this force stood its ground against the advancing Confederates.

Crittenden advanced with Felix Zollicoffer's own brigade in the front. Zollicoffer put the 15th Mississippi in the line of

General Felix Zollicoffer

battle advancing up the road, with the 19th and 20th Tennessee regiments on either side of the road, a little behind the 15th, and his other regiments following. This force was sufficient to force the 10th Indiana and 1st Kentucky Cavalry back off the hill into the woods below. However, the dawn was dark and misty and the Confederates advanced slowly.

After fighting for about an hour on their own, the 10th Indiana and the 1st Kentucky Cavalry were almost out of ammunition and in danger of being overrun. They fell back to a fence bordering a corn field, on a ridge running perpendicular to the road. Here they were finally reinforced by the 4th Kentucky Infantry, and this fence line and ridge formed the basis for the main Federal line throughout the battle. The 10th Indiana fell back a

58

short distance to regroup, and the troopers of the 1st Kentucky Cavalry sent their horses to the rear and fell in beside their infantry comrades in the 4th Kentucky.

Unable to push this force back, the Confederates moved to the right, under the cover of a deep wooded ravine. From here they could approach the Federal lines before engaging them at close range. This infuriated the commander of the 4th Kentucky, Colonel Speed S. Fry, who climbed up on the fence and angrily demanded that the enemy stand up and fight like men.

The Confederates made little headway in the woods to the west of the road. Most of the soldiers had never been in a battle before, and the dark rainy morning, coupled with the smoke and din of battle, produced quite a bit of confusion. General Zollicoffer, sure that his men were fighting another Confederate regiment, rode forward in this road to reconnoiter. There he met Colonel Fry, who had ridden to his right for the same purpose. Neither recognized the other (Zollicoffer was said to have been extremely nearsighted, and his own uniform was covered by a raincoat). Zollicoffer ordered Fry to cease firing on his friends. As Fry moved back toward his regiment, a Confederate staff officer rode up to warn Zollicoffer, firing his pistol at Fry. Fry and the Union soldiers near him immediately returned the fire, and Zollicoffer fell dead in the road.

Colonel Speed Fry

Zollicoffer's death demoralized his troops on that part of the field and they made no more efforts to advance. However the 15th Mississippi and 20th Tennessee launched a series of furious attacks on Fry's position, some of them even reaching the fence where they fought the Federal soldiers hand-to-hand. The Confederate regiments moved ever toward their right, threatening to turn the Federal left flank. However, a section of Federal artillery appeared

Confederate General Zollicoffer slain

and threw shells toward the Confederates, and the 2nd Minnesota and 9th Ohio regiments arrived to bolster the Federal defenses.

For over an hour, the 15th Mississippi and 20th Tennessee battled the Federals almost alone. Rutledge's Confederate battery fired a few rounds, but Crittenden was never able to bring up the rest of his infantry and bring all of his forces to bear. The Confederates were further demoralized by the fact that many of their weapons, most which were obsolete flintlocks, failed to fire in the pouring rain. As the 1st and 2nd Tennessee and 12th Kentucky U.S. regiments arrived on the Federal left, outflanking the hard-fighting 15th Mississippi and 20th Tennessee, the 9th Ohio made a bayonet charge on the right, and the Confederate line crumbled. Most of the men simply turned and ran.

The entire Union line advanced, forcing what was left of the Confederate army back to the top of the hill from which they had attacked. Here, the 16th Alabama and 17th and 29th Tennessee regiments attempted to hold the Federals back. The Confederates retreated and the battle was over by 9:30am.

The Aftermath

The beaten Southerners fled back down the road, many of them discarding their weapons and accoutrements along the way. They rallied at their Beech Grove entrenchments, but General Thomas arrived with his forces in the afternoon and promptly opened a bombardment on the Confederate camp, including the steamboat at the ferry. Recognizing that his men were badly beaten and his position was untenable, Crittenden ordered a withdrawal across the river that night.

The Confederates left behind all their artillery pieces and wagons, and most of their horses and camp equipment. When dawn arrived on January 20 and the Federals moved against the Confederate works, they found the camps abandoned and Crittenden's force safely across the river.

The Federal forces reported 246 casualties of the battle, including 39 killed in action. The Confederates suffered 533 casualties, including 125 killed in action. The fallen were left on the field to be buried in mass graves near the site of Zollicoffer's death.

Coupled with the Confederate losses of Forts Henry and Donelson less than a month later, the Union victory at Mill Springs cracked the Southern defense line in Kentucky and opened up Tennessee to Federal invasion.

*   *   *

ALBERT SIDNEY JOHNSTON

By Dr. Charles P. Roland

Gen. Albert Sidney Johnston

Albert Sidney Johnston, considered by many historians as the No. 1 Confederate field commander at the outset of the Civil War, was born at Washington, Ky., on Feb. 2, 1803. He grew up in this tiny town where his father, Dr. John Johnston, had settled 20 years before. Washington was a village of mud-daubed log huts in a rude stockade. The sources of food were hunting and planting with war whoops ringing in the air. Indian fighter Simon Kenton still led his bands of Kentucky riflemen across the Ohio to keep the Indians at bay.

Dr. Johnston had three sons by his first wife who died in 1793. He then married Abigail Harris and they had six children. Albert Sidney was their fifth child. She died when he was three.

As Albert matured, so did Washington and Mason County. Washington, the county seat, was now a thriving community on the stagecoach route from the port of Maysville to Lexington. Favored with rich soil, a pleasing landscape and energetic people, Washington had the grace of a mature society.

In 1818, after graduating from a private academy, Johnston entered Transylvania University at the age of 15. While there he met eventual Confederacy President Jefferson Davis. In the fall of 1821 Johnston changed his major from medicine to the military, much to his father's chagrin.

After graduating from West Point in June 1826, he served at Sackett's Harbor, New York, in 1826; with the 6th Infantry at Jefferson Barracks, Missouri, in 1827; and as a regimental adjutant in the Black Hawk War.

On January 20, 1829, he married Henrietta Preston. He resigned his commission on April 22, 1834. Henrietta Johnston died on August 12, 1835. Albert Johnston then went to a farm near St. Louis.

In 1836 Johnston moved to Texas and enlisted as a private in the Texas Army. The following year he was appointed adjutant general by Thomas Jefferson Rusk, and on Jan. 31, 1837, he became senior brigadier general in command of the army, to replace Felix Huston. A duel with Huston resulted, and Johnston was wounded and could not take the command.

On Dec. 22, 1838, he was appointed Secretary of War for the Republic of Texas by President Mirabeau B. Lamar, and in December 1839 he led an expedition against the Cherokee in East Texas.

On March 1, 1840, Johnston returned to Kentucky where, on Oct. 3, 1843, he married Eliza Griffin, a cousin of his first wife. They returned to Texas to settle at China Grove Plantation in Brazoria County.

During the Mexican War, Johnston distinguished himself a a member of W. O. Butler's staff at the Battle of Monterrey, Mexico. On Dec. 2, 1849, Johnston became Paymaster in the U.S. Army, and was assigned to the Texas frontier. In the spring of 1856, he was appointed colonel of the newly created 2nd Cavalry Regiment. From 1858 to 1860 he commanded an expedition to suppress an alleged Mormon rebellion.

At the beginning of the Civil War, he resigned his commission in the U.S. Army.

Because of his military successes prior to the Civil War, Confederate President Jefferson Davis appointed Johnston a general in the Confederate army and assigned him command of the Western Department which included Tennessee and Kentucky. In that capacity, Johnston was the second most senior officer in the entire Confederacy. In his first action, Johnston took Bowling Green, Kentucky, issued a call for men, and formed and drilled an army. He knew the weaknesses of his army: its small size, lack of organization, and long line of defense intersected by three major rivers (the Mississippi, Tennessee, and Cumberland) that were heavily navigated by steamboats.

Johnston laid out a line through middle Kentucky, dipping down to the Tennessee River in Western Tennessee. The eastern end was ripped asunder in January 1862 by a Union attack at Mill Springs; in February the western end cracked when Forts Henry and Donelson surrendered. The center could not hold, especially since Foote's Union gunboats were able to penetrate into central Tennessee on the Cumberland and all the way to northern Mississippi and Alabana on the Tennessee. Johnston pulled back into northern Mississippi and finally concentrated his forces.

Battle of Shiloh, Tennessee

Johnston took the initiative against the Union forces that had stopped at Pittsburg Landing on the Tennessee River to reorganize and resupply. Setting off from Corinth, Mississippi, he marched his three Corps toward Shiloh. The Union hadn't posted adequate pickets, and his attack was a surprise. Johnston led from the front, attempting to bore his way to the river and Grant's headquarters. He failed to reach either. He was wounded in the leg, something he did not consider serious enough to slow him down. Unfortunately, he had miscalculated, and bled to death on April 6, 1862.

The two-day Battle of Shiloh was the costliest in U.S. history up to that time. It resulted in the defeat of the Confederate armies and frustrated Johnston's plans to prevent the joining of the two Union armies in Tennessee. A total of 23,746 men were killed, wounded or missing.

Johnston was temporarily buried at New Orleans. By special appropriation, the Texas Legislature in January 1867, had his remains transferred to Austin for burial in the State Cemetery. In 1905 a stone monument executed by noted sculptor Elisabet Ney was erected at the site.

Those who knew Albert Sidney Johnston considered him a gentleman, devoted husband and kind father. Reared in the chivalric tradition of the Old South, he exalted womanhood as above reproach. Those who served under him respected and loved him. He was referred to as "one of the most unselfish men I ever knew," and "an officer of high-bred courtesy which gave him the affection of all who came near him," and "one of the most just and considerate to those under his command."

His actual successes during the war were limited. Albert Sidney Johnston's death early in the war possibly prevented him from gaining the fame that historians say could well have been his due. In fact, his death may have been the turning point in the war. His leadership was crucial for success, and only later would the South realize that any chance of Confederate victory in the west had died with Johnston's passing from the scene.

The Albert Sidney Johnston House at Historic Washington, is open to the public during Living History Weekend in August and the first weekend in December in connection with the "Frontier Christmas" celebration. The house may also be seen by taking a tour from the Washington Visitors Center.

The Mint Julep

The Mint Julep, a fabled favorite of patrician plantation owners, originated with Albert Sidney Johnston. Although he wasn't considered much of a drinker himself, Johnston supposedly originated it to prove to friends that Kentucky whiskey had an appeal all of its own. Here is the original recipe: "Choose a good-sized catnip leaf, hold it along the inside of a water glass and severely bruise it with a spoon. Fill the glass with cracked ice, and pour in Kentucky bourbon to within a half-inch of the top. In another glass filled with water, dissolve two teaspoons of sugar. Add enough of this sugar water to top of the glass filled with whiskey. Finally, stick in three sprigs of catnip with two to three leaves on each. Do not stir, just sip slowly.

* * *

WASHINGTON, KENTUCKY
THIS COMMUNITY'S ROLE IN THE WAR BETWEEN THE STATES

General William "Bull" Nelson, *born in nearby Maysville in 1824, was commissioned a Brigadier-General in the Union Army. Nelson would see his friend Albert Sidney Johnston at Shiloh. Johnston was killed in this battle in 1862. Nelson was to meet an untimely death shortly thereafter at the Galt House in Louisville. After a name-calling fracas, a fellow Union General named Jefferson Davis shot him in the chest. General Nelson's remains are buried in Maysville.*

Slavery Artifacts

Harriet Beecher Stowe Slavery to Freedom Museum
Before her marriage to Mr. Stowe, Harriet Beecher was a young teacher in Cincinnati, Ohio, where her father operated Lane Seminary. One of her pupils was a daughter of Marshall Key of Washington, Kentucky. Miss Key brought her teacher home with her for a short visit, and to entertain her one day, Mr. Key took her to the courthouse lawn to see the slaves being sold on the block. This vivid scene so impressed Harriet Beecher that she never forgot it and over 20 years later she wrote her book, Uncle Tom's Cabin. Her novel became a bestseller in 1852 and created a wave of anti-slavery feelings. President Lincoln, when he met the author, remarked, "So this is the little lady who started the big war?"

Albert Sidney Johnston, *who was to become a famous Confederate General, was born in Washington, Kentucky, February 2, 1803. General Johnston was killed at the Battle of Shiloh and historians agree that his death rather early in the war was a disastrous blow for the south, as he was a military genius.*

The Civil War Living History Weekend *is held annually the second weekend of August. It features: Encampments, Artillery Demonstrations, Ladies' Tea, and Battle Re-enactment.*

Washington is part of the "Civil War Discovery Trail"

Albert Sidney Johnston Museum
This house built in the 1790's was home to Dr. John Johnston and his wife Abigail Harris Johnston. Albert Sidney, who was to become a famous Confederate General was born in the house on February 2, 1803. Many other families resided here after Dr. Johnston's death, among them the family of William "Bull" Nelson, who also gained fame as a General in the Civil War, but on the Union side.

Tours Available Daily
- Historic Washington
- Underground Railroad
- Freedom Trail
- Log Cabin Learning

• Antiques • Specialty Shops • Dining

Maysville-Mason County Tourism
216 Bridge St., Maysville, Kentucky 41056
606-564-9419 • www.cityofmaysville.com

George W. Johnson
Governor of Confederate Kentucky

By Dr. Lowell Harrison

George W. Johnson

Kentucky sentiment was divided when the Civil War began in the spring of 1861. With strong ties to both the North and the South, the state's decision to declare neutrality made a sort of sense, although a state had no more right to adopt neutrality than it did to secede. Elections during the summer of 1861 resulted in clear Union victories, and neutrality ended in early September.

That decision was not acceptable to many pro-Confederate Kentuckians. On October 29-30, a meeting was held in Russellville behind the lines of the Confederate army that had entered the state in September. Led by George W. Johnson, a Scott County planter, the group called for a sovereignty convention to meet in Russellville on November 18 to sever Kentucky's ties with the United States.

At that convention, George Johnson continued to provide leadership. After declaring independence from the United States, the convention formed a provisional government that consisted of a governor and a 10-man council, one from each of the state's representative districts. Bowling Green was declared the state's capitol, but "the Governor and Council shall have power to meet any place other that they deem appropriate." Then the convention recognized George Johnson's leadership by electing him governor of Confederate Kentucky.

Johnson was born near Georgetown in Scott County on May 28, 1811. After attending local schools, he received three degrees from Transylvania University. In 1833 he married Ann Viley, daughter of Captain Willa Viley, a wealthy farmer and horse breeder. Seven of their 10 children lived to adulthood. After practicing law in Georgetown, Johnson decided that he preferred farming, and they moved to a large farm adjacent to Captain Viley's holding. Their large home became a gathering place for prominent leaders of the state.

While Johnson did not indulge, he kept an ample supply of bourbon for his guests. He also acquired a 1,000-acre Arkansas plantation where he raised cotton. He accepted election to the Kentucky House of Representatives in 1838, 1839, and 1840; thereafter he shunned office holding,

although he was deeply interested in politics. Concerned over the slavery issue, in August 1845, he headed the Committee of Sixty that seized Cassius M. Clay's *True American* press and shipped it to Cincinnati.

A firm believer in state's rights, Johnson was convinced that new radical groups and parties were destroying the "Old Union" that he loved. The Republican party, he judged, was "a constitutional faction, united by fanatical and crusading sentiments in a system of aggression on the equal rights of the people of the Southern States." In the fateful 1860 election, Johnson supported the candidacy of John C. Breckinridge. As the election of Lincoln became evident, Johnson opposed secession of the Southern states. The Republicans would not control the Senate or the Supreme Court, and they could be defeated in 1864.

But as the Confederate States of America was formed, Johnson abandoned hope of dealing with the crisis within the framework of the Union. Instead, he decided, Kentucky should secede and join the Confederacy. The two nations would then be so evenly matched as to preclude the possibility of war. They could then negotiate their differences and form a free trade union.

Johnson had an active role in attempting to determine Kentucky's future in 1861. "I have been run nearly to death since I got here," he wrote Ann from Louisville where he was engaged in several conferences and meetings. Late in the summer he was sent to Richmond, Virginia, to secure Jefferson Davis's promise to respect Kentucky's neutrality. Although irked by long waits for interviews, Johnson wrote Ann that "I have not the slightest doubt of our ultimate success."

Johnson and other pro-Southerners held a State Rights Convention in Frankfort on September 10 in a last-minute effort to keep Kentucky from aiding the Union cause. With Richard Hawes presiding, the convention called for the restoration of neutrality and condemned the Federal government for invading the state. Their protests had no effect.

Aware that he might be arrested, Johnson fled the state on horseback. But he went to Bowling Green as Confederate troops entered Kentucky, and he became a volunteer aide to General Simon Bolivar Buckner. He missed his family. "Oh my dear Children," he mourned in an October 20, 1861, letter to Ann. "How I love to see them all once more." He warned Ann not "to give up your property to my creditors. If you do, you will embitter my whole life." Could she get a pass from a Union general to allow her to join him? Except for missing his family, Johnson was content in Bowling Green. Buckner was a personal friend, and he came to admire commanding General Albert Sidney Johnston. "He is eminently a great and good man, and I cannot help loving him."

Johnson deluded himself into believing that the Frankfort government did not represent the true wishes of Kentuckians. Southern orthodox thinking held that if a state wanted to make a fundamental change, such as secession, the state legislature had to call a special convention which could make the change, which might or might not be submitted to a popular vote. Since that procedure was impossible with Unionists in control of the General Assembly, Johnson and his associates appealed to the revolutionary right of the people "to alter, reform, or abolish their government, in such manner as they think proper." They held an October meeting in Russellville that called for a sovereignty convention to convene in that town on November 18.

Johnson was a major figure in the November convention, and the delegates elected him governor of the Provisional Government of Kentucky. On November 21, 1861, Governor Johnson penned a long letter to Jefferson Davis in which he justified their irregular action and asked for admission into the confederacy. Kentuckians had had to resort to the right of revolution, but "We come to you now, when it is honorable to do so, to offer you our assistance in a common cause while peril surrounds us both and to share with you a common destiny." Davis had doubts about the irregularity of the process, but he concluded that "there is enough of merit in the application to warrant a disregard of its irregularity," and on December 10, 1861, the provisional government was admitted into the Confederate States of America.

On November 26, Johnson issued a general address to the people of Kentucky in which he charged abolitionists with the dissolution of the Union. The South could not be conquered, he asserted; the only real solution was to accept two nations that would be united through free trade. He would gladly resign, Johnson continued, whenever "the regularly elected Governor shall escape from his virtual imprisonment at Frankfort." Although he was pro-Confederate in sentiment, Governor Beriah Magoffin denounced the Confederate government which represented only a minority of Kentuckians.

Governor Johnson had trouble hearing family news except for son Matthew, who had enlisted in John Hunt Morgan's cavalry command. In January 1862, he begged Ann to send 15-year old son Junius to him. When the lad "grows old he will love to think that he too did something in the field for our glorious revolution." Ann refused to make the sacrifice.

Johnson tried to establish a working government, but it had no jurisdiction beyond the area held by the Confederate army. While he consulted with the generals, he could do little to raise the 46,000 men for Confederate service as required by an act of the Confederate Congress. Nor did the new government have much success in acquiring funds. Many taxpayers in southern Kentucky refused to pay taxes, and Warren County Sheriff Pleasant J. Potter was one of the Unionist officials removed from office when he refused to turn his collections over to Confederate authorities. Efforts to compel gun owners to turn weapons over to the government also had little success.

Confederate Kentucky could send two senators and 12 representatives to the Congress in Richmond, and an election was held on January 22, 1862. Local officials were appointed to replace Unionists who had fled. They included a number of justices of the peace who had authority to perform marriages. After the Confederates withdrew from the state, a question arose about the legality of marriages that they had performed. (Their legality was upheld.)

By early February, 1862, the Confederate right flank had been crushed at Mill Springs, and Forts Henry and Donelson were in jeopardy on the left flank. After consulting with his chief subordinates, Johnston decided on February 8 that he must withdraw to some point south of the Tennessee River. By mid-February most of the army was in or near Nashville. Johnson lingered in Bowling Green as long as possible. He wrote Ann on February 15 that "I now go with the Army and intend to remain constantly in the field." Still optimistic about the future, he predicted that "We will soon be ready to return." The government caught up with the army, and a New Orleans newspaper of March 12 reported that "the capital of Kentucky [is] now being located in a Sibley tent."

General Johnston proposed to make a stand when his army was beyond the Tennessee River where Union gunboats might sever his line of supply. When rumors circulated that he might relinquish command to General Pierre G.T. Beauregard, Johnson urged his friend to retain command. "We are in the right place, at the right time, and the proudest victory of the war awaits you, unless you commit suicide by yielding up the command of your army when it most needs energy and an active head. You must not do this."

When the Confederates attacked at Shiloh on Sunday, April 6, 1862, Johnson went forward as a volunteer aide to General John C. Breckinridge. When the First Kentucky Brigade became separated from Breckinridge, Johnson assisted Colonel Robert P. Trabue. After his horse was shot from under him during the morning attack, the Governor joined Captain Ben Monroe's Company E, Fourth Kentucky Infantry. "I am determined to share the dangers of the battle with these boys," he explained. "They are my friends and relatives, and I feel better with them." That evening Johnson insisted on being sworn in as a private in Company E. "I will take a night's rest," he said, "and be ready for a good day's fighting."

On Monday afternoon, as the Confederates retreated before strong Union attacks, Johnson was struck by two bullets, one in the right thigh, the other in the abdomen. He lay unattended on the battlefield until Tuesday when he was recognized by Union General Alexander McDowell McCook. They had attended the abortive Democratic National Convention in Charleston in 1860, and they were both fellow Masons. Johnson was carried carefully to the hospital ship *Hannibal* on the Tennessee River, and doctors and a chaplain were assigned to the care of the mortally wounded governor of Confederate Kentucky.

Johnson knew that he was dying, but he had strength enough to dictate several farewell messages. None went to Ann: "My wife knows how well I love her, and she needs no message," he told the attending chaplain. He tried to explain why he had taken the course that he had.

"I wanted personal honor and political liberty and constitutional state government, and for these I drew the sword." He had never joined a church, but the chaplain wrote the widow: "I feel confident that he died a converted man. I have seen many die but never saw any one die more perfectly resigned. It was as if he was falling asleep."

Friends in the Union army had the body packed in salt and shipped to Georgetown by Adams Express. He was buried

Confederate weapons

with Masonic honors in a Baptist church as friends of conflicting political persuasion paid their final tribute. Unionist editor George D. Prentice wrote in the *Louisville Weekly Journal*: "He was a rebel in arms, and he deserved his fate. But we have a kind regard for him. We knew him well, and we cherished for him the highest personal regard. He was noble, generous, and chivalric. Terrible was he deluded, but we have a heart-tear for him."

Johnson and others were successful in creating a provisional state government that gave an illusion of legality and securing its admission into the Confederate States of America. But he could do little to establish a viable administration in the chaotic conditions that existed in southern Kentucky during his brief tenure within the state. The majority of Kentuckians remained loyal to the Union, and only Confederate military domination of the state would have given the Confederate government a fair chance for success.

* * *

Battle of Shiloh Reenactment

MORGAN'S MEN TWICE RAIDED CYNTHIANA

By William A. Penn

John Hunt Morgan

After the fall of Fort Sumter in April 1861, Harrison County responded with six Confederate and two Union companies, along with several Home Guard units. Over 1,400 eventually went to war, split 63% Confederate and 37% Union. At least 28 slaves joined Union companies. In September 1861, the 35th Ohio established Camp Frazer just north of town to guard the railroad. Union troops arrested over 60 local citizens during the war for alleged disloyalty, and some, like State Representative Lucius Desha, were incarcerated for months at Camp Chase, Ohio.

John Hunt Morgan's Confederate cavalry raided Cynthiana twice during the Civil War. The first raid occurred July 17, 1862, when Morgan, with 850 men and two cannons, surrounded Cynthiana about 3pm. Cynthiana was defended by 345 men under Lt. Col. John J. Landram, mostly Home Guards with a 12-pounder. Simultaneous Confederate cavalry charges at the covered bridge (near present day U.S. 27 bridge), Falmouth Pike, and Magee Hill (today called Standpipe Hill) forced Landram's men to withdraw from those locations toward the depot. After making a brief stand, the Federals withdrew on the Old Lair Pike where everyone except Landram was captured.

Two years later, Morgan's Raiders, with 1,200 men, again attacked Cynthiana (June 11-12, 1864). The battle took place in three locations: the covered bridge, Keller's Bridge, and the present site of Battle Grove Cemetery. On June 11, Col. Conrad Garis defended Cynthiana with 300 men of the 168th Ohio and the local Home Guards under Colonel George W. Berry. At dawn, Morgan attacked at the covered bridge and Magee Hill. The Union troops first retreated to the depot, and then fled toward Pike Street, where they fired from buildings. To flush out Union soldiers, and with the excuse he had no artillery, Morgan ordered several buildings to be set on fire. The flames spread rapidly, consuming 37 downtown structures. Col. Garis and his men surrendered after using the Rankin Hotel and courthouse for protection. Col. Berry was mortally wounded at the depot.

That same morning at dawn, unaware of Morgan's proximity, the 171st Ohio under General Edward Hobson arrived by train at Keller's Bridge, one mile north of Cynthiana. The Confederates fought Hobson on the back pastures of the present Switzer farm that lies on the west side of the Licking River. Hobson retreated north to the adjoining hill leaving a deep railroad cut between the two forces. After three hours of intense fighting, Hobson surrendered.

Morgan, despite being outnumbered, low on ammunition, and with the high-banked Licking River impeding a possible retreat, was optimistic he could defeat Gen.

The Morgan Raid into Kentucky –The Fight at Licking Bridge, Cynthiana. Leslie's Illustrated Newspaper, August 16, 1862

Filson Historical Society

Burbridge, who was pursuing the raiders from Paris. Morgan placed his dismounted cavalry about one mile east of Cynthiana on the Millersburg Pike near Poplar Hill, home of John W. Kimbrough, east of the present site of Battle Grove Cemetery. Col. Smith, protecting Morgan's right line, was deployed on Magee Hill, a site overlooking the New Lair Pike near the present Harrison County High School. Burbridge, with 2,400 men and two cannons, arrived at dawn June 12 on the Millersburg Pike and attacked Morgan's position. Morgan's center and left line soon collapsed and they were forced to run for their horses. Col. Smith held Morgan's right line somewhat longer behind a stone wall, but both a determined Union frontal attack and a cavalry flanking movement from the south compelled Smith's last resisting men to retreat. Morgan escaped and those of his men who were not captured dispersed in all directions, ending the last Civil War engagement in Harrison County.

* * *

ORPHAN BRIGADE
THOSE FIGHTING KENTUCKY REBS

By Dr. Marshall Myers

The North had its Iron Brigade, that brave bunch of Midwesterners who fought so gallantly at Antietam and Gettysburg and Petersburg. But the South had perhaps a more colorful and more storied phalanx of men dubbed "The Orphan Brigade." They were an assembly of mostly Kentuckians who so distinguished themselves in battle with gritty determination that their fame among Civil War buffs is legendary.

You may not believe in their cause, but you have to admire them for their spunk, spirit, and sense of purpose.

The Orphan Brigade got its name from at least two sources. First, they were "orphans" because they could not return to their homes since Kentucky had ultimately aligned itself with the Union, furnishing about 80,000 Boys in Blue, while providing only about 40,000 Gray Clads.

Things were so bad for the Orphan Brigade that they risked imprisonment and execution by a firing squad should they return to their native state to visit relatives or to seek volunteers. They were away from home with no home to return to.

Yet, throughout the war, the rugged, and often ragged, brigade clung to the idea that they would return to Kentucky and liberate it for the Confederacy. In fact, many Orphans enlisted because, as historian Kent Masterson Brown explains, they thought "the conflict would be fought over their native state." And they, of course, wanted to be a part of that action.

Another possible source for the sobriquet was a comment made by their most esteemed leader, General John Cabell Breckinridge, who, in the white heat of battle at Stones River, reportedly said in desperation as his brigade suffered great losses: "My poor orphans! My poor orphans! My poor orphans! They have cut it to pieces."

The unit was a motley crew of fun-loving, yet dedicated Kentuckians from all across the commonwealth, from far western Kentucky, the region with some of the most devout

General Simon Bolivar Buckner, C.S.A., wanted to command the Orphan Brigade but was used instead as a division commander.

secessionists, to the southern and central part of the state, including a goodly number from the Bluegrass region. The group mustered into the Confederate army in large part at Camp Boone, Tennessee, near Clarksville. Soon they occupied Bowling Green, Kentucky, the Confederate capital of Kentucky.

One member of the brigade boasts in a letter that the regiment he is part of is "wholly Kentuckian. It was born and educated upon Kentucky soil, and for it... we have come with many of courage to pour out our life's blood for its glorious defense. We feel, as we stand upon our native hills,.... that they are our peculiar birth-rights, heaven heritages for the brave alone."

Several members of the Orphan Brigade had been integral parts of the State Militia, organized and commanded by General Simon Bolivar Buckner, a native of Munfordville, Kentucky. The State Militia was originally mustered in to defend the state's neutrality at the outset of the war. Decidedly Southern in its sympathies, much of the militia headed south, however, when the Kentucky legislature voted solid support for the Union.

But the Orphan Brigade's beloved brigade commander for much of their campaign was General John C. Breckinridge, a former senator from the commonwealth, Vice President of the United States, and candidate for President on the Southern Democrat ticket in the 1860 election against. His opponent was, among others, another native Kentuckian, Abraham Lincoln. Breckinridge, who hailed from the Lexington area, graduated from Centre College and studied at both Princeton University and Transylvania University. He was a masterful orator, the kind that could quickly move men's minds and convince them of the veracity of his subject. Few in his time, or even today, could match his oratory. And perhaps, ancillary to that ability, he knew the men of his command: he knew what motivated them, what was important to them, and how far he could push them to get the most out of them.

"Old Breck," as his men called him, was that rare combination of tact and devotion, who in large part, hovered over his men, cared about them, and asked after their welfare like a father broods and fusses over his children.

Curiously, Breckinridge, in spite of his total devotion to the Southern cause, felt at the outset of the conflict, and several times during it, that the Southern cause was doomed. William C. Davis's book length study of the brigade quotes "Old Breck" as saying, "I go where my duty calls me. It is a hopeless cause."

But it certainly never showed by the way Breckinridge fought and led his men. At the outset, the brigade, officially known as the First Kentucky Brigade of the Confederacy, consisted of around 3,000 men, and included, for a short time, General John Hunt Morgan and his cavalry, although Morgan soon took his men elsewhere. Units from both Tennessee and Alabama also served with the brigade, but the group remained largely Kentuckian for the duration of the war.

Their baptism by fire was Shiloh, at the time, the bloodiest day in American history, the battle that many say presaged the carnage to come in places like Antietam and Gettysburg. Shiloh, Hebrew for "place of peace," is famed for "The Hornet's Nest," that peach orchard on that April day where the whiz of Union bullets sounded like a nest of enraged hornets.

Soon, the brigade proved itself to be a unit to be reckoned with, fighting ferociously against a dedicated enemy. Historian Davis truly captures the fighting spirit of the unit. In the midst of the most intense fighting at Shiloh, Colonel Robert P. Trabue of the brigade's Fourth Kentucky Infantry, asked Confederate General William J. Hardee what to do with the Kentucky Brigade. Hardee quickly responded, "Put it in where the fight is the thickest, sir." Such was the faith and reputation of this group of rag-tag Kentuckians.

In a letter published by an Orphan Brigade historian, Captain John Trice of the brigade's Fourth Kentucky Infantry concluded that the Battle of Shiloh was "very warmly contracted on both sides, all showing a determination to conquer or die."

One Orphan, Johnny Green, in the heat of battle, felt a bullet strike him just above the heart. Green thought the bullet had gone through him, but luckily learned that his copy of the New Testament had saved him. Davis observes, "More than one pierced Bible made its owner a true believer."

General Benjamin Hardin Helm, C.S.A., served for a short time as a commander of the Orphan Brigade. He was killed at the Battle of Chickamauga, Georgia.

As was true for most units on both sides, it was indeed a bloody day. Of the 2,400 Orphans who reported for duty, 844 were either dead or wounded, a truly massive loss for the quickly depleting brigade.

Among the dead at Shiloh was Governor George W. Johnson, the governor of Confederate Kentucky, who suffered wounds in the thigh and stomach and died on April 9 on a Federal hospital ship.

On to Corinth, to Baton Rouge, and then to Vicksburg where, according to Davis, the brigade once again tasted bitter defeat, along with bouts of dysentery, malaria, and diarrhea, probably contracted from drinking water from mud holes and other disease-infested streams and ponds.

Johnny Green wrote that "sickness is playing great havoc" within the unit. Steadily, the brigade began shrinking as more and more of their numbers succumbed to Union bullets and dreaded diseases.

At Vicksburg, another costly battle, the soldiers of the First Kentucky Brigade found that they had another new commander, Breckinridge having been promoted to division commander. The new leader was Benjamin Hardin Helm, one of a series of commanders that included William Preston, Roger Weightman Hanson, Joseph Lewis, and Robert Trabue, as leaders were killed, wounded or replaced.

Helm received his military education at the Kentucky Military Academy and later graduated from the United States Military Academy at West Point, where he ranked ninth in his class. Having served in the Kentucky legislature, Helm was practicing law in Louisville at the time of the war.

What is particularly interesting about Helm was that he was President and Mrs. Lincoln's brother-in-law. Married to Emilie Todd, Benjamin Hardin Helm had turned down a position as paymaster of the Union army offered by the President. Instead, Helm, aligned himself with the South and quickly rose in rank to general.

The next battle for the Orphan Brigade was the famed Confederate victory at Chickamauga Creek, just over the Tennessee line in Georgia, a battle that renewed the fighting spirit of many Confederate soldiers and sympathizers. Helm led his nearly 1,700 men into battle against another Kentuckian, Union General Thomas Crittenden, and the "Rock of Chickamauga," General George Thomas, known for leading his men in blistering attacks on the Confederate

Lincoln, who was very fond of Helm, is quoted as saying amidst his grief, "I feel as David of old did when he was told of the death of Absalom." Mrs. Lincoln was equally moved, and later comforted Helm's widow in the White House.

From Chickamauga, the Orphans marched to Missionary Ridge above the vital trading center of Chattanooga. It was there in "The Battle Above the Clouds" that they suffered defeat once more as they were confronted by an old nemesis, General U.S. Grant, and by what Brown describes as the "tenacious assaults by the Army of the Cumberland," whose merciless onslaught forced the Orphans to give up their position.

The Orphans spent much of the rest of the war trying to slow the juggernaut of Sherman's army as the Union general swept through the South in a merciless display of total war, slashing and burning and destroying anything that could be useful to the Confederacy in continuing the conflict.

Of course, there were lighter moments, too, even in the heat of battle, particularly near Jonesboro, Georgia, as the Orphans charged up a steep hill toward the raging enemy. One of the Orphans, Bill Robb, had only one button holding up his pants, a button, by chance, shot off, but which somehow missed the rest of his body. Brigade historian William Davis continues the story: "Down went his pants. He picked them up again and tried to continue the advance, but could not do much, holding his rifle in one hand and his last link with modesty in the other. Faced with a choice amid all that shot and shell, he finally let go the trousers and finished his part of the battle with more than his steel bare."

By September of 1864, the original 3,000 Orphans had dwindled to a mere 513. Yet despite their radically depleted numbers, even as late as February 1865, the brigade was still full of fight. The brigade adopted a resolution in which they agreed to carry on. In another resolution, they concluded that "We see nothing in the present aspects of affairs to justify a fear of our ultimate triumph, or any excuse for relaxing our effort to conquer independence and peace."

Orphan Brigade Officers

line as they assaulted Thomas's side and rear. Davis concludes that the Battle of Chickamauga was "the most complete defeat ever suffered by a Union army," and that "Major contributions to that defeat were the terrible, though costly, attacks made by the First Kentucky against more than trice their numbers." Many historians disagree, citing the Battle of Richmond, Kentucky, as the worst Yankee defeat.

But it was a hollow victory for the Orphan Brigade, for they lost Helm, who was shot from his horse and rushed to the rear. Davis reports his last words were "Victory! Victory!"

They then turned to a particular: "Although we have been exiles from our homes and separated from those nearest and dearest to us for more than three years, we are not yet willing to return to our native state upon the terms Lincoln may prescribe." The Orphan Brigade, however, was finally forced to face the inevitable; they gave up May 7, 1865, in Washington, Georgia.

Slowly, they worked their way back to Kentucky and reintegrated themselves into the state after a December resolution in the Kentucky Legislature dropped all indictments against them.

Writing on the Orphan Brigade and their heritage, William Davis notes that "not war, nor death, nor even the anguish of orphanhood could rob them of their sense of destiny, of who they were. That the rest of the world might know and applaud their record stood for little moment. What they knew themselves to be was what bound them together through war and on to posterity. They were Kentuckians, Americans."

They were, indeed, one of Kentucky's most valiant forces. They fought in a war that in Kentucky especially, divided brother from brother. The Orphan Brigade's heritage, bravery, and stories will long live on in the memories and history of not only the commonwealth, but also in our country's history.

* * *

Orphan Brigade Reunion at Octagon Hall, Franklin, Kentucky

GENERAL JOHN BELL HOOD

By Sam Hood

Regardless of the subject, it is difficult to find unanimity of opinion among Civil War historians. But when considering the enigmatic career of Confederate General John Bell Hood, historians would probably agree that the life and career of the native Kentuckian was as extraordinary as that of any figure in American military history.

Hood's meteoric rise and precipitous fall paralleled those of the Confederate States of America itself. His remarkable successes as commander of the acclaimed Hood's Texas Brigade in Robert E. Lee's Army of Northern Virginia in 1862 and 1863 made him a star of Richmond society and a favorite of the Confederate government and high command. But the summer of 1863 saw the Confederacy and Hood reach their apex when Lee's invading army was defeated at Gettysburg, and Hood suffered his first serious wound while leading his Texans in their assault on Little Round Top.

Although a commander of Texas troops, Hood was not a native Texan. The dashing and charismatic Hood was born in the Bath County, Kentucky, town of Owingsville on June 29, 1831, and grew up in rural Montgomery County near Mt. Sterling. The son of a scholarly rural doctor, the gregarious young John Bell Hood was heavily influenced by his two grandfathers: one a crusty veteran of the French and Indian War and the other a Revolutionary War

General John Bell Hood

veteran. The adventurous life of a soldier appealed to Hood, who gained an appointment to West Point in 1849. Assigned to the Texas frontier after his graduation in 1853, Hood served in the elite U.S. Second Cavalry Regiment under the command of future Confederate generals Robert E. Lee and Albert Sidney Johnston. The young cavalry lieutenant first demonstrated his combat prowess when, enduring a wound to his hand by an arrow, he led his heavily outnumbered cavalry patrol to victory in a battle with Comanches at Devil's River, Texas, in the summer of 1857.

At the outbreak of the Civil War, Hood resigned his U.S. Army commission, enlisted in the Confederate army, and was reunited with Robert E. Lee in Virginia. Earning rapid promotions, Hood attained the rank of brigadier general on March 7, 1862, and was given command of the Texas Brigade. Repeatedly called upon by Lee, Hood and his Texans were vanguards in the important Confederate victories at Gaines' Mill (Seven Days Battles) and Second Manassas in the summer of 1862. In September 1862, at the bloody Battle of Antietam, although outnumbered six to one, Hood's brigade held the Confederate left flank, saving Lee's army. For his gallantry, Hood was promoted to major general by Gen. Thomas J. "Stonewall" Jackson.

The fortunes of John Bell Hood and the Confederacy began to wane in 1863, as major Union victories at Vicksburg and Gettysburg turned the tide of the war. After recovery from his Gettysburg wound, Hood, now a division commander, was sent west to join the beleaguered Army of Tennessee. While leading his division in the Confederate victory at Chickamauga, Hood was wounded in the right leg, requiring its amputation.

As 1864 dawned, the Confederate States of America and John Bell Hood were both crippled. War had cost Hood half of his limbs, and the Confederacy had lost much of its territory and many of its senior commanders, including Albert Sidney Johnston, Stonewall Jackson, and, by year's end, A.P. Hill, "Jeb" Stuart, Leonidas Polk, John Hunt Morgan, and others.

With Southern resources and manpower depleted, Union armies launched major campaigns against Confederate forces in Virginia and Georgia in the spring of 1864. Hood, now recovered from his leg amputation, was promoted to the rank of lieutenant general and placed in command of a corps in Gen. Joseph Johnston's newly reinforced Army of Tennessee in north Georgia. Union Gen. William T.

General John Bell Hood

Sherman commenced his Atlanta Campaign in May 1864, and by mid-July had advanced 100 miles south, forcing Johnston to retreat to within 15 miles of Atlanta. On July 17, 1864, Confederate President Jefferson Davis, desperate to save Atlanta, relieved Johnston of command of the Army of Tennessee and replaced him with the aggressive and enthusiastic Hood, who was promoted to the rank of full general.

Hood's ensuing failures as an army commander in 1864 would be as notorious as his successes were notable in the war's early years. Now of rank equivalent to that of Robert E. Lee (who was 20 years older), Hood conducted a spirited defense of Atlanta but failed to break the Union siege, and the important city fell to Sherman's forces in September. With an army as crippled as his own body, Hood led a desperate, last-gasp invasion of Tennessee, suffering decisive defeats at Franklin on Nov. 30, and at Nashville on Dec. 16.

Battered and broken, Hood resigned his army command in January 1865, as the Confederate States of America was rapidly collapsing. After learning of the capture of Jefferson Davis, Hood surrendered to Federal authorities in Natchez, Mississippi, on May 30, 1865.

The intriguing story of John Bell Hood had yet another chapter, also ripe with achievement and misfortune. Settling in New Orleans after the war, Hood, in 1868, married Anna Marie Hennen, the beautiful daughter of a prominent Louisiana attorney and planter. Hood prospered in the cotton brokerage and insurance businesses and in ten years of marriage fathered eleven children, including three sets of twins. As with his military career, tragedy lurked.

In the summer of 1878, a yellow fever epidemic befell New Orleans, killing approximately 3,000 people and forcing the closure of the Cotton Exchange. Although Hood's family escaped illness in 1878, his cotton and insurance businesses failed. In the following summer, New Orleans recorded only five deaths from yellow fever, but three occurred in the Garden District home of John Bell Hood. In the last week of August, Hood, his wife, and eldest daughter contracted yellow fever, and all died within a five-day period.

The remarkable life of John Bell Hood ended on August 30, 1879, but his story had one more sad chapter. Not having recovered from the failure of his businesses the prior year, Hood had died destitute, and the ten surviving orphans – all under the age of ten – were forced into adoption. The children were taken by seven different families in five states, from New York to Louisiana.

It would be difficult to imagine a life story, real or fictional, as fascinating as that of Kentucky's own John Bell Hood.

* * *

CIVIL WAR TARGET: CUMBERLAND GAP

By Larry D. Thacker

Few great American icons of history bear the scars of time as grandly as the westward gateway of Cumberland Gap. To summarize this landmark's significance is to embrace the evidence of our region and our country's entire timeline of nation-shaping events – from Dr. Thomas Walker's 1750 trek through the pass, Daniel Boone's forging of an improved migratory route, to the Gap's looming temptation as an American Gibraltar of our War of Rebellion. There are few chapters in our American history not displayed upon the face of this naturally convenient gateway through the obstacle-laden Cumberland Mountain chain.

And now, as the Cumberland Gap National Historical Park applies the finishing human-touches to the work that nature will once again impose upon the our pass, the 20th century closes and another re-opens in a restored 1775 period – characterized by both the romanticism of human movement and the dread of danger and frontier discomfort.

These are perhaps the two most common and influencing threads possessed by the Cumberland Gap, one emphasizing its inevitable draw, the other sending waves of fear and misgiving through the very people making their way to and through its passage.

No event best illustrates this relationship than activities surrounding Union and Confederate occupations of Cumberland Gap during our American Civil War.

Cumberland Gap, though never host to a fully evolved battle and to only limited skirmishing, was nevertheless generally considered a high-profile militarily and politically strategic vantage point during much of the war. The Gap, of well-known "gateway" fame for decades, remained fresh in the minds of a young America engaged in internal strife. The Gap, its geographic and political location, topography, and potential impact upon the emotional side of the conflict, was a natural strategic choice.

As history shows, though capturing the Gap was generally without casualties, defending and surviving garrison in the Gap was, however, almost too logistically difficult to fulfill any dreams of tactical or strategic value. Deeply trampled, rain-sodden passageways were consistently impassable in all directions, rendering a Gap supply route sporadic and undependable. Railroads were nonexistent. Foraging Powell's Valley and the Cumberland Mountain countryside for supplies was difficult at best against a small, politically mixed population. Add to that an ever-present danger of ambushes and skirmishes, near impossible terrain, and, most importantly, limited raw materials. By the time any hints of battle brewed in the region, a garrisoned force was dangerously low on supplies, as well as morale, often resulting in abandonment or fairly non-violent surrender.

Both the North and South desired the Gap as a permanent strategic and tactically-strengthened political possession. Its intact historical reputation, as well as on-site witness, spurred early optimism. President Abraham Lincoln wished, in January 1862, "to seize and hold a point on the Railroad connecting Virginia and Tennesse [sic], near the Mountain pass called Cumberland Gap," and when presented with choices of controlling the population center of Nashville, Tennessee or the Gap, opted for the latter on strategic grounds that, "first, because it cuts a great artery of the enemy's communication, which Nashville does not;" and "secondly, because it is in the midst of loyal people, who would rally around it, which Nashville is not."

Building upon a continued reputation, Colonel James Rains, CSA, the next month advising tactically that "[Cumberland Gap] should never be abandoned," reported the Tennessee side as "almost impregnable" and that, "Its strategic importance cannot be exaggerated."

General George Morgan, USA, addressed the tactical importance of the Gap, calling it "the strongest position I have ever seen except Gibraltar," in May and June of 1862. His decision to abandon the garrison in September 1862, was a difficult one. He was so sure of the site's importance, in fact, that though his men were in dire straits, Morgan was convinced his force could "hold Cumberland Gap 60 days by eating horses and mules."

Major General H.G. Wright, however, upon defending Morgan's quick retreat, expressed an opposing view, that the Cumberland Gap's "importance has …been much overestimated, there being several passes through the mountains which, though less easy, are nevertheless practicable, as is shown by the fact that Kirby Smith, with a rebel force of over 20,000 men, passed into Kentucky through one of them." This, he claims, effectively diminishes the Gap's importance.

Its importance wavered throughout the war. For example, Confederate President Jefferson Davis considered Brigadier General Jonathan Frazer's surrender of the Gap in September 1863 as "inexplicable"after Frazer was expected to hold "at all hazards."

By winter of 1863, however, optimism began to wane permanently as U.S. Western Forces Commander (and soon-to-be Federal Forces Lieutenant-General) Ulysses S. Grant recognized operations in and out of the pass area as becoming logistically impossible. The Army of the Ohio's animals were reported as "nearly all starved" and Grant, before long, was "determined to go [himself] to see if there was any possible chance of using that route in the spring, and if not, to abandon it" and described troops of the area as suffering under "a comfortless condition."

Sizing up the predicament of the valuable pass in person whilst traveling from east Tennessee to Lexington, Kentucky, in early January of 1864, Grant observed that, "The road over Cumberland Gap, and back of it, was strewn with debris of broken wagons and dead animals," and was further discouraged to find the "road had been cut up to as great a depth as clay could be by mules and wagons, and in that condition frozen; so that the ride of six days from Strawberry Plains to Lexington over these holes and knobs in the road was a very cheerless one, and very disagreeable."

By February 1864, Gen. Ambrose Burnside, last major controller of the Cumberland Gap, had all but abandoned the area upon Grant's recognition that the site, though still considered worthy of holding at all costs, was not an ideal invasion route to Richmond. It was relegated to a secondary strongpoint worthy of defense but hoped at the cost of no large event.

Likewise, Confederate forces met with equal frustration in the Gap. Confederate President Jefferson Davis, having been born in Kentucky and knowing full well the potential pivotal value of southeast Kentucky and upper east Tennessee, found the Cumberland Gap just as impossible to hold after gaining possession.

The communities of Powell's Valley and Cumberland Gap as well as the collections of dwellings that are now the communities of Harrogate, Shawanee and Arthur, Tennessee, and Middlesboro, Kentucky, saw Union and Confederate troops in possession of Cumberland Gap no less than twice each. No recognized battles occurred at the pass though a number of artillery exchanges, skirmishing along the lines, major entrenching, and promising tactical troop movement took place.

Generally, after garrisoning the low-land areas and constructing or reinforcing defensive works on the hillsides and ridges on both the Tennessee and Kentucky sides, whether Union or Confederate was in control, they sooner or later found themselves low on supplies, near starving, ill-protected from the elements and disease. All the while they were also threatened by impending enemy forces somewhere in the hills and valleys to the north or south. Commanders of these occupying forces, numbering as little as 1,500 to as many as 7,000 men at one time, consistently deemed the Gap invaluable, yet not worth fighting for. All of this led to the Gap being outright abandoned twice, and retreated from as well as surrendered, with troops destroying as much equipment and supplies as possible just ahead of the arrival of the enemy.

* * *

DUTY, HONOR, AND FAMILY
THE BRECKINRIDGES OF KENTUCKY IN THE CIVIL WAR

By Dr. James C. Klotter

John Fox Jr. had been born during the middle of the Civil War, though he was too young to recall the conflict. Yet, at age 40, in 1903, he wrote a best-selling novel that captured part of the atmosphere and spirit present in those days of turmoil. In *The Little Shepherd of Kingdom Come*, he told how, "when the great news [of war] came, it came like a sword that, with one stroke, slashed the state in twain, shearing the strongest bonds that link one man to another."

And that sword cut a particularly wide swath in Kentucky. As Fox voiced the dilemma: "As the nation was rent apart, so was the Commonwealth; as the state, so was the country; as the country, the neighborhood; the family, so brother and brother, father and son." A man living at the time of war, James Speed of Louisville, expressed the same sentiment: "So many of our giddy young men have gone into the Southern Army that almost any man...knows that he has to fight a neighbor, a brother, a son or father." Kentucky fully earned the right to call the fighting, "The Brother's War."

Nowhere did those divisions strike deeper than in one of the most prominent families in the commonwealth. For family fought family not just from the masses, but also from the upper classes.

The Breckinridges had long been leaders. John Breckinridge (1760-1806) had been a U.S. Senator, then Thomas Jefferson's Attorney General. His grandson, the tall and handsome John Cabell Breckinridge, had been State Representative, U.S. Representative, Vice President (the youngest ever), presidential candidate, and U.S. Senator, all by the age of 40. Only recently, in 1860, he had experienced his first (and only) political defeat – for the presidency – when he lost to another native Kentuckian, Abraham Lincoln. Now, as a senator in Washington, D.C., he faced the choice all Kentuckians did – would he support the Union or the Confederacy?

General John Cabell Breckinridge, C.S.A.

His uncle and father-figure had already made his course known. On the Washington Monument in 1850, Kentucky had carved the words: "Under the auspices of Heaven, and the precepts of Washington, Kentucky will be the last to give up the Union." Robert Jefferson Breckinridge agreed. Like many Kentuckians at the start of the war, he did not see it as a fight against slavery. After all, he owned 37 slaves. (His nephew John C. Breckinridge likely owned none at the time.) Robert, like the commonwealth generally, wanted both union and slavery.

The 61-year old Robert J. Breckinridge had already had a distinguished – and controversial – career. A Presbyterian divine, he had held his church's highest national office. As Kentucky superintendent of public instruction, he rightfully earned the title "The Father of the Public School System." Yet he also had been strongly anti-Catholic and anti-immigrant in words and actions, both before and during the Know-Nothing movement of the 1850s. Now, in 1861, he became one of the most important spokesmen for the Union cause in Kentucky.

To Robert, disunion would destroy what he saw as God's vision for America. He told of the horrors of secession – the reopening of the slave trade, a bankrupt continent, the destruction of the constitution, anarchy, and untold deaths: "If we desire to perish, all we have to do is leap into this vortex of disunion." Robert's course took a clear and forceful direction.

The decision came harder for his nephew John C. Breckinridge. Like his uncle, he began to warn of horrors also, only in this case, ones connected to the federal government. He predicted that the abolitionists would gain control and let loose on the land hordes of free blacks. Calling Lincoln's early wartime actions unconstitutional and dictatorial, Breckinridge argued that cherished national principles soon would be further destroyed. He feared a military despotism, a "war of extermination," an "endless, aimless, devastating war." Still a U.S. Senator months after Bull Run, Breckinridge now was called a traitor in the midst of Unionists. Later in the year, he made his decision: "I exchange with proud satisfaction a term of six years in the United States Senate for the musket of a soldier." He would go on to be a Confederate general and fought across the South – at Shiloh, Port Hudson, Stone's River, Chickamauga, Chattanooga, New Market, and Winchester. Near conflict's end he became Confederate Secretary of War. In all areas, he served well.

Yet, he could never free himself from the harsh realities of a war that so haunted him. At a banquet at the Confederate capital, he was asked if he had spent a nice evening. With the gaiety and laughter all around him, John C. Breckinridge solemnly answered, "I do not know. I have asked myself more than once tonight, 'Are you the same man who stood gazing down on the faces of the dead...?' The soldiers lying there, they stare at you with their eyes wide open. Is this the same world?" Breckinridge knew war and disliked what he knew.

His decision to join the Confederacy did not prove to be the last defection within Robert J. Breckinridge's Unionist ranks. All around the Reverend Breckinridge, families had divided. Mary Todd Lincoln, the Kentucky-born wife of President Lincoln, saw a brother, three half-brothers, and then husbands of three half-sisters all fight against the cause her husband led. Another of her brothers and a half-sister remained loyal to the northern cause. One Crittenden son became a Union Army general, another a Confederate one. In Robert's own family, of his four adult sons, two rode north, two south. His house had divided against itself.

Robert Jefferson Breckinridge in later life

In fact, wartime events sorely tested Robert's own loyalties to the Union. He had supported a constitutional union, not an immediate end to slavery. Lincoln's actions toward ending "the peculiar institution" stunned Breckinridge. Finally, he compromised his beliefs for the greater good of the nation, but in doing so, he became an even fiercer advocate of the cause. In 1864, he served as temporary chairman of the Republican convention that renominated his friend Lincoln. His body bent by age, but with still eloquent voice, the "Napoleon of the Pulpit" rose to stress that the Constitution must be maintained and the Union should "put to death friend or foe who undertakes to trample it underfoot." Then, this man whose nephew and two sons fought for the Confederacy cried out that "the only

imperishable cement" of free institutions had been the "blood of traitors."

Back in Kentucky, Breckinridge endorsed ever harsher actions. When told of possible illegal arrests by Unionists of innocent people, he recalled how a French Catholic leader in earlier times had killed some heretics during a religious war: "He was appealed to by certain persons – declaring that his men were mistaken, they were killing many who were good Catholics. To which he replied: 'Kill them *all*; God knows his own!' And," said Breckinridge, "this is the way we should deal with these fellows; treat them all alike and if there are any among them who are not rebels at heart, God will take care of them and save them at last." That interesting approach earned him few friends in the South.

And it created even deeper emotional wounds in his family. His most talented son, William Campbell Preston "Willie" Breckinridge, had tried to remain neutral – like Kentucky – at first. After all, as a newly-wed, he had promised to sustain his wife, "alleviating pain with love, driving away care with tenderness." He told her he knew not the future, "but nothing can take out of my heart the memory of your love & trust & confidence."

But soon the young attorney would leave all that behind, and not see her again for the rest of the war. On July 15, 1862, he told his father of his decision to join the raiders of John Hunt Morgan. Later he became a colonel in the 9th Kentucky Cavalry.

Yet, in that strangest of American wars, father and son continued to tell of their love for each other, even as they spoke and fought for opposite causes. In March 1864, Willie had written to Robert: "I pray God that we may both survive this war long enough for you to know that I loved you as a son ought." And to his wife, Willie explained that his father's harsh speech meant little to him: "Nothing he can say or do can make me forget that he is my father & was a loving, kind, indulgent father, to whom I owe more than I can repay."

Robert, in turn, might speak of death to traitors in his talks, but in the end, family won out over philosophy. Love drove away hate. When his namesake Robert Jr. was captured by Federal forces and seemed ready to go to the prison camps where the death knell rang almost daily, Robert J. Breckinridge Sr. saw to it that he went instead to a penitentiary in Ohio, the only Confederate prisoner there. And when Union soldiers seized Robert's son-in-law and threatened to kill him as a guerrilla, Robert took pen in hand

and asked the Union general not to hang his son-in-law, but to treat him as a prisoner of war. The U.S. Attorney General personally wrote to tell Robert that his wish would be followed.

On the other side, when Confederate soldier Willie Breckinridge learned that his Union brother Joseph Breckinridge had been captured in a fight not far from him, Willie rode through the night to see his sibling. They talked, Willie gave him some gold coins to help secure "favors," and both Willie and Robert worked – successfully – to get Joseph exchanged and out of prison. And, in fact, all four Breckinridge sons (and the son-in-law) returned safely from the war, as did John C. Breckinridge. Few Kentucky families could say that.

In Confederate Secretary of War Breckinridge's case, however, war's end did not bring immediate peace. Fearing arrest and imprisonment – as happened to Jefferson Davis – he fled through the wilds of Florida. Mosquitoes, ticks, flies, and other bugs tormented him as he went south. Alligators threatened. Hunger held sway. Risking death, he and a few others made a heroic crossing in a small boat to Cuba. From there, he toured Europe and the Holy Land, and then settled in Canada, awaiting the amnesty that came only in 1869.

As he finally made his way back to Kentucky, crowds cheered him all along the route. The scene filled him with emotion. He said, almost to himself, "Nearly eight years ago." It had been that long since he had seen his beloved Kentucky. Breckinridge later practiced law and engaged in business, but the war and the exile had exacted their toll. He died, at age 54, in 1875.

The war went on for Robert J. Breckinridge also, long after Appomattox. The victorious Unionist welcomed his wayward rebel son Willie back from the war, "without reproach or censure; without patronage or evidence of triumph – the welcome of one who was gentleman as well as father."

It seemed, as novelist Fox later wrote, "When the war was over, the hatchet in Kentucky was buried at once and buried deep. Son came back to father, brother to brother ... and the sundered threads, unraveled by the war, were united together fast."

But not all proved so willing to forget the past. Willie's wife had been angry over her father-in-law's harsh words, and had not let him see his granddaughter during the war. In one unexpected instance, as Robert walked down a street one day, he recognized a servant who had his granddaughter with her. He had placed the little girl on his lap and cried out, "God bless the child. She is the prettiest thing I ever saw." Then she was taken away, for the duration.

Even after the war had ended, Willie's wife refused to let Robert see that grandchild, or another that was born. Finally, after the birth of a third grandchild, almost three years after the war had ended, she relented. On the back of the envelope bearing the news that he could see them at last, Robert wrote in his feeble scrawl something that appeared on no other letter in his surviving correspondence: "Important. Important."

Robert had their company less than a half-decade. He died in December 1871. Willie Breckinridge lived on for more than three decades, until his death in 1904, at age 67. In that time he became a five-term congressman, earned the sobriquet "The Silver-Tongued Orator from Kentucky," and later served as editor of the *Lexington Herald*. In one of his talks, Willie Breckinridge concluded that "He who follows truth for truth's sake as it is given him to see it will follow duty, be accompanied by honor, and crowned by God." In the wartime years, all the Breckinridges had followed duty and honor, as they each had perceived it. Yet, even though time had only slowly healed the emotional wounds of war, in the end the Breckinridges had also followed the ties of family that bound them all together stronger than any cause. Knowing that, they had faced with confidence a postwar world – and the unknown future.

* * *

THE BATTLE OF RICHMOND
AUGUST 29-30, 1862

By Robert C. Moody

The Herndon House (built around 1824) was at the center of Phase I of the Battle of Richmond and was used to treat the wounded during and after the battle. Blood stains can still be seen on the floor in a second-story room. The house will be used as the central facility in Battlefield Park.

The battle of Richmond had its origin in a Chattanooga hotel room on July 31, 1862. As a flickering kerosene lamp illuminated a Kentucky-Tennessee map pinned to the wall, Confederate generals Braxton Bragg and E. Kirby Smith devised a plan to thwart Gen. Don Carlos Buell, whose Union army was threatening Chattanooga. Bragg commanded the Military Department No. 2 and Smith commanded the Department of East Tennessee. The two Confederate commands were independent of each other; however, their territorial responsibilities overlapped.

The plan developed by Bragg and Smith presupposed that thousands of Kentuckians would rally behind the Confederate colors when an organized Confederate army entered Kentucky. John Hunt Morgan had practically assured the two generals that this would happen. Such would more than replenish the depleted Confederate ranks occasioned by their Shiloh losses. In the end, the Kentucky invasion did not achieve that result.

The plan called for Bragg to assemble his army at Chattanooga and for Smith to move his and take the strategically important Cumberland Gap, which was held by the Federals and threatened Knoxville. Smith was then to return to middle Tennessee and link up with Bragg, where

they would begin a joint assault on Buell. On paper, this was a simple, workable plan.

On August 14, Smith left Knoxville, but he soon deviated from the plan, there being no military requirement that he adhere to it. He bypassed Cumberland Gap, leaving his First Infantry Division, commanded by Gen. Carter Stevenson, to surround that Union redoubt. He then proceeded north to the Bluegrass with his other three infantry divisions and cavalry brigade. His army, now called the Confederate Army of Kentucky, proceeded along Old State Road (now U.S. 25, Ky. 1912, and U.S. 421) to Barbourville, London, Mt. Vernon, and Big Hill in Madison County.

Smith used his cavalry brigade as the army's spearhead. It arrived at Big Hill on August 23 and immediately fought a small engagement with Union cavalry. The victorious Confederates sent a delegation to demand surrender of Union-occupied Richmond. When the Union commander in Richmond declined, the Confederate cavalry retired to Rockcastle County to await Smith's orders.

Smith's infantry arrived at Big Hill on August 29, led by Gen. Patrick R. Cleburne's Fourth Infantry Division. General Smith ordered him forward five miles to a place on the old state road called Bobtown. Gen. Thomas J. Churchill's Third Infantry Division trailed at a distance and Gen. Henry Heth's Second Infantry Division was in reserve at a great distance and played no active part in the Battle of Richmond. The 15-day trek by those mostly barefoot soldiers, through the mountains from Knoxville to Big Hill, was made with sparse provisions and little or no water. Their tramp, in the sweltering August heat and through unsympathetic territory, brought them to Big Hill spoiling for a fight. They didn't have long to wait.

Union intelligence revealed the Confederate move north and defensive preparations were made. Gen. William "Bull" Nelson was charged with defending the area. He assembled 6,500 men into two brigades, one commanded by Gen. Mahlon Manson and the other by Gen. Charles Cruft. The governors of Ohio and Indiana, in response to emergency pleas, sent Nelson untrained conscripts, some of whom had been in the military but two weeks. General Nelson also had at his disposal some cavalry and artillery units. His strategic plan was to establish a defensive line at the precipitous Kentucky River palisades at Clay's Ferry in Fayette County. He issued appropriate orders and repaired to Lancaster where various units had been sent to prepare to strike Smith's western flank. Those orders did not reach Manson and Cruft in time for them to act or they were simply ignored. Those brigades had moved to Richmond on the 29th and precipitated some minor skirmishes on Old State Road south of the city, and at Rogersville and at Bobtown.

On the morning of the 30th, about five miles south of Richmond, General Manson established a defensive line of regiments perpendicular to and crossing Old State Road even with, and somewhat south of, Mt. Zion Church. General Smith ordered General Cleburne out of his Bobtown bivouac, to the village of Kingston, some three miles north. As one of his Tennessee units cleared the town, a Union artillery shell cracked overhead and rolled down the road. He placed his regiments in lines on the east side of Old State Road north of the east-west, Lancaster-Irvine mud road (Crooksville Road/Ky. 499) with an artillery battery forward in the center. A counter-battery artillery duel followed from 8am to 10am. Smith ordered Cleburne to conserve his artillery ammunition and to avoid a general engagement until Churchill's trailing division arrived. Cleburne slowed the fighting. Churchill arrived in Kingston about 8am. and immediately began an encirclement of the Union right. It was at this point in the battle that General Cleburne's

tactics provided the advantages which won this stage of the battle and ultimately the entire battle.

He sent a company of sharpshooters west of Old State Road to soften up the Union artillery near the church. This tactic succeeded. He personally selected the sites for his artillery batteries. They were extremely effective. (Most Civil War generals had little knowledge of the proper use of artillery). Cleburne noticed that the Union commander, Manson, was attempting to turn the Confederates' right flank. Cleburne was able to sense this by interpreting sounds of battle. Manson had indeed pulled his troops from the middle of his line and moved them to the left. It was then that Cleburne threw his Shiloh veterans against the weakened center and the whole Union line collapsed.

To the west of Old State Road, Churchill turned Manson's right and captured many Union prisoners west of the church. He skillfully used a ravine and tall cornfields to conceal his soldiers and surprise the Federals.

By early afternoon, those Union soldiers who had fled the line near the church established another defensive line where present-day Duncannon Lane intersects Old State Road. The Confederates quickly pursued and intense combat ensued, mainly on the west side of the Old State Road, with Churchill's somewhat-rested Confederate division carrying the fight. Here again, the Union line collapsed and fled north toward Richmond. Sensing a rout, Smith ordered his cavalry to skirt west of Richmond to trap the exhausted Federals. This was readily accomplished.

The bedraggled Union army again retreated some three miles north and set up yet another defensive line in the Richmond Cemetery behind a fence. The Confederates pursued and the battle resumed. The experienced Confederates' battle tactics panicked the green Union units which became utterly disorganized. General Nelson arrived from Lancaster about 2pm and attempted to rally the Union troops. About this time, from his horse, the corpulent Nelson uttered his famous line, "Boys, if they can't hit me they can't hit a barn door." He was hit at once, and seriously wounded. Nelson failed to reestablish a fighting force from the disorganized units. He was captured, but later escaped in the darkness. The Confederates routed the Union forces in the cemetery, who abandoned their equipment and broke and fled northwest on Richmond's Main Street. This military debacle in the Richmond Cemetery essentially concluded the Battle of Richmond, although some minor mopping-up actions occurred north of the city.

KENTUCKY'S CIVIL WAR MAP

Linda Doane

Kentucky's Civil War Map

1. Columbus-Belmont State Park/Museum/Walking Tour
2. Downtown Paducah Walking Tour
3. General Lloyd Tilghman Historic Home
4. William Clark Market House Museum
5. Fort Smith Walking Tour
6. Fort Heiman
7. Ft. Donelson National Battlefield/Driving Tour
8. Kentucky/Ohio River Civil War Heritage Trail
9. Battle of Sacramento Driving Tour
10. Jefferson Davis Monument State Historic Site
11. Octagon Hall and Old Stone Jail
12. Bowling Green Driving Tour
13. Riverview at Hobson Grove
14. Fort Williams
15. Hart Co. Museum/Walking Tour
16. The Lincoln Museum
17. Abraham Lincoln Birthplace National Historic Site
18. Hardin County History Museum
19. Elizabethtown Downtown Walking Tour
20. Old Bardstown Village Civil War Museum
21. Women of the Civil War Museum
22. Spalding Hall
23. Bullitt Co. Civil War Heritage Trail
24. Fort Duffield
25. John Hunt Morgan—Meade Co./Ohio River Crossing
26. John Hunt Morgan Heritage Trail
27. Frazier Historical Arms Museum
28. Cave Hill Cemetery
29. Pewee Valley Confederate Cemetery
30. National Underground Freedom Center
31. Roebling Suspension Bridge
32. Behringer-Crawford Museum
33. Battles of Cynthiana Driving Tour
34. Cynthiana-Harrison Co. Museum
35. Kentucky Military History Museum
36. Kentucky History Center
37. The Leslie Morris Park on Fort Hill
38. Frankfort/Greenhill Cemeteries
39. Cardome Centre/Georgetown-Scott Co. Museum
40. Hunt-Morgan House
41. Lexington Cemetery
42. Mary Todd Lincoln House
43. Camp Nelson Heritage Park and National Cemetery
44. Perryville Battlefield State Historic Site
45. Lebanon Driving and Walking Tour
46. John Hunt Morgan in Kentucky Heritage Trail
47. Tebbs Bend Battlefield/Driving Tour
48. Civil War Walking Tour of Campbellsville
49. Mill Springs Battlefield/Zollicoffer Park
50. Battle of Richmond Driving Tour
51. Battle of Camp Wildcat Walking Tour
52. Cumberland Gap National Historic Park
53. Ivy Mountain Battlefield Interpretive Site
54. Middle Creek National Battlefield
55. Samuel May House
56. Mason County Museum
57. National Underground Railroad Museum
58. Harriet Beecher Stowe Slavery to Freedom Museum

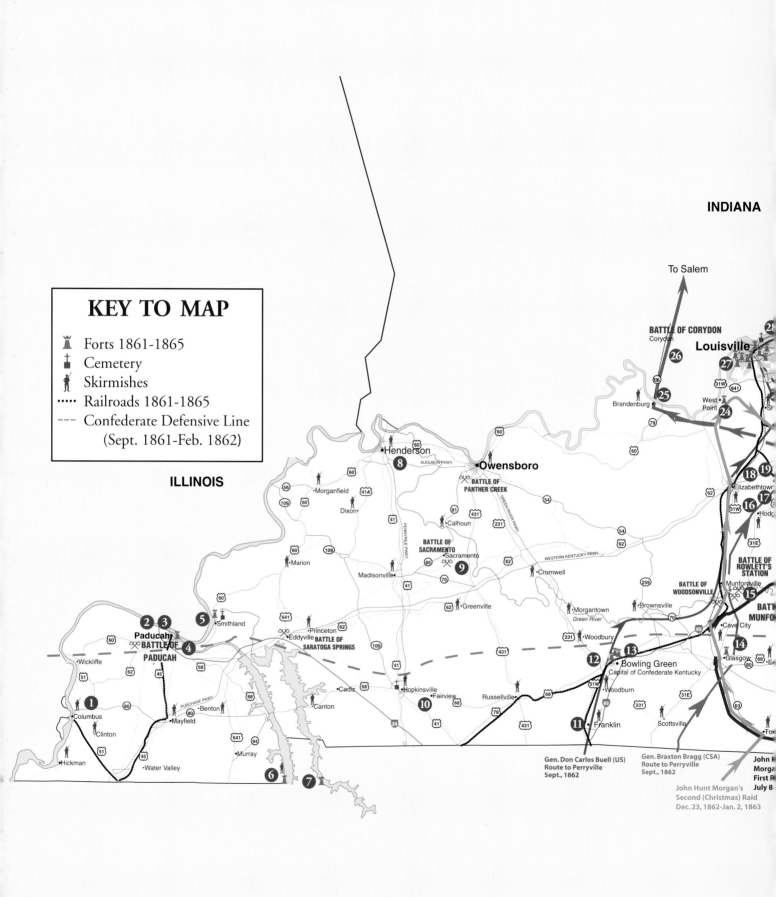

KEY TO MAP

♜ Forts 1861-1865
✝ Cemetery
🏃 Skirmishes
••••• Railroads 1861-1865
– – – Confederate Defensive Line
(Sept. 1861-Feb. 1862)

ILLINOIS

INDIANA

To Salem

BATTLE OF CORYDON
Corydon
26
Louisville
25
Brandenburg
27
West Point
24
841
79
23

Henderson
8
AUDUBON PKWY.
•Owensboro
BATTLE OF PANTHER CREEK
60

56
•Morganfield
41A
109
60
Dixon
41
431
81
•Calhoun
231
54
54
60
109
BATTLE OF SACRAMENTO
85
•Sacramento
62
9
WESTERN KENTUCKY PKWY.
US 62
•Marion
•Madisonville
70
•Cromwell
259
BATTLE OF WOODSONVILLE
Munfordville
18 **19**
•Elizabethtown
62
31W
16 **17**
•Hodg
31E
BATTLE OF ROWLETT'S STATION
15
41
•Greenville
62
BATT MUNFO
•Morgantown
Green River
•Brownsville
70
65
•Cave City
14
60
641
•Princeton
62
•Eddyville **BATTLE OF SARATOGA SPRINGS**
109
431
231 •Woodbury
13
12
•Bowling Green
Capital of Confederate Kentucky
•Glasgow
68
80
Paducah•
BATTLE OF PADUCAH
2 **3**
5
•Smithland
4
•Wickliffe
60
45
68
PURCHASE PKWY.
68
•Cadiz
68
•Canton
41
•Hopkinsville
•Fairview
Russellville
79
31W
•Woodburn
231
31E
63
51
62
80
1
•Benton
24
10
•Franklin
•Scottsville
11
•Columbus
•Clinton
641
94
•Murray
6
7
Gen. Don Carlos Buell (US) Route to Perryville Sept., 1862
Gen. Braxton Bragg (CSA) Route to Perryville Sept., 1862
John H Morga First R July 8
•Hickman
51
45
•Water Valley
•Tor
John Hunt Morgan's Second (Christmas) Raid Dec. 23, 1862-Jan. 2, 1863

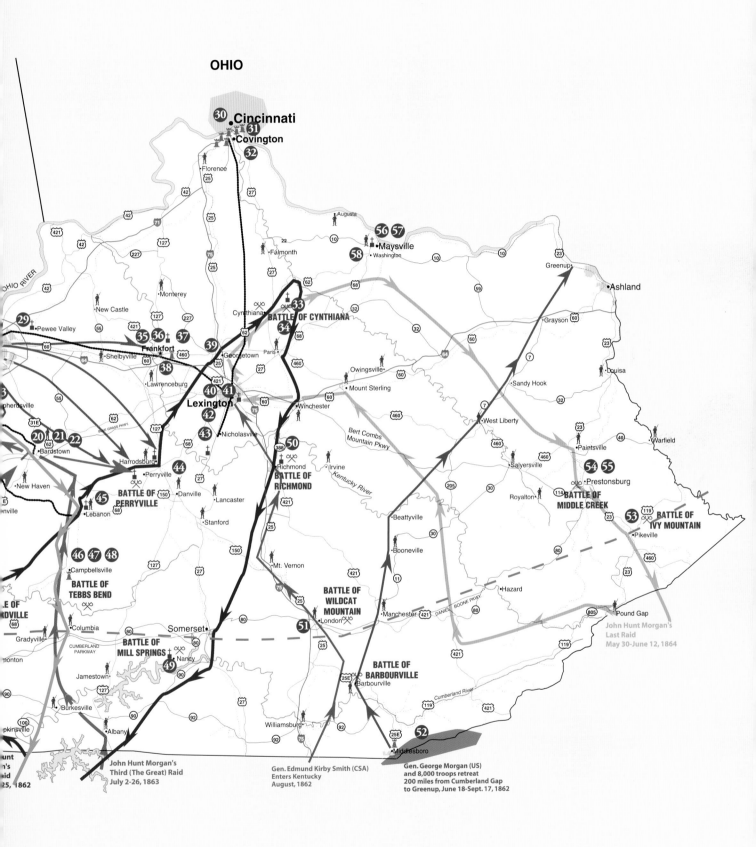

OHIO

③⓪ •Cincinnati
③① •Covington
③②
•Florence
㉕
㊷
•Augusta
㊳ •Falmonth
②② 🔟
⑤⑥⑤⑦
•Maysville
⑤⑧ •Washington

OHIO RIVER

•New Castle
•Monterey
Cynthiana• ③③ **BATTLE OF CYNTHIANA**
③④
•Paris
②⑨ •Pewee Valley
③⑤③⑥ ③⑦ ③⑨
Frankfort
•Shelbyville
③⑧
•Lawrenceburg
•Georgetown
④⓪④① •Winchester
•Mount Sterling
•Owingsville
herdsville
⓶⓪ ②① ②②
•Bardstown
Lexington
④②
④③ •Nicholasville
⑤⓪
•Richmond
BATTLE OF RICHMOND
•Irvine
Bert Combs
Mountain Pkwy
Kentucky River
•West Liberty

•New Haven
•Harrodsburg
④④
•Perryville
④⑤
•Danville
BATTLE OF PERRYVILLE
•Lebanon
•Stanford
•Lancaster
•Beattyville
•Booneville
•Royalton
④⑥④⑦④⑧
•Campbellsville
BATTLE OF TEBBS BEND
•Mt. Vernon
BATTLE OF WILDCAT MOUNTAIN
•Manchester
⑤①
DVILLE
•Columbia
•Somerset
•Gradyville
CUMBERLAND PARKWAY
BATTLE OF MILL SPRINGS
•Nancy
④⑨
•Jamestown
BATTLE OF BARBOURVILLE
•Barbourville
•Burkesville
•Albany
•Williamsburg
⑤②
•Middlesboro

•Sandy Hook
•Grayson
•Greenup
•Ashland
•Louisa
•Salyersville
•Warfield
•Paintsville
⑤④⑤⑤
•Prestonsburg
BATTLE OF MIDDLE CREEK
⑤③ **BATTLE OF IVY MOUNTAIN**
•Pikeville
•Hazard
DANIEL BOONE PKWY
•Pound Gap
John Hunt Morgan's
Last Raid
May 30-June 12, 1864
Cumberland River

**John Hunt Morgan's
Third (The Great) Raid
July 2-26, 1863**

**Gen. Edmund Kirby Smith (CSA)
Enters Kentucky
August, 1862**

**Gen. George Morgan (US)
and 8,000 troops retreat
200 miles from Cumberland Gap
to Greenup, June 18-Sept. 17, 1862**

Battle of Richmond Reenactment

Reenactment photos by Frank Becker

The Battle of Richmond was Kentucky's second-largest Civil War battle. Of the 6,500 Union men involved, 5,353 were killed, captured, or wounded. Accordingly, it was the most overwhelming Confederate victory in the entire Civil War. Of the 6,000 Confederate infantry and 800 cavalry engaged, 600 were killed, captured or wounded. This western theater Confederate victory got very little contemporary press attention as it occurred on the same day as Second Manassas in the eastern theater.

The Battle of Richmond had many interesting sidelights. A Confederate artillery battery commander was arrested for allowing his men to ride on his gun carriages. A wounded Confederate soldier was discovered to be a female by a treating Union surgeon. A Confederate general suffered a wound by having a minié ball enter his wide-open mouth. A rare occasion occurred when a single artillery spherical shot shell killed two Confederate artillerists. The Federals captured a mountain howitzer from the Confederate cavalry. It was then fired at the Confederates until it was recaptured along with most of the Union equipment and supplies. The battle records and local traditions are replete with examples of the many kindnesses extended to the wounded of both sides by local citizens. One family treated a wounded soldier from each side.

The Battle of Richmond raged on and off for more than ten hours on August 30, 1862, with the result being a tremendous victory by hardened veterans over untrained conscripts. For a battle not meant to be fought when and where it was, it created a tremendous morale boost for the Confederates. The advantages gained by the lopsided victory were subsequently squandered away by their commanders' indecisiveness before, during, and after the later Perryville battle and the withdrawal of their forces from Kentucky.

* * *

'THE BIG BULL IS DEAD'

By Dr. Marshall Myers

On September 29, 1862, Union General William "Bull" Nelson lay on a bed near death in Louisville's Galt House, his own blood staining his white vest. He was a mountain of a man: six feet four or five inches tall and 300 pounds, with curly brown hair and a matching beard. He commanded and received respect for his size alone.

Union general, fellow Kentuckian, and life-long friend Thomas Crittenden, was staying in the same hotel and rushed to Nelson's side.

"Tom, I am murdered," Nelson told him. Nelson requested a clergyman; he had never been baptized. Rev. J.J. Talbott of Calvary Episcopal Church was summoned. Dr. Robert Murray, Major Gen. Don Carlos Buell's Medical Director, was asked to assist in the medical treatment, but there was little the physician could do. Within the hour, General William "Bull" Nelson was dead.

Nelson's murder is a complex story that stretches from Camp Dick Robinson to Shiloh, to the Battle of Richmond, and finally to Louisville and the panic that gripped that city in the fall of 1862.

He was born on September 27, 1824, to a prominent Maysville, Kentucky, family who counted the Crittendens, Clays and Beckinridges as friends. Nelson studied at Norwich Academy in Vermont, followed in 1840 by the United States Naval Academy. At the height of the Mexican War in 1847, he served in support of General Winfield Scott's troops at Vera Cruz. By 1855, Nelson had reached what was then the prestigious rank of lieutenant.

When Lincoln was elected in 1860, he appointed Thomas Nelson, William's brother, as minister to Chile, while William also volunteered his services to the newly-elected president. Lincoln respected William "Bull" Nelson, a man who earned his sobriquet for his blaring, authoritative, foghorn voice, the kind of sound that causes men to snap to and pay attention.

Lincoln sent Nelson on a delicate mission. Trying to respect Kentucky's self-imposed neutrality and also to save it for the Union, Lincoln asked Nelson to assess the Union sentiment in Kentucky and the need for arms, but he didn't want to tip the state's citizenry toward the South and secession. Kentucky was a key state to the Union, vastly more important than just as the geographical shield to the states below her.

General William "Bull" Nelson

Kentucky Historical Society

Kentucky had two competing military organizations, both supposedly bent on defending the state's neutrality. The State Guards, headed by Simon Bolivar Buckner, who along with his men were decidedly Confederate in sympathies, and the Home Guards, who generally leaned toward the Union. While they may have differed in their political sympathies, both groups needed one thing: guns, and lots of them.

Nelson easily persuaded Lincoln that the guns should go to those who supported the Union, and they were secretly distributed around the state, using key people in Union Kentucky politics, among them, friends of Lincoln like Joshua Speed, James Harlan, and Charles H. Wickliffe.

Historian Lowell Harrison remarks that Nelson, with his booming voice and gruff manner, was "one of the most unusual undercover agents of the Civil War." But Nelson accomplished his mission, earning the respect of both Lincoln and his supporters across the state. July, 1861, Nelson was given 10,000 arms, six cannon, and a generous supply of ammunition and ordered to raise five Union regiments from within the state. Nelson soon set up a recruiting camp, first at Crab Orchard and later at Camp Dick Robinson in Garrard County.

When he found out about it, Kentucky's Southern-leaning governor, Beriah Magoffin, was furious, arguing in a long letter to Lincoln that such a recruitment was in gross violation of Kentucky's neutrality. Sensing Kentucky's political winds were decidedly blowing toward the Union, based on a recent general election in Kentucky, Lincoln's reply to Magoffin's protests was polite, but hardly an attempt to mend political fences. Amid all the controversy at the highest levels of government, Lincoln rewarded Nelson by commissioning him a brigadier general of volunteers in the Army of the Ohio. Out of state, Nelson and his men fought at Shiloh, Corinth, and Chattanooga, where Nelson earned a reputation as a tough taskmaster, reportedly rallying his troops by hitting the men on the shoulders with the flat part of his sword, all the while bellowing in that deep, resonant voice.

Yet it was within the state that Nelson set in motion the events that would eventually lead to his death. General William Tecumseh Sherman, who had assumed command of the state volunteers from the ailing General Robert Anderson, ordered Nelson on September 15, 1861, to relinquish his duties at Camp Dick Robinson and go to Maysville to organize a campaign to drive Confederates out of eastern Kentucky and to open the way to East Tennessee and its many Union recruits, supplies and supporters.

Particularly troublesome to Sherman were Confederate troops occupying Hazel Green, West Liberty, Prestonsburg, and Pikeville. With four incomplete regiments from Ohio, plus some Kentucky volunteers, Nelson headed south, swiftly driving an under-armed and ragged lot of 2,000 Confederate forces from Hazel Green and West Liberty. Learning of the Union advance, Confederate Colonel Andrew Jackson May abandoned Prestonsburg and began falling back to join a larger Confederate force in Pikeville under Colonel John S. Williams. On the way, May sought to slow down Nelson's advance by taking the defensible position where Ivy Creek and Levisa Fork joined at the foot of Ivy Mountain, where the 700 Confederates, they thought, would have the advantage.

On November 8, 1861, after a tussle of about 80 minutes with Nelson's Union forces, the Confederates retreated, unable to deal with the larger and more thoroughly trained Yankee forces. The following day, Nelson and his troops marched toward Pikeville, occupying it on November 10.

Ultimately, it was at the Battle of Richmond that events would be set in motion that led to Nelson's demise.

"Don't engage the Confederates south of the Kentucky River, unless you are sure of success," were the orders General Horatio G. Wright, commander of the Union forces from the Department of the Ohio in Cincinnati, gave Nelson. Wright understood keenly that the troops Nelson commanded in Lexington were hardly well-trained and that the Kentucky River, with its sheer cliffs, would be highly defensible, but south of the river the terrain was much more to the Confederates' advantage. So when Confederate Gen. Kirby Smith crossed into Kentucky at Cumberland Gap and made for the Bluegrass, according to battle expert Warren Lambert, the only thing stopping him and his 6,850 men, were 6,500 green Federal troops on the south side of the Kentucky River.

Nelson, however, was not there, and never relayed Wright's message to Brigadier General Mahlon D. Manson, Union commander of troops around Richmond. By the morning of August 29, 1862, skirmishing had begun around Richmond, at Big Hill, Kingston, and Bobtown. Fierce fighting continued the next day at Mt. Zion Church, White's Farm, and finally at the Richmond Cemetery – largely without Nelson, who, late on the second day, rushed from Lexington to meet the battle. True to his nickname, Nelson assumed command, bellowing orders and spouting scathing epithets, as James Lee McDonough in *War in Kentucky*, notes, "cursing, shouting, and berating the men as cowards, [riding] among the troops, trying to rally the panic-stricken, knocking some down with his fist, using the flat of his sword to strike others."

By late afternoon, the battle had turned into a stunning Confederate victory. There is little to prevent most of the blame for the "Second Yankee Skedaddle," after Bull Run, to be placed in large part, at Nelson's feet. While Manson may have been too eager to taste battle, Nelson should have been more forthcoming with Manson about Wright's orders and should have been there for the duration of the battle itself. Instead of humbling himself, Nelson assumed his usual brusque and brassy manner. On September 25, for example, he boldly ordered a progress report on fortifications from General Jefferson C. Davis, a man who not only had an unfortunate name, but also called Indiana home. (A number of sources cite Nelson's deep dislike of all things Hoosier.) According to historian Kirk Jenkins, Davis and Nelson got into a heated exchange, with Davis demanding "the courtesy due my rank!" "I will treat you as you deserve. You have disappointed me... You are relieved from duty here, and will proceed to Cincinnati and report to General Wright," Nelson barked back. Four days later, with the Indiana governor in tow, Davis again challenged Nelson at the Galt House. "General Nelson," Davis sneered. "I want to know why you disgraced me by placing me under arrest?" "Do you know who you are talking to?" Nelson barked. Davis repeated the question. "Go away, you damned puppy. I don't want anything to do with you!" Nelson snapped.

Davis grabbed a calling card from the hotel desk, wadded it up and threw it in Nelson's face. Nelson then slapped Davis with the back of his hand and headed toward his room, eyes afire. Davis quickly secured a pistol and followed Nelson up the stairs. "Not another step farther," Davis demanded, and looked into Nelson's eyes and fired from about a yard away, striking Nelson just above the heart.

Amazingly, in spite of this obviously cold-blooded murder of a Union general in time of war, and in spite of a number of eye-witnesses, Davis was never prosecuted. Whether it was Governor Morton's considerable political pull in Washington, or the honor afforded a military officer to avenge an insult, or just military exigency in a time of panic, Davis was never punished.

* * *

The shooting of General Nelson

THE BATTLE OF MUNFORDVILLE

By Bryan Bush

Battle of Munfordville

In August 1862, Confederate General Braxton Bragg, commander of the Army of the Mississippi, and Confederate General Edmund Kirby Smith, commander of the Army of East Tennessee, decided upon a plan to maneuver the Federals out of Alabama and Tennessee, and possibly take Kentucky. In September, General Smith was the first to enter Kentucky and took Lexington. Smith had been successful in routing the only serious Federal force in the state at the Battle of Richmond. General Bragg was soon to follow Smith into Kentucky. Bragg's first battle would occur at a place called Munfordville.

On September 8, 1862, Union Col. John T. Wilder assumed command of the forces at Munfordville. He immediately set about building fortifications for the defense of the railroad bridge over the Green River. Wilder's force of over 4,000 men (mostly from Indiana companies), consisted of three regiments and one company of cavalry, and four pieces of heavy artillery. On September 9, the railroad bridge at the Salt River was burned by the Confederates and no supplies were able to reach Wilder's men. He had only one day's rations, so he set about collecting flour and bacon from the surrounding area, bought bread from Bowling Green, and was able to collect 15 days' worth of rations. At the same time, Wilder ordered all Home Guard companies and recruits for the 33rd Kentucky who were not equipped with

arms, to act as scouts. It was the 33rd Kentucky that informed Wilder of Confederate General Braxton Bragg's arrival into Kentucky from the Cumberland River.

With the scouts watching Bragg's approach, Wilder learned Bragg's numbers, pieces of artillery, and his direction. On Saturday, Sept. 13, Col. John S. Scott, of the 1st Louisiana Cavalry and a battery of five mountain howitzers, came down the north side of the river from Greensburg and at 8pm demanded that Wilder surrender Fort Craig. Wilder refused. That night, Brig. Gen. James Chalmers' Mississippi Brigade, which was comprised of the 7th, 9th, 10th, 20th, 29th, and 44th Mississippi, and Capt. James Garrity's and Scott's Louisiana batteries, arrived and at 3:00 o'clock the next morning, Scott's and Chalmers' men fired on Wilder's pickets. Chalmers sent three regiments against the western Union stockade and two regiments against the eastern blockhouse. Capt. William Ketchum's Confederate battery was brought up.

At daybreak a furious attack was made on the pickets on the south side of the river by a large force of infantry. Wilder sent Company K, 74th Indiana, out to a belt of woods about a quarter mile in advance, to act as a reserve for the pickets to rally on. They held their ground until surrounded and fell back only when ordered by Major David Cubberly of the

Harper's History of the Great Rebellion, Harper's Weekly

89th Indiana, who had charge of the pickets and skirmishers on the south side of the river. Wilder's advance line fought the Confederates for an hour, until the line was called back into the fort by Col. Wilder. At 5:30am, the fighting broke out along the whole line. The Confederates advanced within 200 yards of Wilder's works. An hour later, when the Confederates advanced in battleline upon the west, or main work, Wilder ordered his men to fix bayonets and prepare for an assault. The Confederates came screaming into the works. When the Confederates came within 30 yards, Wilder ordered his men to fire. Wilder said that a "very avalanche of death swept through the ranks," causing the Confederates to first stagger and then run in disorder to the woods in the rear, having left their field officers on the ground either killed or wounded. The regiments that made the charge were the 7th and 10th Mississippi and 7th Alabama.

Another attack was made on the redoubt by the 9th and 29th Mississippi and a battalion of sharpshooters. Wilder reported that the Confederates were "murdered by a terrible fire from the gallant defenders of the work."

Maj. Augustus Abbott sprang upon the parapet, with his hat in one hand and a drawn saber in the other, urging his men to stand by the works, until he was shot dead under the flag he was defending. The flag had 146 bullet holes shot through it and the staff was struck 11 times.

Lt. Tyler Mason, of the 13th Indiana, commanding the artillery, was riddling the Confederates with grapeshot and canister, when the Confederates broke and ran in all directions, fleeing the scene. Wilder sent Col. Frank Emerson, of the 67th Indiana, with one company, to reinforce the redoubt and to take command. The Confederates rallied, and kept up a constant fire. They charged again, but were repulsed. At 9:30am. Chalmers sent in a flag of truce, and sent a message to Wilder. The note said, "You have made a gallant defense of your position, and to avoid further bloodshed I demand an unconditional surrender of your forces. I have six regiments of infantry, one battalion of infantry sharpshooters, and have just been reinforced by a brigade of cavalry, under Colonel Scott, with two battalions of artillery. I have

Col. Thomas White, of the Ninth Mississippi Infantry, participated in the Battle of Munfordville. Thses are two views of his sword's handle.

Col. Thomas White's Sword

two regiments on the north side of the river, and you can't escape. The railroad track is torn up in your rear and you can't receive reenforcements. General Bragg's army is but a short distance in the rear." Wilder wrote back: "Your note demanding the unconditional surrender of my forces has been received. Thank you for your compliments. If you wish to avoid further bloodshed keep out of the range of my guns. As to reenforcements, they are now entering my works. I think I can defend my position against your entire force; at least I shall try to do so." Chalmers then asked if he could remove the dead and wounded from the field. Wilder gave him permission to do so.

Wilder's telegraph line was still uncut and he immediately called for help. At 9am. Wilder was re-enforced by six companies of the 50th Indiana, under Col. Cyrus Dunham, who had come down on the railroad from Louisville. Six miles from Munfordville, the train was thrown off the track. Luckily, Dunham and his men arrived at the works with only one man lost.

By this point, Chalmers had become frustrated with the situation. He came to the conclusion that the fort could not be taken by infantry or light artillery. He also was deceived by reports saying that there were only 1,200 to 1,800 men in the fort, that the strength of the works was only rifle works, and that the Union troops could not be re-enforced. But in reality, there were 2,500 men; their works were extensive and complete and mounted with heavier guns than Chalmers had, and Col. Dunham, with his six companies, had arrived. As night was falling upon the battlefield, Chalmers and Wilder collected their dead and wounded. Wilder had lost 37 men on the Union side. The Confederate loss was three officers and 32 men killed, 28 officers and 225 men wounded, including Lt. Col. James Bullard, Col. Robert Smith, Lt. Col. James Moore.

With the arrival of Dunham, the whole force amounted to 4,076 men. Since Dunham was Wilder's superior, he took command of the Fort. Bragg was prepared to attack, but was talked out of attacking the town by Confederate General Simon Buckner, who was a native of Munfordville. By this time Confederate General Leonidas Polk, of Bragg's command, had crossed the river 10 miles to the North, with the right wing of Bragg's army. Polk's force took up a position on the hills on the south side. Bragg had to take Munfordville quickly before Union General Don Carlos Buell's army caught up with him.

Munfordville

Buell was at Bowling Green, approaching Bragg's west flank. Confederate Major General William Hardee's men were placed in front of Fort Craig. On September 16, Bragg asked for Dunham's surrender. Dunham refused at first, but then asked if he could consult with his superiors. General C.C. Gilbert telegraphed instructions from Louisville removing Dunham from command and Wilder was put back in command. Wilder wrote to Bragg that after a consultation with his officers it was agreed that if satisfactory evidence is given of Bragg's ability to make good on his assertions of largely superior numbers, so as to make the defense of this position a useless waste of human life, Wilder would entertain terms of an honorable surrender. Bragg wrote back that he had 20,000 men that were ready to attack. He gave Wilder one hour in which to make his decision.

Confederate General Simon Buckner, who once lived in Munfordville, asked if Wilder would meet with him under a flag of truce. Wilder agreed and met with the commander. Buckner showed Wilder some of the Confederate positions, pointed out superior gun emplacements and the extent of the besieger's lines. Wilder was told that he would get no help from Louisville, that his ammunition for small arms was running out and his men were worn out by constant work and fighting four days and nights. Being satisfied that further resistance was "no less than willful murder of the brave men who had so long contested with overwhelming numbers" and, after counting 45 cannon and being surrounded by 25,000 men, Wilder decided to surrender at 2am, September 17, 1862. At 6am, Wilder and his men marched out of the works with "all the honors of war, drums beating and colors flying, we being allowed

Col. Thomas White's uniform

Swords and uniform photos by Bryan Bush, courtesy of the Old Bardstown Village and The Civil War Battles of the Western Theater Museum, Bardstown, Kentucky.

by the terms of surrender our side arms and all private property and four days rations." Officers and men were paroled and they started for the Ohio River. Wilder and his men reached Louisville.

Bragg left Munfordville on September 20 to join Smith, but by this time, Buell's army had moved north to reinforce Louisville and Bragg missed Smith. By taking time to capture Munfordville, Bragg had lost time, supplies, and an opportunity to seize an important military objective: Louisville.

* * *

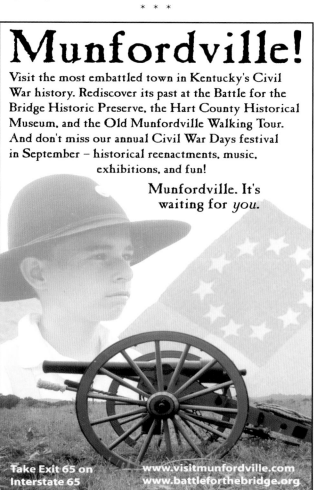

NORTHERN KENTUCKY UNIVERSITY AND THE COMMUNITY
WORKING TOGETHER.

Archaeology and history students and faculty from Northern Kentucky University are teaming up with the City of Fort Wright and Behringer-Crawford Museum to restore and display Battery Hooper, one of Northern Kentucky's few remaining Civil War defensive fortifications.

Thanks to an NKU University-Community Partnership grant, Regents Professor James A. Ramage is leading the effort to excavate and restore the battery and create a museum on the 14-acre site, which was donated to the NKU Foundation by Fern Storer and purchased for a park by the City of Fort Wright. Jeannine Kreinbrink, Adjunct Professor of Archaeology at NKU, is directing archaeological excavation.

In addition to preserving the site for future generations, this project is providing NKU students practical experience in archaeological excavation, historical research, and museum administration. Archaeological excavations include NKU students and citizen volunteers, and on September 30, 2004, about 150 fifth grade and high school students participated in "Battery Hooper Day," featuring "hands-on" learning in archaeology and Civil War history.

Other NKU students are involved in researching Battery Hooper, Union lines of defense and William Hooper, the prominent Cincinnati businessman for whom the battery is named, and creating the museum that, according to Dr. Ramage, "will provide visitors a model of what a community can accomplish working together in a threatening crisis comparable to terrorist attacks today."

Battery Hooper was one of several batteries in the ten-mile line of fortifications and rifle pits that defended Covington, Newport, and Cincinnati from Confederate attack.

NKU NORTHERN KENTUCKY UNIVERSITY

QUALITY-MADE, COMMUNITY-DRIVEN

FRANKFORT
KENTUCKY'S CAPITAL TORN BY DEBATE

By Nicky Hughes

Frankfort, the capital city of Kentucky, is usually a fairly quiet place. These days, the worst battles take place in the chambers of the Capitol, or sometimes in City Hall. However, that has not always been the case. Bitter debates about Kentucky's role in the Civil War happened here in 1860 and 1861, and twice during the war the town became an actual battleground.

It can be argued that the most important events of the Civil War in Kentucky took place not on any battlefield, but in Frankfort. Caught between the two warring sections during the secession crisis, Kentucky state government faced an extraordinarily difficult decision in 1861. Loud voices called for Kentucky to leave the Union, while others insisted that the Commonwealth remain one of the United States.

As happens on many issues, the governor and the legislature took opposing positions. Governor Beriah Magoffin would have taken Kentucky out of the Union and into the Confederacy if he could have found a legal way of doing so. However, during this period, voters elected a General Assembly in which a majority were loyal Union men. Unable to resolve this stalemate, Kentucky state government adopted a policy of neutrality. Kentucky would join neither side. Both the North and the South respected this peculiar stance for several months, fearing that angering Kentuckians would push the state into the opposing camp.

The General Assembly slowly pared down Governor Magoffin's authority, while the military situation came to favor the Union cause. Working in the Capitol in less formal settings all across Frankfort, advocates of the Union carried the day. The government of the Commonwealth of Kentucky remained loyal to the United States. Instead of a defensible northern border on the Ohio River, the Confederacy faced Union troops on the farmlands along the Tennessee/Kentucky state line. Kentucky foodstuffs, horses, manpower, and other resources that might have strengthened the Confederacy were lost to the Southern cause. Just as the war started, Unionist Kentuckians inflicted a blow of strategic significance to the Confederacy without firing a shot.

In the summer of 1862, Frankfort gained the distinction – unwanted by many of its inhabitants, but welcomed by others – of becoming the only pro-Union state capital captured by the army of the Confederate States of America.

After their success at the Battle of Richmond, Confederate troops from the command of Edmund Kirby Smith occupied the town. State government moved to Louisville, leaving just before the Confederates arrived. Members of Col. John Scott's Louisiana Cavalry Regiment hung their flag on the dome of the State House. Unionist citizens lay low, while supporters of the Confederacy greeted the gray-clad troops as liberators.

The climax of this Southern triumph came when General Braxton Bragg arrived in Frankfort. He oversaw a colorful ceremony in which Richard Hawes, Confederate Governor of Kentucky, was installed in the Capitol. Before the planned inaugural ball could be held – and before the Confederate state government could accomplish anything worthwhile – uninvited guests in blue uniforms appeared on the hills overlooking downtown Frankfort from the west. Union soldiers lobbed artillery shells into the capital. Now it was the Confederates' turn to abandon Kentucky's seat of government. The main Confederate force evacuated the town, leaving cavalrymen to skirmish with Union troopers on the approach roads and downtown streets. A few days later, after the Battle of Perryville, the Confederate Army abandoned Kentucky. The Commonwealth's star remained firmly affixed to the flag of the United States for the rest of the war.

Frankfort's next episode of wartime combat occurred almost two years later - June 10 and 11, 1864. During his last raid into Kentucky, a detachment of John Hunt Morgan's cavalrymen attacked the capital. Unlike Scott's men in 1862, they were not able to ride unopposed into the town. Thomas Bramlette, Kentucky's staunchly pro-Union governor, called out the local militia when he became aware of the possibility of a raid on Frankfort. Each citizen-soldier received a .69 caliber musket, ammunition, and accoutrements at the State Arsenal. Many of the men took positions on the walls of Fort Boone, an earthen fort on a high bluff (now known as Fort Hill) overlooking downtown Frankfort. Bramlette, who had raised and commanded an infantry regiment early in the war, took a musket and a place on the wall himself.

Late on June 10, the Confederates made a dash toward the fort. Firing continued until dark, and the militiamen kept the attackers out of Fort Boone. Early the next morning, the

Confederates changed the direction of their assault. They appeared on the south bank of the Kentucky River and demanded the surrender of the capital. State and local officials refused to surrender, and shooting broke out back and forth across the river. The cannons at Fort Boone, two 20-pound Parrot rifles and three 6-pounders, joined in the fighting. Frankfort residents long would remember the sparks and rush of shells flying over downtown rooftops. The amateur gunners put a few shots into the very houses they were trying to defend. Their defense of their hometown was successful, however, and late on June 11 Morgan's men rode away. The number of Confederate casualties is unknown, and only three Frankfort defenders were wounded.

The 1864 Frankfort skirmish had no strategic military significance, but it was important to future generations of Frankfort citizens and Kentuckians. If the raiders had gotten into downtown Frankfort, it is likely that they would have destroyed everything belonging to state government to which they could put the torch. With its Frankfort buildings in ruins, state government might have left town – as advocates of a capital at Lexington, Louisville, and other communities urged many times during the 19th century. In that event, the fate of Frankfort would have been very different – and so might have been the conduct of state government.

To insure the safety of Frankfort, United States Army engineers built another fort – a formidable redoubt on the summit of Fort Hill. Its guns never fired a shot in anger, but they burned off 300 blank rounds to celebrate General Lee's surrender in April, 1865.

Today, much of Civil War Frankfort remains. The Old Capitol, site of those critical political deliberations, is restored to its mid-19th century appearance. Across the Kentucky River stands the New Capitol. In its rotunda are heroic-scale statues of Kentucky's native sons, Abraham Lincoln and Jefferson Davis. The State Arsenal, where militiamen received their weapons in 1864, is now the Kentucky Military History Museum. Fort Boone's earthen ramparts and the nearby New Redoubt still stand in the Leslie Morris Park on Fort Hill. Frankfort is still Kentucky's Civil War capital.

* * *

Old State Capitol from the Kentucky Military Institute 1859 Class Album.

RICHARD HAWES, 1797-1877

'OUR CAUSE IS STEADILY ON THE INCREASE'

By Dr. Lowell Harrison

Richard Hawes was born in Caroline County, Virginia, on February 6, 1797, but his family moved to Kentucky in 1810. Most of his education was in Samuel Wilson's Jessamine County school. He read law with two prominent attorneys and was admitted to the bar in 1818.

Six years later he moved to Winchester where he practiced law and invested in a rope walk and a bagging factory. In 1843 he decided to make his home in Paris, where he enjoyed moderate prosperity. In 1860 he was listed as having 16.5 acres of land and 13 slaves. An active Whig, Hawes was elected to the state House of Representatives in 1828, 1829, and 1836. For two terms (1837-41), he represented Henry Clay's famed Ashland District in U.S. Congress. In 1848, Hawes supported Zachary Taylor for president, and his relationship with Clay cooled. When the Whig party dissolved in the 1850s, Hawes became a Democrat who supported the candidacy of John C. Breckinridge for president in 1860.

During his first term in Congress, Hawes was described as being of "middling stature, good size... rather spare. His visage is oval, keen and fair... with a remarkable high, retreating forehead and corresponding features... all set off with a sparkling deep blue eye. His countenance is animated and pleasing; and with the eye denotes genius and talent of the first order. In refinement of manner Mr. H. will lose nothing by comparison with the first gentlemen of the Atlantic Cities."

Hawes was much concerned over the sectional controversy and the election of Abraham Lincoln in 1860. While he loved the Union, he saw it being destroyed by radical Northern groups and parties. In May, 1861, he, John C. Breckinridge and Gov. Beriah Magoffin were the Southern Rights respresentatives on a six-man committee asked to recommend a course of action for Kentucky in the hour of crisis. Rebuffed in their demand for a state convention to determine the appropriate stand (opponents feared that a convention might vote for secession), the committee recommended neutrality, and that became the state's policy for several months.

In late July, Hawes and other Democrats issue a broadside address to "The People of Bourbon County." They accused the Republicans of starting the war, they denied the right of the federal government to coerce a state into remaining in the Union, and they warned that the Lincoln administration would wage war upon slavery. Hawes and his associates

called for a halt to the fighting, recognition of the Confederate States of America, and an equitable division of the national debt and federal property.

Hawes was among the pro-Confederates who fled the state when Kentucky's neutrality ended in September, 1861. His 64 years and limited military experience made him a poor candidate for active service, but he sought and received a commission as major, and was assigned as brigade commissary in the command of Brigadier General Humphrey Marshall in eastern Kentucky and western Virginia. Because of his isolated position, Hawes was not involved in the formation of the Confederate government of Kentucky, and he rejected its offer of state auditor in order to remain with the troops.

Hawes was not an ideal subordinate. He felt free to ignore the chain of command and to deal directly with such high ranking officials as Secretary of War Judah P. Benjamin and Adjutant General Samuel Cooper. His troubled relationship with Marshall was eased when Hawes wrote President Jefferson Davis on January 25, 1862, that Confederate Governor George Johnson was "most urgently requesting my presence at Bowlinggreen [sic] to aid him in the state government."

A bout of typhoid fever delayed his departure, and when Hawes joined the state government, it was in exile. He joined it as its second governor, for Johnson had been killed fighting at Shiloh, and Hawes had been elected as his successor. On May 31, 1862, council members Josiah Pillsbury and John Burnham attested that "this day, Richard Hawes Governor Elect of the Provisional Government of the State aforesaid appeared before us and took the oath required by the Constitution and laws of the State."

Governor Hawes added to the burdens of President Davis by recommending a number of Kentuckians for civil and military positions. He was encouraged by military prospects in the summer of 1862 as Generals Braxton Bragg and E. Kirby Smith led invasions into Kentucky.

The exiled Confederate government endorsed the moves and recommended that such prominent Kentuckians as John C. Breckinridge be sent into the state to encourage enlistments. The Governor and Council made plans for assuming the powers of state government once the Federal forces had been defeated. Prospects appeared good. Smith almost destroyed a Union army of 6,500 near Richmond on

August 30, 1862, and occupied Lexington on September 1 and Frankfort two days later. Frankfort thus achieved the distinction of being the only state capital captured by the Confederacy during the Civil War. Bragg bypassed heavily fortified Bowling Green but captured a Federal force of over 4,000 at Munfordville. Bragg's wagon train carried some 20,000 arms to equip the expected Kentucky volunteers for Confederate service. But there were few volunteers – and too many of them wanted to start as cavalry captains – and Bragg complained, "Unless a change occurs soon we must abandon the garden spot of Kentucky to cupidity."

A possible solution was to install the Provisional Government in power and apply the Confederate Conscription Act of April 16, 1862. The Provisional Government had followed the troops into Kentucky, and Bragg met Hawes and Kirby Smith in Lexington on October 2. They went to Frankfort by train the next day to install Hawes as governor of the Commonwealth.

A crowd packed the state house on October 4. It heard Bragg promise to defend the state, then introduce Governor Hawes. In his lengthy partisan remarks, Hawes gave his asssessment of the causes of the war, detailed complaints of Kentuckians against the Unionist government of the state, and promised to hold elections as soon as possible. When he discussed slavery, Hawes declared that "emancipation would be the most unmitigated curse that could be inflicted upon the slave race." In concluding, Hawes declared that "we have now no civil law of government in Kentucky; and it is the purpose of the provisional government, to institute as far as possible such civil institutions, as will protect persons and property, until the people in their sovereign capacity can establish a permanent Government founded on the will of the majority."

If his listeners were encouraged by Hawes' predictions, they were soon disillusioned. By early afternoon, Union forces were within artillery range of Frankfort, and the elaborate ceremonies planned for the governor's inauguration were abandoned. A reporter wrote that "Richard Hawes is said to have displayed the locomotive capacity of youth in his departure."

The Confederate invasion of Kentucky ended after the Battle of Perryville on October 8, and the provisional government returned south with the army. Hawes continued to make recommendations and offer suggestions to President Davis and other members of the Confederate government. Despite the army's recent withdrawal from Kentucky, Hawes remained optimistic about the future. "Our cause is steadily on the increase" in Kentucky, he assured Davis in March, 1863. The governor also devoted time and effort in attempts to secure some funds that had been collected in Kentucky before the early 1862 withdrawal and the $1,000,000 appropriation of the Confederate Congress in August 1861 that was designed to help the state resist efforts of the federal government to control it. Davis rejected the claim because, he argued, Kentucky forfeited its claim to the money when it was admitted into the Confederate States of America.

During the summer of 1864, he received disturbing charges against General John Hunt Morgan. Col. R.A. Alston of the 9th Tennessee Cavalry Regiment denounced the crimes and depredations committed by Morgan's command during his unauthorized raid into Kentucky in June, 1864. Alston asked the Governor to assist in bringing about an investigation. Hawes did not have to take a stand, for on August 10 Morgan was suspended from command pending a hearing at Abington, Virginia, on September 10. Morgan was surprised and killed by Union troops at Greeneville, Tenn., on Sept. 4, 1864.

The end of the Confederacy came in the spring of 1865, and the provisional government of Kentucky died with it. There was no formal surrender of the Confederate States of America. Starting with the Army of Northern Virginia, armies surrendered one by one. Many smaller units simply dissolved, and the men went home. Since no records are known to chronicle the last days of the Confederate government of Kentucky, we can only assume that it dissolved with the close of the long conflict.

As the armies surrendered, the postwar treatment of Confederate leaders was in doubt. Should they be punished for their crimes against the United States? Some prominent Kentuckians, including John C. Breckinridge, fled the country for safety. Richard Hawes remained at Nelly's Ford until the summer of 1865 when he considered it safe to return to his home in Bourbon County. On September 18, 1865, he appeared before A.J. Ballard, Clerk of the Federal District Court in Louisville, and swore that "I will henceforth faithfully support and defend the constitution of the United States, and the Union of the States thereunder; and that I will in like manner abide by and faithfully support all laws and proclamations which have been made during the existing rebellion with reference to the emancipation of slaves." This document was forwarded to Washington for the approval that would allow Hawes to resume his pre-war occupation.

Hawes became master commissioner of the circuit and common pleas courts, a position he held until his death on May 25, 1877, at his Paris, Kentucky, home. He retained his interest in politics, and as late as 1871 he was mentioned as a possible Democratic candidate for governor. His funeral was described as "one of the largest and most impressive occasions of the kind ever witnessed in the county." In his eulogy at a public meeting, W.E. Simms asserted that "His acts and his deeds while here, must now abide the judgment of posterity."

* * *

BATTLE OF BARDSTOWN
FIGHT AT THE FAIRGROUNDS

By Dixie Hibbs

When the sun rose in Bardstown, Kentucky, on the morning of October 4, 1862, most of General Braxton Bragg's Army of Mississippi was already on the move on the roads to the east. After resting and gathering provision for 10 days, the orders were given to move out.

On October 3, Gen. Leonidas Polk had called a council of Wing and Divisional commanders to discuss Bragg's order to proceed to Frankfort by way of Bloomfield. This controversial meeting was used in the testimony during the review of the Perryville Campaign.

Bragg's orders to Polk were to "move with all available force via Bloomfield to Frankfort to strike the enemy..." But when Polk received information that Buell was closing in from Louisville, he called his Division and Wing commanders who unanimously endorsed his views to move on the route (previously) indicated by Bragg toward Camp Breckinridge. So he moved the army toward Danville-Harrodsburg, via Springfield.

The movement of more than 26,000 troops was slow but deliberate. The supply train alone reached a 10-mile length. Colonel Joseph Wheeler's Cavalry was ordered to follow and cover the rear of the Left Wing of the army which was moving toward Glenville in Washington County. Every turnpike, county road or trail was used. The army vehicles and foot traffic churned up dust, then mud after the rain. Fords were used as well as the bridges.

Pickets and rear guards were notified of the move and proceeded to slowly withdraw back from the north on the Louisville Road and from the west toward Boston. Colonel

John A. Wharton, on the Louisville Road with the 8th Texas Cavalry known as Terry's Texas Rangers, had been scouting and skirmishing this front since the beginning of the Bardstown occupation when he replaced General Nathan B. Forrest. He penetrated as far as Fern Creek in Jefferson County before withdrawing south toward the main army. His job was to procure intelligence and protect from surprise attack.

On October 4, he was within four miles of town gathering intelligence on Buell's movements from Louisville when he realized he had been flanked. The following report was filed by George G. Garner, A.A.G., from Harrodsburg, Oct. 7, 1862:

"The General commanding (Polk) takes pleasure in bringing to the notice of the army under his command the gallant and brilliant charge made by Col. John A. Wharton, commanding the Cavalry of the Right Wing, against a large force of the enemy near Bardstown, Ky., on the 4th Inst. Being posted four miles on the Louisville Pike, which, as he believed, Col. Wharton occupied and guarded the town of Bardstown and its approaches, Col. Wharton received sudden intelligence that the enemy in force were within half a mile, to the east of the pike between him and Bardstown. Immediately ordering his battery to follow after as soon as possible, he put himself at the head of the Texas Rangers and rode at half speed to the point of danger."

Garner continued: "In 30 minutes he passed the four miles and then found the 1st and 4th Kentucky, 3rd Ohio and 3rd Indiana regiments of Cavalry — four times his own number — drawn up on the road and behind houses to receive him. In the rear, but not in supporting distance, was a battery of artillery and a heavy force of infantry. The enemy's Cavalry was partially drawn up in columns of eight, prepared for a charge and the rest as a reserve. The enemy was allowed to approach within 40 yards, when Col. Wharton ordered a charge. The fearless Rangers responded nobly to the order, and in a few minutes the whole force of the enemy was drawn in confusion from the field with a loss of 50 killed and 40 prisoners, among the latter a Major" (Maj. Watts of Bardstown).

But a more personal account was told 30 years later in the *Confederate Veteran* magazine by L.S. Ferrell, a solder in Co. K, 4th Tenn. Cavalry, who was in the fight:

"When within a mile or two of Bardstown, a rumor reached us that a heavy force of Federal Cavalry had slipped in between us and the town. Of citizens who passed us some said there were no Federals between us and the town and others reported 'a Yankee line of battle across the pike at the fairgrounds.' To settle the question, Gen. Wharton directed Capt. Anderson to take his company and ascertain the facts. We went at a gallop, and soon found them in line and 'ready for business.' Sending a courier hurriedly back to Gen. Wharton, Capt. Anderson called at the top of his voice, 'Form fours, my brave boys!' This was to mislead the enemy and gain a few precious moments of time. Meanwhile, the Yankees began firing. They shot over our heads at first, but soon secured good range."

Col. John A. Wharton

"The captain ordered the fence on our right pulled down so we could pass into a growth of timber. I sprang from my horse and lowered the fence. As the boys rushed through, one rode between me and my horse, and I was forced to turn him loose. The company kept right on and left me, striking the enemy's flank. Just then I wished that horse was somewhere else and I honorably with my wife and babies. Forty kingdoms would I have given for a horse, for my own little roan. I secured him with nerve, and just as I caught him I heard the hoofbeat and muttering roar of Wharton's column as it advanced down the pike in a headlong charge. 'Rough riders' they were, sure enough."

Ferrell continues: "Standing on his stirrups, bareheaded, his hair streaming behind, and whipping his gray mare 'Fanny' across the withers with his hat, Gen. Wharton led the charge, shouting, 'Charge 'em, boys!' I fell in with the Texans."

"When the head of our column struck the enemy, the rail fence on our left went down in a moment and we charged through an open woodland. Capturing a prisoner, Col. Tom Harrison ordered me to take him up behind me, and carry him to headquarters. As we had to retrace our steps and get on the pike to find headquarters, and as our forces had moved on and the Yankees were expected every minute, I thought it foolhardy to risk my prisoner with the advantage he would have behind me and for once disobeyed orders and made my prisoner double-quick (run alongside). We had not proceeded very far when we encountered another Reb having charge of another prisoner. He asked me what I was going to do with my Yank. 'Take him to headquarters,' I replied. 'Yes, and we will both be captured. I'm going to kill mine right here,' he rejoined. At this the prisoner began begging for his life. I told Johnnie not to do so cowardly a deed as that, and requested him to turn his man over to me. 'Take him and go to h--- with him!' he shouted, and putting spurs to his horse, was quickly out of sight, leaving me with both prisoners, who readily ran until we were out of danger."

"By this headlong charge of Wharton's, the Federals were scattered like chaff, and I think they lost about 15 killed and wounded, and perhaps 25 or 30 prisoners. We had but one man wounded and that was slight. After the battle of Perryville, we rode into Stanford. As we drew up in front of the hotel, there were a group of paroled Federals on the verandah. Soon one of them sprang up, exclaiming, 'Yonder's my man!' He ran to me and seizing my hand, seemed as glad as if he had found a long-lost brother. He was one of the Bardstown prisoners."

L.S. Ferrell's story continued about an episode before the Battle at the Fairgrounds as they protected the rear of the army. "On our way to the front we met one of the 8th Texas, who had a bullet hole in his forehead from which the blood flowed freely. He presented a ghastly sight to beginners. As he passed us, he pointed exultingly to his wound and wanted to know of Capt. Paul Anderson if that would not entitle him to a furlough. This was R.K. Cheatam of Texas, who lived many years afterward, carrying the bullet to his grave."

The Federal advance was so swift that Col. Joe Wheeler was almost cut off by the Federals as he supervised the rear guard actions on the west side of town for Bragg's Army. He waited until nearly dark, then circled the town to avoid capture and rejoined the army.

On October 5, General Don Carlos Buell and staff passed through Bardstown at 8:30 in the morning. During this time a wounded Confederate soldier, Lt. H.W. Reddick of Florida, was housed in a school on the Main Street and wrote of watching Buell's army pass through. "I counted 110 flags," carried with the Union troops who streamed into town less than eight hours after the Confederates had left.

* * *

Perryville:

The Bloody Tide-Turning Battle, the Aftermath, and Modern Preservation

By Stuart W. Sanders

In the summer of 1862, Confederate authorities in East Tennessee desperately sought a way to prevent Union forces from reaching the vital railroad junction of Chattanooga. To halt the Union advance, Confederate generals Braxton Bragg and Edmund Kirby Smith devised plans to invade Kentucky. Bragg and Smith hoped that their Kentucky campaign, which Smith called "a bold move, offering brilliant results," would pull Federal troops away from Chattanooga and would induce Kentuckians to rally to the Southern cause. Furthermore, it was hoped that the occupation of Kentucky could lead to an invasion of Indiana or Ohio. For these Southerners, a Confederate Kentucky seemed within their grasp.

Kirby Smith struck first. Moving through the Cumberland Gap, Smith's army barreled northward, where they whipped 7,000 Union troops at Richmond. His soldiers then captured Lexington and Frankfort, which was the only pro-Union capitol to fall into Confederate hands during the Civil War. After watching Smith's success unfold, Bragg's army feinted toward Nashville and moved into the Bluegrass State. Entering Kentucky near Glasgow, Bragg's soldiers captured a Union garrison at Munfordville and then advanced on Louisville. Never before had Confederate armies found such success in the Commonwealth.

Union Major General Don Carlos Buell refused to allow the Confederates to have free reign in Kentucky. Buell rushed into the Commonwealth from Nashville, where he shadowed Bragg's army. When Bragg's Confederates spent several days besieging the Munfordville garrison, Buell hastened his men to Louisville. By the time Buell reinforced his army with tens of thousands of recruits, Smith's Confederates were scattered around Lexington and Frankfort, and a portion of Bragg's army was at Bardstown.

Buell sent 20,000 Union troops toward Frankfort as a diversion, and the remainder of his army, nearly 58,000 strong, was deployed against Bragg's command at Bardstown. When these tens of thousands of bluecoats approached, Bragg's troops withdrew to Perryville, where they halted. The quiet town became a focal point for the armies because of adequate water sources, an extensive local road network, and because the Confederates wanted to stay between the Union army

and a supply depot they had established in Garrard County.

Water played a heightened role during the campaign. A severe drought plagued central Kentucky for months, and local streams, creeks, and wells were completely dry. Because of this lack of water, soldiers had to drink out of stagnant, fetid ponds. Many troops recalled driving hogs out of muddy, polluted water before filling their canteens. One Federal noted that as he procured water from a pond, his fellow troops washed their feet and socks from the same water. To his disgust, a dead mule floated at the other end of the pool. Illness quickly broke out in the ranks. Thousands of soldiers suffered from dysentery, typhoid, and other maladies.

By October 7, Bragg's 18,000 Confederates were camped in Perryville. West of the village, on a farm owned by Jacob Peters, they stationed an advance unit on a hill that overlooked Doctor's Creek, a small waterway that wound around the ridges outside of town. As the Union soldiers approached, it was rumored that Doctor's Creek held water. To take the creek and hold the high ground above it, Union soldiers attacked Peter's Hill and drove back the Confederates. The first shots of the battle had been fired.

Despite this encounter, Bragg, who was in Frankfort inaugurating a new Confederate governor of Kentucky, was fooled by Buell's diversion. When Bragg learned that Union soldiers were moving on the capital, he wrongly assumed that this was the main body of Buell's army. He believed that the force encountered at Perryville was a minor one. Bragg then ordered his troops in Perryville to brush aside the Union forces there before marching to Versailles, where he hoped to link his command with Kirby Smith's army. Confederate officers in Perryville, however, realized that they faced more than a minor force. These troops disobeyed orders and held a defensive stance. At this point, 58,000 Union soldiers were forming north, west, and south of town.

Bragg rushed to Perryville when he learned that his men had not attacked the enemy. Still believing that he faced a small force, he realigned his army for the attack. When these 18,000 soldiers marched northwards, they kicked up immense clouds of dust. Union troops outside of town saw

Battle of Perryville

these dust clouds and mistakenly believed that the Southerners were retreating to Harrodsburg. Their officers would regret this mistake.

Bragg's attack plan was a typical 19th century strategy. He first hoped to strike the left flank of the Union army, located at the northern end of the Federal line. Then, the attack would continue from north to south. The Confederate army hoped to push back both ends of the Federal line until it snapped.

At 2pm on October 8, Major General Benjamin F. Cheatham's Confederate division struck the left flank of Union Major General Alexander McCook's corps, which had deployed on the ridges northwest of Perryville. These Northern troops thought that the Confederates had retreated and were surprised by the attack. Although Cheatham's assault was initially checked by immense Federal musketry and artillery fire, the Confederates doggedly pushed back McCook's left flank. Many of the Union troops in this sector were new recruits, and some of them had never before fired their rifles. It was a brutal baptism of fire.

Confederate Private Sam Watkins later recalled the Southern assault. "Such obstinate fighting I never had seen before or since," he wrote. "The guns were discharged so rapidly that

it seemed the earth itself was in a volcanic uproar. The iron storm passed through our ranks, mangling and tearing men to pieces… Our men were dead and dying right in the midst of this grand havoc of battle."

To the south, the center of the Union line held firm as Federal troops repelled the Southern assault with concentrated artillery fire. Federal cannon commanded by Captain Peter Simonson and Captain Cyrus Loomis held a steep ridge with their 12 guns and infantry support. Although two Confederate brigades tried to dislodge these troops, the Federals repulsed consecutive attacks. Only when the Union right fell back did the center of their line crumble.

While the battle raged, left and center, on the Federals, the fight opened against the Union right flank. Confederate brigades led by Bushrod Rust Johnson, Patrick Cleburne, and Daniel Adams crossed Doctor's Creek, passed the whitewashed farmhouse of local farmer Henry P. Bottom, and savagely attacked the Union right. The Northern troops held for several hours, but the Southern momentum forced them back for more than a mile. Although the Federals were driven away, one Union officer declared that "The numerous dead bodies found upon the ground in front of the position I occupied shows that the enemy were severely punished."

Linda Doane

In pushing back both ends of McCook's battle line, the Confederates won a tactical victory. However, they encountered a strategic defeat. Although they whipped a portion of the Union army, they eventually withdrew from Kentucky. Their invasion was over and the hopes for a Confederate Kentucky were permanently dashed. Furthermore, the Southern dream of procuring thousands of recruits was also destroyed. The Confederate army had hauled 20,000 rifles into the state, but only 2,500 Kentuckians joined their cause. One Southerner complained that Kentucky citizens were "too well off to fight." Never again was there a concerted effort to hold the Commonwealth for the Confederacy.

The Aftermath

When daylight broke on October 9, the lives of Perryville residents were forever changed. The Commonwealth's most ferocious Civil War battle had raged around them; cannonballs had smashed through the roofs of their homes and knocked gaps in the siding of the town's covered bridge. Within hours of the fight, nearly every home, church, stable, barn, and business had become field hospitals for the thousands of wounded and sick soldiers. Residents' clothes were shredded for use as bandages; food and livestock were taken, and fences and furniture were burned for firewood. During this chaos, the town's 300 inhabitants and the residents of other nearby communities were left to bury the dead, heal and feed the wounded, and repair their homes and farms during months of post-battle occupation.

The battlefield presented heartbreaking scenes to the soldiers who toured the ground. One Confederate from the 3rd Florida Infantry informed his mother that "the night was a splendid moonlight night and I had an opportunity of seeing a battle field as I have read of it ... never will I forget it ..."

The carnage repelled a member of the 8th Tennessee Infantry, who helped dozens of wounded soldiers after the fight. "Amid these painful scenes I remain till sometime after dark. My hands and clothes are besmeared with blood. The noise of the battle has died away. Nothing is heard but the rumbling of ambulances, groans and cries of sufferers, the slash of the surgeon's knife, and the harsher sound of the saw."

George W. Potter of the 80th Indiana Infantry was surprised when he witnessed camaraderie between enemy soldiers. "I was sent on the battlefield the next morning to take water to the wounded that was on the field and it was an awful sight to see," Potter wrote. "There was men torn all to pieces with cannon balls and bomb shells. The dead and wounded lay thick in all directions, friends and foes side by side. Some of the wounded talking with each other, asking questions in regard to the fight, how many they had and where they was from, talking as friendly as if they was the best of friends."

The Federal troops reformed their battle lines near a house owned by local farmer John C. Russell. Here, as night fell, the Union army blocked the Confederate advance. Near this house, however, Northern soldiers suffered some of their heaviest casualties. According to Union Colonel Michael Gooding, whose 22nd Indiana Infantry Regiment lost nearly 70% of its strength, the battle "raged furiously; one after one, my men were cut down... Fiercer and fiercer grew the contest and more dreadful became the onslaught. Almost hand-to-hand [my men] fought at least five times their own number ..." Although the Federal army slowed the Confederate offensive, Union General McCook later admitted that his force "was badly whipped."

The Confederates were victorious in the fighting north of town, but they quickly learned that they were outnumbered. Nearly 40,000 Union troops had not participated in the battle. While McCook's corps received the brunt of the Southern attack north of town, a lone Confederate brigade of about 1,400 men attempted to assault Union forces west of Perryville. These troops quickly retreated when they realized they were facing nearly 20,000 enemy soldiers. Furthermore, south of Perryville, Confederate cavalry skirmished with Union troops and discovered that 20,000 Federals were in this area. Outnumbered, the Confederates withdrew to Harrodsburg, leaving their dead and most of the wounded behind. The Battle of Perryville killed and wounded nearly 8,000 men.

The thousands of casualties lay scattered over hundreds of acres. "We found that the Rebels had left during the night," wrote a Federal cavalryman. "We marched over the battlefield. It was a horrible sight. For four miles the fields are strewn with the dead of both parties, some are torn to pieces and some in the dying agonies of death. The ambulances are unable to take all the wounded … A large pile of legs and arms are lying around that the Rebel doctors cut off."

Hundreds of amputations occurred without the benefit of anesthesia. Union surgeon J.G. Hatchitt visited the home of John C. Russell, which had been commandeered as a hospital. Here, Hatchitt wrote, he "found about 150 wounded, most of them lying on the ground in the yard … [the surgeons] had labored all night as best they could. No supplies reached this hospital, they were compelled to amputate without chloroform." The surgeon noted that the drought had taken its toll on hospital sanitary conditions. He remarked that doctors couldn't find enough water to wash the blood from their hands for two days. This lack of sanitation likely led to scores of deaths from medical complications.

Residences, businesses, schools, and churches quickly filled with the wounded. The Ewing Institute, a noted antebellum girls' school, was a hospital for six months after the battle. All of the school's fencing was burned, window glass was smashed, stoves destroyed, interior paint and floors ruined, and desks were cobbled together to create bunks for wounded men. Local churches were similarly abused. The Perryville Christian Church lost fencing and pews, which were burned for firewood. Federal authorities placed Confederate wounded in this church, and according to local resident Sue Vandaripe, "a good many died while there." The Presbyterian Church lost $1,000 in damages when Union wounded filled their sanctuary. In this house of worship pews and shutters were destroyed, floors soiled, and plaster damaged. Pews from the Methodist Church were dismantled to make coffins.

Perryville residents lost thousands of dollars worth of property as a result of the battle. John C. Russell, whose home was a hospital for 17 days, lost four horses, 40 barrels of corn, 2,000 bundles of wheat, and 1,000 pounds of hay. Henry P. Bottom, who buried most of the Confederate dead, suffered more than any other resident. The soldiers confiscated or destroyed nine head of Bottom's cattle, 30 sheep, 8,000 pounds of pork, 4,500 pounds of bacon, 320 cords of wood, 3,000 bushels of corn, two horses, 50 bushels of oats, and 22 tons of hay. For the first time ever, the Bottom family had to buy food to eat.

Because of the sacrifices made by the soldiers and civilians who endured Kentucky's largest Civil War battle, in 1991, the Perryville Battlefield Preservation Association (PBPA) was formed to preserve and interpret this historic battleground. Through partnership formed with federal, state, and local agencies, the PBPA has become one of the most active battlefield preservation organizations in the nation.

The Future
All of this important progress has been made thanks to the involvement of many individuals and the continued support of several state, federal, and local organizations. Using public-private partnerships, the PBPA Battlefield Commission, Boyle County Fiscal Court, Danville-Boyle County Convention and Visitor's Bureau, the Kentucky Department of Parks, Kentucky Heritage Council, Kentucky Transportation Cabinet, and many other agencies have worked hard to sustain this project.

With a preserved and interpreted battlefield and town, it is certain that Perryville will become one of the preeminent tourist destinations in the Commonwealth. This heightened visitation will have a beneficial economic impact on the region. Because Perryville is such a rich cultural resource, the combination of Kentucky's fiercest Civil War Battle with the vibrant commercial history of antebellum Perryville makes this area a focal point for learning about 19th century military and civilian life.

* * *

Parson's Battery Reenactment

97

GEN. PATRICK R. CLEBURNE
'STONEWALL OF THE WEST'
TWO KENTUCKY BATTLES, TWO WOUNDS

By Robert C. Moody

Patrick Ronayne Cleburne was one of the more competent generals in the Confederate army. He was born in Ireland, appropriately on St. Patrick's Eve, in 1828, the son of a physician. Orphaned early, he emigrated to the United States in 1849 and settled in Helena, Arkansas, with an intermittent stop in Cincinnati, Ohio.

He was naturalized in Helena, became a drug-store manager and owner, newspaper owner, and lawyer. Cleburne dabbled in politics and became Master of his Masonic lodge. He was a chess enthusiast and frequently entered oratorical contests. Among Irish immigrants, he was that rare commodity, a protestant teetotaler.

Gen. Patrick Cleburne

Cleburne owned no slaves, but when the war clouds formed, he felt his allegiance was to the state and region which had provided him with so many opportunities.

In 1860, Cleburne organized a militia company in Helena, known as the Yell Rifles. When it came to close-order drilling, training and "spit and polish," his three and a half years in the British army served him well. Cleburne was elected captain of that unit which was later integrated into the Confederate army. Subsequently, he was commissioned a colonel and commanded a regiment. He was promoted to brigadier general on March 4, 1862, in Tennessee. There, he had successfully executed a rear guard action for the Confederate army evacuating Bowling Green, Kentucky, and Columbus, Mississippi, after Forts Henry and Donelson fell to Federal forces.

Cleburne's first intense combat occurred at Shiloh. He acquitted himself well when his brigade was part of an unfortunate attack in which it suffered 38 percent casualties. His unit fought as the advance unit which won day one of the battle, but lost day two, after which the entire army withdrew and his unit was ordered east to Knoxville. Shiloh was a great learning experience for Cleburne.

The Kentucky invasion plan was devised on July 31, 1862, in Chattanooga. Cleburne's 3,000-man division was detached

from Braxton Bragg's army and attached to Kirby Smith's. His 4th Infantry Division of the Confederate Army of Kentucky had entered Kentucky at Roger's Gap on August 14, 1862. On the night of August 29, Cleburne and his division "slept on their arms" at Bobtown in Madison County. A strong Federal force was reported north of them and south of Richmond. The next day's battle demonstrated Cleburne's improving generalship.

On the morning of the 30th, Cleburne proceeded about three miles to a strategic point one-half mile north of the small town of Kingston. There, he more or less precipitated stage one of the Battle of Richmond. He demonstrated great skill in the use of his artillery and wreaked havoc on the Federals with his newly-formed sharpshooter company. While the Federals were withdrawing from the center of the skirmish line to attempt to "turn" Cleburne's right flank, he charged the weakened Union center with his seasoned Shiloh veterans. As a result, the newly-recruited Union soldiers broke and ran.

This recurred twice later in the day until nearly all of the Union army was either killed, wounded or captured. Cleburne himself was wounded in stage one and retired from the field. One account has it that a minié ball entered his open mouth and took out several teeth. He recuperated for two weeks in Madison County then rejoined his brigade, somewhere between Georgetown and Shelbyville. His leadership at the Battle of Richmond helped earn his army a citation from the Confederate Congress.

Cleburne's second Kentucky combat experience was at Perryville on October 8, 1862. He was then a brigade commander in Buckner's division, again under Gen. Hardee in Bragg's Army of the Mississippi. At first, Cleburne's brigade was in reserve, but it soon entered the fray.

His men, who were wearing blue Union army trousers captured at Richmond, came under a Confederate artillery barrage. Cleyburne halted his advance while he secured a cease-fire from those cannoniers. Cleburne adopted a new tactic to fit the Boyle County terrain. He utilized widely-spaced skirmishers advancing on a hill crest to purposely draw enemy fire. Then, Cleburne poured his main line (which had been 10 paces behind) through his advance line with devastating results. A Cleburne aide riding near him was shot and killed, and Cleburne's horse "Dixie" was shot from under him and killed. Cleburne suffered a severe leg wound but continued the charge on foot. The Federals in front of Cleburne retired from the battlefield.

Because of perceived overnight Union reinforcements, Bragg ordered a withdrawal which ultimately began on October 13. Cleburne was again reduced to being on "sick call," nursing his leg wound. Nevertheless, when the retreat reached Big Hill in Madison County, he was required to use more than gentle persuasion on malingering soldiers. He forced them to practically carry the wagon trains up Big Hill. Cleburne was out of Kentucky and in Knoxville by October 26, 1862.

Cleburne participated in the Tennessee and Georgia battles at Murfreesboro, McLemore's Cove, Chickamauga, Missionary Ridge, Bald Hill, Jonesboro (Atlanta Campaign), and Ringgold Gap, to name a few. For the latter, he received another citation from the Confederate Congress. In all of those battles, he displayed his military genius. Such was his ability that no less an authority than Jefferson Davis dubbed him the "Stonewall of the West."

Cleburne was promoted to major general on December 12, 1862, partly as a reward for his outstanding performances at Richmond and Perryville and in salvaging the army's trains at Big Hill.

Gen. Cleburne later held numerous command positions normally filled by full generals, and he performed them with distinction. He was, however, never promoted to that rank, partially because of his advocating the use of slaves as soldiers in 1864. In return for their service, they were to be given their freedom at the end of hostilities. This proposal was rejected and even hushed up by President Davis, but later re-proposed by Robert E. Lee.

In Tennessee in 1864, rumors and innuendos spread in the units that Cleburne's commander, Gen. J.B. Hood, held himself responsible for Union units "slipping by" on November 29, 1864. Militarily, prevention of such would have been Hood's responsibility.

Cleburne sought an audience with the commanding general to explain the circumstances, but none was granted. On the next day, Hood ordered a desperate attack on well-defended Franklin, Tenn. That attack was thought by some to be in the form of punishment. Gen. Cleburne was killed in that assault on November 30, 1864, along with four other Confederate generals. He was buried in Rose Hill Cemetery in Columbia, Tenn., and reburied in nearby St. John's churchyard, and finally removed to Helena in 1869.

Gen. Cleburne was by nature fearless and as a result he was awarded the Confederate Medal of Honor for his bravery at the Battle of Franklin. He developed so much esprit de corps within his division that his was the only one in the Confederate army allowed its own flag. It had a white circle in a blue field and was much feared when seen by the Union troops in a skirmish line.

Gen. Cleburne's Kentucky combat involvement was brief, and his two main battles, Richmond and Perryville, left him with two serious wounds. His short combat stint in Kentucky was definitely instrumental in his development into one of the Confederacy's more competent field generals.

Patrick Ronayne Cleburne was one of only a handful of Civil War soldiers to rise in rank from private to general officer. His meteoric rise was well earned. His keen military sense combined with his faultless personal traits combined to make him an extremely competent field general. His knack of battlefield analysis along with his innate ability to quickly devise a battle plan on the field, allowed him to defeat superior opposing forces on many occasions. In many regards he was an innovator in the Confederate army.

He justly deserved the sobriquet, "Stonewall of the West."

* * *

Battle of Richmond Reenactment

'...A VERY GOOD CAMPING PLACE...'
NEW HAVEN AND THE CIVIL WAR, 1861-1865
NOTES FROM A SOLDIER'S DIARY

By Charles R. Lemons

The full-time Union occupation of New Haven, Kentucky, began on the 17th of October 1862 with the arrival of the 78th and 91st Regiments of Illinois Volunteer Infantry. The two regiments had started their trip to New Haven from Louisville, where the Federal army had been concentrating troops for the protection of the Commonwealth.

General Don Carlos Buell's army had already marched out to engage the Confederate forces under General Braxton Bragg in Perryville, and the two regiments had arrived too late to take part in the campaign. After performing picket duty in Louisville, the two regiments were ordered to march towards New Haven.

Leaving Louisville on October 6, they took the road to Shepherdsville, arriving in that small town on October 7, after a 21-mile march through a "flat and poorly cultivated" countryside. The Louisville & Nashville Railroad bridge located there had been burned two days before and work had already begun on a replacement. The troops camped up river from the town, about 30 rods (165 yards) from the railroad bridge and river, posting pickets around the campsite on both sides of the river. The river was so dry that you could walk across it and not get your feet wet. They remained on the outskirts of Shepherdsville until October 14, when they took the road south following the railroad.

The units reached the "lovely town" of Belmont that same day, and camped overnight. The next day, they continued down the railroad and, turning east at the Lebanon Junction, proceeded to the L&N bridge over the Beech Fork of the Salt River, east of Boston. On October 17, the two regiments moved out along a road that followed the railroad line. Later that day, they "stopped at the meadow of an old Sesech named Beeler, on the bank of the Rolling Fork, opposite to and a little below the town of New Haven." The country was described as of a "rather better character" than they had been seeing, with a large number of pitch pine trees, cedars, and chestnuts – some being "tolerably large."

Bridge Fortifications

There were six significant bridges along the Lebanon Branch of the L&N Railroad, one across the Beech Fork at Boston, one across Wilson's Creek, one across Pottinger's Creek, and three bridges across the Rolling Fork, including the one at New Haven itself. To protect these bridges, the two regiments were expected to construct such works as were necessary to preserve their safety. The 91st Illinois Regiment (less one company left at the Rolling Fork Bridge) was sent down to the L&N Railroad bridge over the Beech Fork and began construction of works to protect that bridge. In the meantime, the 78th Illinois, under the command of Col. William H. Benneson, had begun construction of protective works at the Rolling Fork bridge and at New Haven. These works were completed by October 21.

Morgan's Men Come to Call

December 25 marked the day when the news arrived that the Confederates were coming. December 27, heavy firing could be heard from the direction of Elizabethtown. In response to the news, the members of H Company 78th Illinois renewed their work on the stockade. "...strength was added to our already strong works by means of banking up dirt as high as could be done." The firing stopped by nightfall, but work on the stockade continued. But the feared attack failed to materialize for several days.

By December 28 Morgan's forces had captured Elizabethtown and burned the L&N bridges on Muldraugh's Hill – taking captive both the 91st Illinois Infantry Regiment and the two companies (B & C) of the 78th Illinois sent to help them. More gun and cannon fire was heard on December 29, this time from the direction of Boston. This gunfire was the sound of Morgan's command defending itself from a superior Union force that had caught them on the wrong side of the swollen Rolling Fork River near Boston. They were able to escape, but not without some casualties.

That very same evening Confederate cavalry were observed crossing the railroad line, north to south, about a mile to the west of the stockade. Because the troops were in a column of fours, the men of the 78th Illinois were able to ascertain that there were between 150 and 200 men in the enemy force. Captain Allen ordered that the stockade be cleared for action and the men went to work dismantling and stacking the many conveniences which they had worked so hard to install.

The best description of the Battle of New Haven comes from Sgt. James McNeil, a member of Company H, who was assigned a position in the stockade during the battle. The soldiers manning the stockade woke early on the morning of December 30 to a light rain. It wasn't very long after that the Confederates, whom the soldiers had glimpsed the evening before, finally made their appearance.

"About 7am we discovered, up the Bardstown Pike, a flag of truce accompanied by three cavalrymen. They were met at the farther extremity of the railroad bridge by Captain Allen and a Lieutenant Beers. They presented a formal demand for the surrender of the fort. It stipulated that if we would surrender, private property would be respected; that we were surrounded by cavalry and artillery; that any agreement made with Captain Housley, the bearer of the demand, would be respected, etc. and was signed 'John Morgan, Brigadier General.' Colonel Benneson replied that he 'respectfully declined.'"

This scene was witnessed by a number of the townspeople, and Sgt. McNeil noted in his journal that "A great many citizens came in the morning to see the battle, but also, as I said, to see us paroled. The adjoining hills were filled with them. Poor fellows were destined to be disappointed in seeing Company H paroled. When the flag of truce came in the morning, the citizens flocked to see the surrender, which at the time was hardly even ready for a reply. .... We've not had our flag up before that morning for several weeks on account of it being torn. But it was brought out and run up that morning. As it opened with its folds to the morning breeze, it floated gloriously over us. We thought afresh of the secret promises we made to the fair dames when we made the pledge we made them on the presentation - 'With it to live, with it to die.'"

Nearly an hour and a half passed before the Confederate troops finally made their appearance on the wooded ridge line to the northwest of the stockade. A single 12-pounder mountain howitzer was moved into position in a small meadow some thousand yards distant, accompanied by a battle line of mounted cavalry, made up of three companies of the Confederate 9th Kentucky Cavalry.

As the attack began, the Union forces manned their defenses. Fifteen soldiers under the command of First Sergeant Thomas Scott occupied the rifle pits, while the rest of the force manned their designated areas in the stockade and in the colonel's headquarters. The men fell in at their designated defensive positions, some in each of the circles making up the corners of the stockade, as well as at the four walls. In addition there was also a reserve force of ten men placed at the center of the stockade.

At about 9am the battle began, or as Sgt. McNeill noted, "The Ball opened." The Confederate gun began its bombardment of the stockade, firing a solid shot from 1,000 yards away. Sgt. Scott, since he was outside of the walls of the stockade, was designated to give the warning of attack and as the gun opened fire, he yelled out, "Look out, here she comes!" As Sgt. McNeil recorded, "...every fellow found his hiding place." The shot came buzzing in, landing 50 yards short of the stockade, but in a direct line with it. The solid shot bounced into the air, over the stockade, and buried itself in the east bank of the Rolling Fork.

A few moments later a second round, this time a fuzed shell, came over making a "doleful whiz" and exploding just short of the stockade walls. The shrapnel from the shell showered down amongst the men, but failed to hit anyone. When the men discovered that no one had been hurt, they took off their hats and cheered as if it were the Fourth of July. A third shot passed between the stockade and the Adjutant's tent, burying itself into the ground 10 feet from the south wall. More direct firing followed, to little affect.

The howitzer now moved to a second position about a quarter-mile south of its first position and "some closer to us." All this time the cavalry, which was drawn up in a long battle line to the rear of the battery, had done nothing but watch. However, when the howitzer moved to its new position, "a company of their cavalry deployed and came sweeping down near where they had taken their second position with the battery." The battery was now some 800 yards distance from the stockade. The men in the stockade and rifle pits, who had been just aching to get into the fight, were finally given the order to open fire. Interestingly, when the Union troops finally opened up, the enemy cavalry finally dismounted and lead their horses back to the Howell

house, which was close by. There they placed them out of harm's way behind the building and returned to the fences, where they opened fire with carbines.

Captain Allen urged his men to "pour it into them," and the infantry opened a rapid and incessant fire, which they maintained for about half an hour. "And it growing too hot for them, they (the Confederates) ingloriously fled up the hill much faster than they came down..." The gunners were driven from their gun, returning only to withdraw it off of the field. As the retreat began, some of the cavalry, which had been held back, crossed the tracks and, passing the Johnson house, moved down the road and field near the river below the stockade.

The men in this column were screened from the stockade by the raised railroad bed which towered an average of 10 feet above the farmer's fields. Upon seeing this new development, Colonel Benneson sent a few men over the top of the railroad bed to prevent the Confederates from taking the ford, but shots from Sgt. Richards, who had planted himself on the bridge abutment overlooking the ford, sent the Confederates packing.

The Confederate records of the skirmish are sketchy and no report of casualties from the affair appears in the official records. The colonel commanding the Union forces noted that the information available from sources after the battle reported that the Confederates suffered casualties of 2-3 dead and 10-12 wounded, all of which had been removed from the field during the retreat. Both sides agreed that the skirmish was a decided defeat for the Confederates, as there were no casualties to Union forces or defenses.

The town of New Haven, on the other hand, received damage to several buildings due to the poor marksmanship of the Confederate gunners. It was fortunate that, although several rounds fell into the town, no civilian casualties were reported. One round "struck the Mansion house, passing through the wall and into the basement story, and fragments from another passed through the New Haven Hotel causing no material damage."

* * *

15TH KENTUCKY INFANTRY REGIMENT

By William E. Matthews

The gallant 15th Kentucky Infantry Regiment which fought on the front lines for three years for the Union included many Shelby Countians in its ranks. In fact, companies A and B of the regiment consisted almost entirely of Shelbyville and Shelby County residents. Company B was commanded by Capt. Abraham (Abe) Rothschild of Shelby County who, after the war, founded a clothing store on Main Street which was to last nearly 100 years. His unit included many sharpshooters from the Mt. Eden and Southville neighborhoods.

For most of the war the infantry regiment was commanded by Col. Marion C. Taylor, distinguished attorney-soldier from Shelbyville. Earlier, he was Captain of Company A. These Shelby County soldiers battled from Perryville to Atlanta, and participated in Sherman's famous march through Georgia.

Casualties were high. Of 888 men (over 100 from Shelby County) who helped form the regiment in 1861, over 400 were killed or wounded. Many of these casualties were Shelby County men, including Capt. James A. McGrath, Commander of Company A, who died at Perryville. Col. Taylor was wounded at least twice.

The history of the 15th Kentucky was provided in a speech after the war by D.N. Sharp from Shelbyville, who had served throughout the war as a lieutenant. Other information has been obtained from a scrapbook of newspaper clippings collected by George Petry, who served as a captain of the regiment. The regiment was organized in Louisville in August 1861, and at first consisted of about 90 raw recruits from the Louisville area. The group failed in its first mission which was to intercept a wagonload of weapons that were being shipped from Lexington to the Confederacy.

A train took the troops to Beard's Station where they were to intercept the wagons hauling the weapons. But the Louisville officers were unfamiliar with the county roads, their scouts disappeared, and the raw troops did not stay together. About midnight the troops found themselves about three miles from Shelbyville. At daylight the soldiers were spread out from Shelbyville to Middletown, only three men completing the 40 mile, all night hike. The stragglers were picked up by wagons. The Shelbyville group in the 15th was first called the "Shelby Zouaves." They were part of a regiment made up of men mostly from Shelby, Spencer, Henry, Bullitt, Kenton and Jefferson counties. Most were farmers or store clerks.

Many of the Shelby men started out as privates or non-commissioned officers, but won battlefield commissions. Those who won commissions included George Deering, Richard Whitaker, Joseph and Henry Lyle, Joseph Atherton, Dan Spaulding, Jourd Ballad, George Petry, John and Henry Tilden Tom Baker, Joseph McClure, Frank Todd, Irvine McDowell, Ezekiel Forman, Lud Luckett, and D.N. Sharp.

In February 1862 the regiment marched to Bowling Green, the Confederates fleeing the city as the Union soldiers moved in. The local men remembered the incident because they captured a large supply of salt beef and rye bread which was a treat from their regular army rations.

From there the troops marched to previously-captured Nashville where they found the bridges destroyed. They crossed by steamboats, and some of the veterans said later that the steamboat trip was among their most pleasurable memories of the conflict. After arriving and staying at Huntsville, Alabama, for about six months, the Kentuckians took part in the famous race back to Louisville when Union troops dashed to beat the invading forces of Confederate General Braxton Bragg. In the final lap of this race, the 15th Kentucky started at dawn two miles from Elizabethtown and marched to Louisville, over 40 miles, before daylight the next day. This was considered quite an achievement for "foot cavalry."

At Louisville the 15th Regiment was stationed with veterans from Ohio. The officers of the Kentuckians had been stressing neatness and marching drills, so the new arrivals were quickly christened "The Paper Collar Regiment" by the crusty Ohioans. The name stuck, even after the war. But the locals soon had an opportunity to prove themselves in battle. Within a few days they were at Perryville, where their losses were severe. When the battle started the regiment was lined up behind a rail fence and log barn. In front, across the road, was a stone fence. The Confederates marched up to the stone wall, took positions behind it, and started firing at the 15th. The rail fence was shattered and the barn set on fire by Confederate guns. But the 15th held, despite heavy losses. Sixty-three were killed and over 200 wounded. The dead included Lt. McGrath. The regiment's colors were riddled and nine soldiers holding the standard were killed. As each went down, another grabbed the standard.

The next major battle was at Stone River, Tenn. Again the 15th was ordered to hold a road until the retreating Union artillery could get by. The regiment held the road but lost 81 men, either dead or seriously wounded, including the regiment's commander. A few weeks later, in January 1863, Captain Taylor was promoted to colonel and commander of the 15th, D.N. Sharp was made adjutant, and Woodford Hall, a Shelbyville private, was made quartermaster.

Shelby Countians were also engaged at Missionary Ridge and Chickamauga near Chattanooga. One night they had lonesome duty on top of a ridge where they could hear, all night long, the Confederate troops in the valley below. They worked on fortifications within range of the enemy's guns on Lookout Mountain and became besieged. Food ran short, but the soldiers were ordered to "hold the place till we starved," Lt. Sharp recalled in his memoirs. He adds, "The promise was kept, for we did hold the place, and we starved."

After hearing of Gen. Hooker's victory at Lookout Mountain, bedlam broke out amongst the local troops. Sharp recalls, "The whole army yelled as if with one impulse. After weary days of fasting and short rations, we were once again restored to a full supply of bacon, crackers, beans, and potatoes."

Out of action for some time, the 15th Kentucky later joined in the siege of Atlanta where, according to Sharp, "they burrowed around the city for about 30 days." The Kentuckians were then called upon to join Gen. William Tecumseh Sherman's "March to the Sea." At Atlanta, the 15th had faced Confederate General Joseph Lewis's Kentucky Brigade, which included several Shelby Countians. When members of the 15th were pulling back, the Confederates called from their lines, asking where they were going. Told that they had been ordered out, the Rebels yelled back, "All right, we will hull your acorns for you some day soon." The 15th's badge was an acorn.

Later, near Jonesboro, the Confederate Kentuckians were overrun by Union forces, and many were captured. Soldiers from the 15th visited the campground where the prisoners were being held, and Col. Philip Lee of the Confederates came to Colonel Taylor, shook his hand, and said, "Well, Colonel, we have come over to hull those acorns." Col. Lee was also from Shelby County, and after the War served for many years as Commonwealth's Attorney for a multi-county region. Shelby Countians took part in Sherman's methodical destruction of the South's railroads leading from Atlanta to Macon, Georgia. They saw little action after that, returning to Louisville on Christmas Day in 1864. They were mustered out on Jan. 14, 1865, having served exactly three years, three months, three weeks, and three days.

* * *

THE 6TH KENTUCKY VOLUNTEER INFANTRY

By Joseph R. Reinhart

Union troops reaching the crest of Missionary Ridge, November 25, 1863

Historian William C. Davis has called the 6th Kentucky Volunteer Infantry Regiment "one of the finest fighting regiments of the Yankee army in the West." While the soldiers of this gallant combat unit would not have considered themselves "Yankees," they would undoubtedly have agreed with Davis's assessment of their military skills. Recognized by William F. Fox in his "fighting 300 regiments" of the Union army, the 6th Kentucky is also noteworthy for its large contingent of German immigrants. Four of its ten companies consisted of Germans principally from Louisville. The remaining companies comprised mainly native-born farmers from Henry, Kenton, Oldham, and Shelby counties. Some natives of England, Ireland and Scotland also served in the unit.

Brig. Gen. Walter C. Whitaker

The 6th Kentucky resulted from the consolidation of three separate organizations, each of which had hoped to become a separate regiment but which could not raise 10 companies in a timely manner. Walter C. Whitaker, a fiery, 38-year-old lawyer, farmer and state senator from Shelbyville who controlled five companies, was elected colonel of the new regiment. George T. Cotton, a friend of Whitaker's from Versailles, was chosen lieutenant colonel, and William C. Hailman, who headed three of the German companies, was elected major. John R. Pirtle, who originally commanded two companies, resigned after learning he would not become the major.

The consolidation was a marriage of convenience and ethnic tensions were immediately apparent. Three of the German companies had planned to become part of a German regiment and many in their ranks could not understand English (although the company officers could). Pvt. Alford H. Sampson of Shelby County wrote to his family shortly after the regiment assembled at Camp Sigel near Louisville: "the German and American Soldiers . . . can't under Stand one Another[;] they seem to be suspicious of each other. . . . I think it would be better to have them Separate." Many of the Germans felt the same way. Despite cultural differences and mutual ethnic prejudices, the 6th's officers and men united on the battlefield and forged a record second to none of Kentucky's 60 other Union regiments.

The new regiment arrived at Camp Wickliffe in Larue County, Kentucky, on January 7, 1862, where it joined the 19th Brigade, 4th Division, Army of the Ohio. Col. William B. Hazen, a disciplined West Point graduate who demanded the very best from his troops, commanded the brigade. The regiment arrived in Nashville, Tennessee, on February 25, and at Pittsburg Landing on the Tennessee River on April 6. On April 7 the regiment received its brutal baptism of fire at the battle of Shiloh. Shiloh was the bloodiest battle to date in the war and the 6th suffered 103 casualties. The regiment then participated in the capture of Corinth, Mississippi, before moving mostly by foot to

Murfreesboro, Tennessee, for garrison duty. The 6th joined in its army's rugged march to Louisville in September 1862, arriving Sept. 26. The regiment marched out of Louisville with Maj. Gen. Don Carlos Buell's army on October 1 but was not ordered into the hotly contested battle of Perryville, fought on October 8. The 6th and its brigade, however, led the pursuit of the withdrawing Confederate armies as far as London, Kentucky.

Hazen's brigade next marched to Nashville, Tennessee, where its army was concentrating under Maj. Gen. William S. Rosecrans. Rosecrans had superseded Buell not long after the battle of Perryville and reorganized the Army of the Ohio. The army was renamed the 14th Army Corps but soon became known as the Army of the Cumberland.

On December 31, 1862, the Confederate Army of Tennessee attacked Rosecrans' army near Murfreesboro, and in savage fighting drove back the Federal line like a door on a hinge. The hinge was a small, slightly elevated copse of woods called the "Round Forest" located on the Federal left flank. Hazen's brigade (the 110th Illinois, 9th Indiana, 6th Kentucky, and 41st Ohio), posted at the edge of the Round Forest, repulsed four separate attacks across the Cowan farm and was the only Federal unit that did not give ground during the fighting that day. Had the Round Forest's defenders been driven off, the Federal line would have collapsed and resulted in a resounding defeat. The 6th Kentucky fought courageously on December 31, 1862, and again on January 2, 1863 (the final day of combat of the battle of Stones River). Almost one-third of the regiment's 361 infantrymen engaged in the battle became casualties, including 20 who lost their lives. Among the slain were Lt. Colonel George T. Cotton and Capt. Charles S. Todd (of Shelbyville). Eight of the slain Kentuckians are buried near the massive Hazen Brigade Monument in Round Forest.

The 6th Kentucky next shed significant blood in Georgia at the Battle of Chickamauga (Sept. 19-20, 1863). Although the 6th and its brigade fought stubbornly in the Brock field, at the Poe house, and the Brotherton farm on the first day of the battle, and at the Kelly field and Snodgrass Hill on the second day, Rosecrans' army had to retreat into Chattanooga because of a Confederate breakthrough elsewhere in its long battle line. The regiment was almost shattered in the fighting; 118 of the 302 men taken into the battle were killed, wounded or missing. Col. George T. Shackelford of Richmond, who had assumed command of the 6th in July after Colonel Whitaker received a general's star and a brigade command, was seriously wounded on the first day of the battle and never returned to the regiment. Command of the greatly battle-shrunken unit devolved to General Whitaker's younger brother, Maj. Richard T. Whitaker.

Led by Major Whitaker, the 6th participated in an amphibious attack at Brown's Ferry, the extension of the Union line to Orchard Knob, and was among the first regiments to reach the crest of Missionary Ridge on November 25, 1863 – a stunning victory that broke the strangling Confederate siege at Chattanooga. Battle casualties were 24. The regiment was dispatched to Knoxville on November 28, 1863, and spent the next three and a half months camping and marching around in East Tennessee. Although there was little contact with the enemy, the men suffered terribly from long periods of extremely cold weather, and the lack of adequate clothing, shelter and rations.

The regiment embarked on the grueling Atlanta campaign in early May 1864 and, by August 22, when it was pulled from the entrenchments in front of Atlanta to guard a vital railroad, had suffered another 56 men killed and wounded and 3 captured. Capt. Isaac N. Johnston of Pleasureville commanded the regiment after Major Whitaker resigned on May 11.

On January 2, 1865, the regiment's last company was mustered out of service. During its three years of existence, almost one half of the 937 men who served in the regiment were wounded. A total of 95 members lost their lives due to combat and 82 more died from disease. Wounds and non-combat disabilities caused 248 men to be discharged or transferred to the Veteran Reserve Corps.

* * *

Hazen Brigade Monument
Stones River National Battlefield Park

JOHN HUNT MORGAN'S CHRISTMAS RAID

By Tim Asher

Union Brigade at Muldraugh's Hill

In December 1862, the Confederate army was back in Tennessee after its disappointment at Perryville, Kentucky. The Confederates found themselves under constant pressure from the growing Union presence in Tennessee directed by Gen. William Rosecrans. All indications were that the Union general was planning a winter campaign as soon as adequate supplies were collected in Nashville. Understanding his situation, the Confederate commander, General Braxton Bragg, decided to stop, or at least delay, the flow of war materials into Nashville as best he could. To do this, he called upon his newly promoted brigadier general and Kentucky native John Hunt Morgan to break Rosecrans' L&N supply line.

The L&N railroad carried food, forage, and supplies from Louisville through the uneven terrain of Kentucky to the Union army's depot at Nashville. Reports were the L&N tracks were heavily guarded to prepare for the push on Bragg in Chattanooga. But an ever confident Morgan believed that, regardless of the fortifications, a weakness could be found just north of Elizabethtown in an area known as Muldraugh's Hill.

Muldraugh's Hill is an escarpment rising from the Ohio River to an elevation of over 400 feet in just five miles and

crisscrossed by streams and gorges. Morgan's knowledge of the area probably came from the experience of his brother-in-law and second in command, Colonel Basil Duke, who walked through the area avoiding Federals in Elizabethtown. He had noticed the two huge wooden trestles elevating the tracks above deep gorges, both about 90 feet high and 500 feet long. These trestles, located in very difficult country, became the primary targets of the Christmas Raid.

December 22, 1862, dawned bright and sunny in Alexandria, Tennessee, where the Christmas Raid began. Morgan kissed his new bride, Mattie, good-bye and, after her carriage disappeared from sight around a curve, he passed orders to Duke: "Forward march!" Morgan moved the largest Confederate force he had ever commanded, approximately 4,000 strong, toward Tompkinsville. They reached the town by nightfall of the 23rd. As they camped that night, the men were glad to be on their native soil once again. Approximately 90% of Morgan's command were Kentuckians who had not been home since they'd enlisted. One of Morgan's officers, Lt. Col. James B. McCreary, put his emotions into words as he confided to his diary: "Tonight we are camped on the sacred soil of Kentucky, and it fills my heart with joy and pride."

The next day was Christmas Eve and they continued to Glasgow under gray clouds and a cold wind that cut through the men. They arrived at Glasgow about mid-afternoon and dispatched the Federal garrison stationed there. They continued on across the Green River on Christmas Day, quickly moving Federal forces out of their way as they went. That night they camped in a cold rain just outside of Upton where a Union stockade and blockhouse guarded the track.

The next morning, in a move to keep the Federals from guessing his true objective, Morgan sent a detachment south to burn the Bacon Creek Bridge. About 100 men were fortified in a blockhouse and put up a brief but ferocious fight that resulted in the destruction of the bridge for the third time in the war. The men tore up track and burned crossties on their way back to their Upton camp. During this raid, protracted resistance was rare. Most of the stockades that were challenged quickly surrendered after Duke, "gave them a look down the barrel of his artillery."

In Upton, Pvt. George "Lightning" Ellsworth went to work by cutting into the telegraph line and began sending confusing information about Morgan's whereabouts, his troop strength, and intentions, to all of the Federal officers in the area.

The morning of the 27th dawned cold but the sky was clearing as Morgan and his regiment rode toward Elizabethtown.

John Hunt Morgan

Upon arriving, Morgan threw a cordon around the town and set his artillery on a hill commanding the entire area. The Federals had set up a strong resistance near the railroad by fortifying a number of brick warehouses, complete with loopholes though which to fire muskets. Stockades were under construction but not completed when Morgan arrived.

About 650 soldiers of the 91st Illinois Vol. Infantry commanded by Col. Harry S. Smith were garrisoned in the town. Col. Smith knew the hopelessness of his situation but was determined to give Morgan his best effort by first attempting to fool the Confederate commander into believing that a huge Federal host occupied the town. He did this by marching his men in a "double file" loop across the brow of a hill in full view to give Morgan the impression that he commanded much greater numbers. Next he sent to Morgan word that a Federal force had him surrounded and that he should surrender immediately. Neither ruse worked, and after repeated requests that Smith surrender, Morgan gave the town 30 minutes to evacuate the women and children, and the Battle of Elizabethtown was on.

Col. Smith was at a tactical disadvantage with his men scattered among the various warehouses and downtown buildings and could not affect much of a coordinated resistance. On the other hand, General Morgan used his 6-to-1 advantage of men and seven pieces of artillery to perfection, quickly overpowering the occupiers of the town.

With his artillery commanding Cemetery Hill, he sent Col. Duke's brigade to the right and Col. William Breckinridge to the left where they would make, as Morgan phrased it, "a street fight out of it." As the Confederates moved into town, the artillery shells screamed over their heads. They waded through the freezing, waist-deep water of the rain-swollen Valley Creek, holding their muskets above their heads. Morgan's artillery kept most of the Federals under cover. Col. Smith could only attempt to delay the inevitable.

Major Joseph Palmer, Morgan's head of artillery, described the accuracy of the artillery fire as, "nearly every shot striking the houses occupied by the enemy."

With the missiles doing their deadly work, Duke and Breckinridge flushed out the isolated Federals in house-to-house fighting. Soon handkerchiefs, bed cloths, and anything white began emerging from windows and doorways all over town. Col. Smith, who was wounded by flying shrapnel, was furious at the unauthorized surrender. Nonetheless, as Duke recalled years later, "Smith was not ready to surrender, but his men were not going to wait on him and ran out of the houses and threw down their arms."

In general, Confederate sympathies in Elizabethtown were strong and the residents were glad to throw off the yolk of Federal occupation for awhile. The invaders were treated like conquering heroes and afforded whiskey, Christmas goodies, and entertainment.

On the morning of December 28, Morgan moved his men up the railroad, tearing up tracks as they went. Five miles from Elizabethtown, on Muldraugh's Hill, were the two huge wooden structures over Sulphur Fork and Broad Run, the main objectives of the raid. The trestles were about a mile apart and the Federals were in the process of constructing defensive positions consisting of earthworks and artillery platforms. At the time of Morgan's arrival, however, the positions were not complete and the defenders had no artillery. Lt. Col. Courtland Matson commanded both positions. When he saw the Confederates arriving in force he called all of his 560 men to Sulphur Fork in an effort to turn Morgan back. Matson held out for eight hours due primarily to the patience of Morgan. Morgan repeatedly demanded Matson's surrender. On the second attempt, Morgan offered to take the Federal commander out of his position to view the hopelessness of his situation. To this Matson replied that it was his and his men's "duty to fight" and that they would do so "until the last." At 3pm Morgan began shelling the position and the surrender occurred about an hour later. Morgan then burned the trestles and the unfinished stockades.

The Christmas raid was Morgan's most successful. He captured and paroled over 1,800 prisoners, inflicted 150 casualties, burned a total of 2,290 feet of railroad bridgework, destroyed 35 miles of track and telegraph line, and destroyed three depots, three water stations, several culverts and cattle guards, and large quantities of Federal stores. In doing this, Morgan suffered 26 casualties: 2 dead and 24 wounded. The railroad was closed for five weeks from December 28, 1862, when Morgan burned the bridge over Bacon Creek, to February 1, 1863, when the damage was repaired and the tracks were reopened.

* * *

MORGAN'S RAIDS MAP KEY

- **1** Preparing for Morgan's Cavalry
- **2** Morgan in Scottsville
- **3a** Morgan's Command Organized
- **3b** A Family Divided
- **3c** Fort C.F. Smith
- **3d** The Confederate Monument
- **4a** Morgan's Cave City Raid
- **4b** Morgan Burns Train
- **5** Morgan Sworn In
- **6** McMillan's Landing
- **7** Battle of Tompkinsville
- **8a** Attack on Fort Williams
- **8b** Morgan in Glasgow
- **8c** Defending Glasgow
- **8d** General Joseph H. Lewis
- **9** Fight in Bear Wallow
- **10** The Raider-Morgan Sworn In to CSA
- **11** Bacon Creek Bridge
- **12** Morgan Surprised Union Outposts
- **13a** The Cannonball
- **13b** Morgan Shuts Down the L&N
- **13c** Make a Street Fight Out of It

- **14** Lebanon Junction
- **15** Battle of the Rolling Fork
- **16a** Damned Yankees
- **16b** "A Pretty Close Call"
- **17** A Fight at New Haven
- **18** Confederate Crossing at Neeley Ferry
- **19** Rebel Crossing at Burkesville Ferry
- **20** Skirmish at Norris Branch
- **21** Civil War Camp at Marrowbone
- **22a** The Door Left Open
- **22b** Frank Lane Wolford
- **23** Camp Billy Williams near Neatsville
- **24** A Night at Cane Valley
- **25** Tebbs Bend Battlefield Tour
- **26a** General E.H. Hobson
- **26b** Home of General E.H. Hobson
- **27a** Redman's Tavern
- **27b** Rebel New Year's Eve Party
- **27c** Rebel Guerrillas on Main Street
- **27d** Raid on Hiestand-Chandler House
- **28a** Morgan Held Prisoner at Pleasant Hill
- **28b** Morgan's Revenge

- **29a** Death of Tom Morgan
- **29b** Union Commissary Building
- **29c** The Battle of Lebanon
- **29d** Morgan's Headquarters
- **30a** Washington County
- **30b** Morgan in Springfield
- **30c** A Busy Day in Springfield
- **31** Morgan in Mackville
- **32** Camp Charity
- **33** Stockade at Belmont
- **34** Action at Bardstown Junction
- **35** Fort DeWolf
- **36** West Point
- **37** A Rest at Otter Creek
- **38a** Capture of the Alice Dean
- **38b** Crossing the Ohio

HARDIN COUNTY HISTORY MUSEUM

In Elizabethtown

View displays about the L&N Railroad, Morgan's Raid, Custer's long stay in Elizabethtown and other interesting stories about the history of the area.

Museum and Gift Shop Hours: Wed - Sat 10 a.m. - 2 p.m. / located at 201 West Dixie Avenue, on the corner of Mulberry Street and Dixie (Hwy 31W) in downtown Elizabethtown.

HISTORIC DOWNTOWN WALKING TOUR

In Elizabethtown

Every Thursday night during the summer famous characters from Elizabethtown's history come to life to recreate life as it was in "days gone by." Come and see our history's colorful characters such as General George Custer, Carry A. Nation, P.T. Barnum and hear Jenny Lind sing "My Old Kentucky Home."

Tours begin at 7 p.m. in the Elizabethtown's downtown square area. The season begins in June and runs through the end of September each year.

CAMP NELSON

A FORTIFIED UNION SUPPLY DEPOT, RECRUITMENT CENTER, AND AFRICAN AMERICAN REFUGEE CAMP

By Dr. W. Stephen McBride

Camp Nelson Barracks

Camp Nelson was an important Union quartermaster and commissary depot, recruitment center, and hospital facility located in Jessamine County, Kentucky. It was the largest depot and permanent encampment in Kentucky outside of Louisville and served a critical function to the Union war effort by providing supplies, livestock, and troops for the Army of the Ohio. Besides its general everyday supply functions, Camp Nelson was also critical in the support of a number of offensive campaigns into Tennessee and Virginia.

The greatest national significance of the camp, however, was as one of the largest recruitment camps for African-American troops. Eight regiments of U.S. Colored Troops, as the African American regiments were designated, were founded at Camp Nelson, and five others served there. A refugee camp for these soldiers' families was also established within Camp Nelson.

Camp Nelson, as a recruitment and refugee camp for ex-slaves and as a recruitment camp for whites from slave-holding Kentucky and Tennessee, represents a microcosm of the social and political issues that divided the nation and brought on the Civil War. Camp Nelson as an encampment allows us to examine the more typical day-to-day lives of the soldiers who, after all, spent very little of their total enlistment time in battle.

Construction of Camp Nelson was begun in June, 1863, following orders from Major General Ambrose E. Burnside, commander of the newly formed Army of the Ohio. Burnside wanted a large and secure supply depot and encampment for his planned campaign to capture Knoxville, Tennessee, addressing President Lincoln's longstanding promise to free Pro-Union sections of East Tennessee from Confederate control. The southern tip of Jessamine County was chosen because of its location on a major turnpike and river, and because of the natural defenses provided by the 400- to 500-feet high limestone palisades of the Kentucky River and Hickman Creek. Camp Nelson was named after the late Major General William "Bull" Nelson, founder of

Camp Dick Robinson, the first Union recruitment camp in Kentucky.

Camp Nelson contained over 300 wooden buildings, numerous tents, and nine forts. The core of the camp covered over 800 acres on either side of the Lexington-Danville Turnpike (U.S. 127). The structures included 20 warehouses to store two million rations, clothing, and equipment; stables, cribs, barns, sheds, and corrals for thousands of horses and mules and their feed. There were six industrial-sized workshops to build and repair wagons and ambulances, make and repair harnesses, shoe horses, and provide lumber for construction. Two ordnance warehouses and a large powder magazine housed cannons, small arms, ammunition, and powder. Administrative buildings included the camp headquarters, quartermaster and commissary office, provost marshal's office, and other small offices. Also there were two barracks, many mess (dining) houses, two taverns, sutler stores, and a bakery. The camp also contained a large hospital facility which included 10 large wards, the "Soldiers Home," and a prison.

Over 2,000 civilians – carpenters, blacksmiths, wagon makers, harness makers, teamsters, cooks, clerks, and laborers, and many impressed slaves - were employed here. Camp Nelson was generally garrisoned by 3,000 to 8,000 soldiers. It provided supplies for soldiers stationed in Central and Eastern Kentucky and East Tennessee. Camp Nelson was also the staging ground and supply center for three important campaigns. These were Major General Ambrose E. Burnside's August-November 1863 Knoxville campaign, Major General Stephen G. Burbridge's October 1864 Southwestern Virginia campaign, and Major General Burbridge's wing of Major General Stoneman's December 1864 Southwestern Virginia campaign.

One of the missions of Camp Nelson was to recruit and train soldiers. Early regiments or companies organized at Camp Nelson include the 47th and 49th Kentucky Mounted Infantries, Battery E of the 1st Kentucky Light Artillery, Companies E-K of the 8th Tennessee Infantry, the 8th

Tennessee Cavalry, Companies B and C of the 9th Tennessee Cavalry, Companies A and D of the 11th Tennessee Cavalry, and Batteries B and E of the 1st Tennessee Light Artillery.

Camp Nelson's great significance as a recruitment center, however, is most closely tied to its being Kentucky's largest recruitment and training center for U.S. Colored Troops (USCT). Because of Kentucky's situation as a Union slave-holding state, the Federal government delayed the recruitment of African-American troops, which would free them from slavery. This delay was the result of fear of violent retaliation or even secession on the part of the Commonwealth. It was not until the passage of the Conscriptive Act of February 1864, that enlisting of slaves and free blacks began over the entire Commonwealth.

In the spring of 1864, the recruitment of Kentucky's African-Americans greatly accelerated and a flood of slaves and free blacks began arriving at Camp Nelson. Many had risked great peril to reach the camp and attain their freedom and fight for the freedom of others. By the end of 1865, about 10,000 men, or 40 percent of Kentucky's African-American soldiers, had passed through Camp Nelson. The regiments formed at Camp Nelson included the 114th, 116th, 119th, and the 124th U.S. Colored Infantry; the 5th and 6th U.S. Colored Cavalry; and the 12th and 13th U.S. Colored Heavy Artillery. The 72nd, 117th, 120th, 121st, and 123rd U.S. Colored Infantries were also stationed at Camp Nelson for a time. African-American men continued to be enlisted at Camp Nelson as a means of emancipating them until December 1865 when the 13th Amendment was ratified.

At Camp Nelson, many enlistees got their first taste of freedom, although one tempered by army life. Life in the army could be difficult, but as Sergeant Elijah Marrs of the 12th USCHA stated: "I can stand this, said I …this is better than slavery, though I do march in line at the tap of a drum. I felt freedom in my bones, and when I saw the American eagle with outspread wings, upon the American flag, with the motto E Pluribus Unum, the thought came to me, 'Give me liberty or give me death.' Then all fear banished."

The Camp Nelson USCT was involved in a number of larger battles and campaigns. The 5th and a portion of the 6th U.S. Colored Cavalry were involved in both battles of Saltville, Virginia, (October and December 1864), where the main salt works for the Army of Northern Virginia was located. In fact, these regiments took the highest casualties at the first battle of Saltville and about 45 of its wounded and captured soldiers were murdered by Confederate Tennessee soldiers after the battle, which was a Confederate victory. On the way down to Saltville, the USCT experienced some taunting and verbal abuse by the white troops, but on the return trip things were different, as Colonel James S. Brisbin, commander of the 6th USCC, reported:

"On the march the colored soldiers, as well as their white officers, were made the subject of much ridicule and much insulting remarks by the white troops… These insults, as well as the jeers and taunts that they would not fight, were borne by the colored soldier patiently… Of this fight [first Saltville] I can only say that the men could not have behaved more bravely. I have seen white troops fight in 27 battles and I never saw any fight better… On the return of the forces, those who had scoffed at the colored troops on the march out where silent."

When African American recruits entered Camp Nelson they were often accompanied by their wives and children, who were also looking for freedom and opportunity. These family members lived either with the recruit or in hastily built shanties. Initially, the army did not know what to do with these family members and had no clear policy. In November 1864, Brigadier General Speed S. Fry, the commander of Camp Nelson, ordered 400 refugees out of camp on a bitterly cold day. The order was eventually countermanded, but 102 refugees died of exposure and disease. The political uproar which followed led directly to the March 1865 Congressional Act which freed the families of the recruits and to the establishment of a home for the refugees. The refugee home was administered jointly by the army, with Captain Theron E. Hall as superintendent, and the American Missionary Association, particularly the Reverend John G. Fee.

In June 1866, the army finally abandoned Camp Nelson, ending the military occupation of the area. The school and other administrative buildings were administered by Abisha Scofield, John G. Fee, and Gabriel Burdett of the American Missionary Association, and the cottages continued to be lived in by the African American families.

In 1866, the main Camp Nelson cemetery was designated a National Cemetery. The original sections of the cemetery contain the remains of 1,615 soldiers, including 837 USCT, and even some civilian employees who died at Camp Nelson. In the summer of 1868, 2,203 Union dead from Perryville, Richmond, Frankfort, London, and Covington were reinterred at Camp Nelson National Cemetery. Since that time, veterans continue to be buried at the cemetery.

The remainder of Camp Nelson, except for the cemetery, returned to its residential and agricultural use. The civilian houses used by the army were reoccupied, generally by the original owners, and the land returned to pasture or cropland. It remains much the same today.

* * *

Colored Troops from Kentucky
Proud to Serve and Served Proudly

By Dr. Marshall Myers

During the Civil War, few Kentucky slave holders felt compelled by patriotism to allow their eligible male slaves to join the Union army. In fact, many were openly adamant about losing what landowners saw as private property. After all, the Emancipation Proclamation, issued January 1, 1863, didn't apply to Kentucky, because she was not one of the states "in rebellion," so the terms of the document did not lawfully free a single slave in Kentucky.

George Prentice, editor of the powerful, pro-Union *Louisville Journal*, even published articles specifically designed for black preachers to "set themselves earnestly, zealously, and energetically to explain" to fellow bondsmen that the Emancipation Proclamation did not apply to Kentucky slaves. Yet slaves quickly got the message that the "peculiar institution" was soon to be a thing of the past.

Corporal Andrew Jackson Smith, 55th Massachusetts Infantry

The occupation of Kentucky by Union armies naturally encouraged slaves to flee to the military camps to escape bondage. According to Marion Lucas' excellent multi-volume *A History of Blacks in Kentucky* Union commanders had mixed reactions to the slaves that congregated around military fortifications and camps. Some welcomed the runaways into their midst, while others turned away those so desperate to be free.

General William Tecumseh Sherman, training and commanding Union troops in Kentucky, perplexed by all these new mouths to feed, finally decided that his troops would "have nothing to do with them [runaways] at all," cautioning those below him on the command ladder to not let the blacks "take refuge in camp." But slaves who were accepted as "contraband" of war by other commanders were often put to work doing menial tasks like chopping wood and repairing railroad lines destroyed by Confederate guerrillas.

In the early years of the war, Lincoln remained firm in his decision not to use black soldiers, noting, "To arm the Negroes would turn 50,000 bayonets from the loyal Border States against us that were for us." Later he expanded on his reasons: "If I were to arm the colored I fear that in a few weeks, the arms would be in the hands of the rebels." As the war wore on,

however, the Union needed more manpower, and the slaves remained an untapped source of willing soldiers, men who truly had a stake in the outcome of the war.

Lincoln had to be cautious, though, because he did not want to antagonize Kentucky, a state he felt was key to the war efforts. According to Benjamin Quarles in *Lincoln and the Negro*, Kentucky had "shown its temper" in mid-year of 1863 when the administration had proposed a sweeping draft order to include Kentucky. General Ambrose Burnside fired off a telegram to Lincoln cautioning the President on the implications of such an order: "We will lose a much larger number of good white volunteers and give the secret enemies of the Government a weapon to use against it."

According to Lucas, Lincoln next ordered a census of Kentucky to record the number of "eligible colored people" in the state, while, at the same time, pressuring Kentucky Governor Thomas E. Bramlette to help fill his draft quotas. The census revealed that there were 40,285 eligible black males in Kentucky, and only 1,650 free blacks available for service in the Union army. With some hesitation, Governor Bramlette relented to Lincoln's wishes and allowed the recruitment of blacks to meet the state's draft quota for March, 1864.

There were, however, certain stipulations that only applied to Kentucky. Those Union supporters who surrendered slaves for the Union army were given certificates that guaranteed compensation as high as $300 per recruit, and property (slaves) seized would be returned after the war. Perhaps most importantly, no slaves would be stationed inside the Commonwealth, a promise not always honored. Some slaves were paid by their owners to serve as substitutes for them, a practice especially popular, as Lucas notes, toward the end of the war. Black soldiers saw this opportunity as a way to escape slavery, see more of the world, and fight for a cause they most sincerely believed in. As an added incentive, in the first part of March of 1865, Federal law freed the families of black soldiers, prompting a spate of marriages and further encouraging slaves to sign up.

But many whites in the state did not react favorably to the idea of "colored" soldiers in Kentucky. A mob in Boyle County attacked a number of black soldiers, while black recruits of from Green, Taylor, and Adair counties were the subjects of severe whippings. As Lucas observes, Hancock County officials had to lock black recruits in the county jail to protect them from angry whites. Yet by March of 1865, 71 percent of blacks in Kentucky were free.

From recruiting stations in Louisville, Covington, Paducah, Bowling Green, Lebanon, Louisa, London, and Camp Nelson, black soldiers and other refugees ended up at Camp Nelson in Jessamine County, eight miles from Nicholasville, where they would receive their training.

Camp Nelson was, unfortunately, not a safe place to be. Lucas concludes that the military installation "created some of the worst living conditions of the Civil War." Never, "have I seen any cases which appealed so strongly to the sympathies of the benevolent as those congregated in the contraband camp at Camp Nelson," one member of the humanitarian United States Sanitary Commission concluded. Pneumonia was prevalent, and death was a constant companion of those brave enough to volunteer for service.

In the days of 19th century medicine, common childhood diseases – measles, mumps, and the more serious diseases like pneumonia – spread quickly through the camp, claiming the lives of countless soldiers huddled together in close quarters. At another camp with similar conditions, a Union soldier from a Maine company, quipped, "though we enlisted to fight and die, nothing happened to us so serious as the measles."

With so much time on their hands, black recruits thought of their families back home. Many of these former slaves could not read and write, prompting them to seek out literate whites and blacks to transcribe their thoughts to their loved ones so far away. As Lucas notes, one chaplain "wrote 150 letters to soldiers' families in a single month...while Sanitation Commission authorities estimated that its associates at Camp Nelson wrote 5,000 letters for black soldiers." Sgt. Elijah P. Marrs, a literate black soldier (b. 1840 Shelby County), was kept busy writing letters for his comrades.

So keen was the interest in writing and reading, that Richard Sears, author of *Camp Nelson, Kentucky*, observes that by November of 1864, under the leadership of John Fee, 13 volunteers agreed to hold classes at Camp Nelson to assist soldiers who wanted to be literate. One student of John Tyler's school for blacks in another state remarked that he wanted "to be able to read the Bible before I die."

Black soldiers from Kentucky often were, technically, members of the regular U.S. Army. They were organized into infantry and artillery units under white commanders, rather than being organized by states, as many of the white Union soldiers were. According to the adjutant general's report from Kentucky, there were 19 regiments of infantry and artillery soldiers, sub-divided into various companies, with white commanders.

The 114th U.S. Colored Infantry from Kentucky served in places like the siege at Petersburg, Richmond, then Appomattox. The 107th was active in the Carolinas, eventually occupying Raleigh, North Carolina, while the 110th occupied Nashville, and other parts of Tennessee. The 8th U.S. Colored Heavy Artillery showed great bravery in action in the Paducah area against the former slave trader, millionaire and Confederate cavalry leader, General Nathan Bedford Forrest.

Despite his earlier resolution against using black troops, Lincoln appeared to re-evaluate his position on the issue by 1864. According to psychologist and Lincoln biographer Charles B. Stozier, President Abraham Lincoln went far beyond his political companions to claim blacks should have "the rights of life, liberty, and the pursuit of happiness for Negroes in America - a radical statement, for it was more than they enjoyed at the time." Lincoln's later conversations with the great black leader, Frederick Douglass, impressed Douglass so much that the former slave called Lincoln "one of the most meritorious men in America," noting Lincoln's "entire freedom from popular prejudice against the colored race." Speaking of meeting Lincoln, Sojourner Truth, the powerful, ex-slave orator, concluded that she "felt that I was in the presence of a friend."

What the war was really about, however, seemed quite clear to Edward Francis, a black Union soldier from Richmond, Kentucky, serving in the 114th U.S. Colored Infantry. Francis keenly understood that he was fighting for a just and noble cause. At one point, in a letter to his wife from Vanceburg, he notes: "I do hope we shall be spared to see this cruel war over and the fetter[s] of every slave snapped asunder [.] It will be a blessed day for the Child of God."

After the war ended, black soldiers were often the last to be mustered out. Private Francis, for example, was not released from the service until June 8, 1867, more than two years after the close of the war.

In the end, according to Michael Jones of the Kentucky Historical Society, Kentucky furnished more black troops than any other state except Louisiana, with many of them, like Francis, spending the bulk of their enlistment stationed near Brownsville, Texas. In spite of overwhelming prejudice from commanders and their leaders in Washington, the black soldiers had, on more than one occasion, proved themselves to be able and effective soldiers, the pride of not only their race, but also the pride, ultimately, of the whole nation.

* * *

CONFEDERATE GENERAL LLOYD TILGHMAN

'AS A MAN, A SOLDIER, AND A GENERAL, HE HAD FEW IF ANY SUPERIORS.'

By Bryan Bush

The words used to describe Lloyd Tilghman are "brave, heroic, patriotic, loyal," and "totally devoted to the cause he believed in." Confederate Colonel A.E. Reynolds once said of Tilghman that "as a man, a soldier, and a General, he had few if any superiors."

He also has been described as a strict disciplinarian who abided by the military rules and regulations of the army. Many volunteer officers who did not understand military rules and regulations, did not get along well with Tilghman. This, and his surrender at Fort Henry, played a large part in casting Tilghman in a negative light. After the surrender of Ft. Henry, Tilghman was used as a scapegoat for the bungling of others. With these facts taken into account, and Tilghman's brave stand at Champion's Hill, Tilghman must be remembered as a general who was brave and totally devoted to his cause.

Gen. Lloyd Tilghman

Tilghman was born January 26, 1816, near Claiborne, Maryland, and came from a family steeped in military tradition. His ancestors played an important role in the early history of our country. His grandfather was part of the Continental Congress and was a Senator. Because of Tilghman's family background, he was admitted to West Point. While at West Point, Tilghman would be brevetted 2nd Lieutenant of the 1st Dragoons, September 1836.

At West Point, Tilghman would learn the skills to be an engineer, a career that was very highly sought after in the American market, especially by the ever-expanding railroad industry. Tilghman graduated from West Point on October 1, 1836, but resigned his commission in the military and decided that he would try his luck in the civilian sector.

Tilghman worked as an engineer on several different railroads from 1837 until he decided to join the Army in 1845. The Mexican War had broken out and he felt it was his personal duty to fight for his country. Tilghman arrived at Corpus Christi, Texas, in September 1845 and became a sutler supplying the army. Once the army found out that Tilghman had been a Lieutenant in the Dragoons, he immediately became the aide de camp for General David Twiggs, who commanded the 2nd Dragoons.

During the Mexican War, Tilghman helped make reconnaissances of enemy positions, fought in the battle of Monterrey, was placed in command of a partisan corps of 20 men and fought the enemy at La Mesa, La Puerta, and Sueesties. By 1847 Tilghman was at Matamoros and helped build the defenses and fortifications around the city. Later that year, Tilghman became a captain and commanded a light artillery battery of six guns to serve with the Maryland and District of Columbia Volunteer Light Artillery. He was stationed with his battery at Jalapa. In 1848 he made several expeditions to Montego, and at Mantoosco he and his 100 men came to the rescue of Captain Robert Wheat, who was surrounded by 600 men. The Mexican War ended on February 2, 1848. Tilghman learned valuable lessons during the Mexican War, honing his skills as an engineer and a leader of men.

After the Mexican War, Tilghman returned to civilian life, serving as Chief Engineer for many railroads. In 1852 he moved to Kentucky to help build the Paducah branch of the Mobile and Ohio railroad. In Paducah, Tilghman bought a beautiful 10-room mansion and became an official resident of the state of Kentucky. He had several children by his wife Augusta Murray Boyd. He was at the top of his profession and life was good.

In December of 1860 Tilghman decided to join the Kentucky State Guard. Confederate in sympathy, it became known as one of the best militia organizations in the United States. Tilghman became a major in the Paducah Southwest Battalion. Then, shots were fired at Fort Sumter in April of 1861. The country was at war. Tilghman was commander of the western division of the Kentucky State Guard, which included the Paducah and the Columbus areas in Kentucky.

Tensions in the state quickly came to a boil. Tilghman had to make his decision: would he stay loyal to the Union or join the Confederacy? The decision could not have been an easy one, but on July 5, 1861, Tilghman and the 3rd Kentucky Infantry, Company D, joined the Confederacy. He and his commander of the Kentucky State Guard, Simon Buckner, felt strongly that the government was not following the constitutionality of State Rights. They saw the Union forces invading their state against the will of the people to remain neutral. This one event would change Tilghman's life forever and lead to a series of events that would influence the outcome of the Civil War.

After Tilghman resigned from the Kentucky State Guard, he became commander of the 3rd Kentucky Infantry, C.S.A. He had the almost impossible task to arm his men with weapons, clothes and accouterments.

On September 6, 1861, Brig. Gen. Ulysses S. Grant entered the city of Paducah. Grant says that when he entered the city Tilghman and his army had left. Grant took the city without firing a shot. After leaving Paducah, Tilghman and his 3rd Kentucky fell back to Camp Boone, Tennessee. On October 18, 1861, he was promoted to Brigadier General and was sent to Hopkinsville, Kentucky, where he trained 3,000 men, although getting arms for these men was a massive undertaking.

On October 27, 1861, Tilghman wrote to Gen. Albert Sidney Johnston that "a vast deal of suffering exists, owing to the condition of the men. I have made arrangements for 200 women to work on clothing, and hope for a better contribution of blankets and clothing from the society at this place." He also mentions in the letter that he was sorry to hear about the "inefficient condition of things at Fort Donelson." At the end of the letter, Tilghman made a plea for artillery, wagons, mules, harnesses, forage, and horses for artillery commands. During this time most of the arms and ammunition being made in Nashville, Tennessee, and the surrounding area was being sent east to supply the Army of Northern Virginia.

On November 17th, 1861, Tilghman was sent to take control of Forts Henry and Donelson in Tennessee and their defenses. With Tilghman's military experience and engineering skills, it seemed that he was the perfect man for the task. But the forts were not equipped and were in poor shape. He had 1,000 unarmed men. Tilghman wrote to Confederate General Leonidas Polk, the district commander, that he needed more manpower to complete the forts, but none came. Tilghman was loyal to the Confederacy and would try and make the best of the situation. He worked diligently in building earthworks, rifle pits, and securing the approaches to the forts. By January, 1862, Tilghman felt that work on the forts had progressed, but he had 2,000 men that were unarmed and he knew that the Union troops would soon arrive to try and take the forts.

Fate now worked against Tilghman. Fort Henry had been built on low ground and the fort was quickly filling with water from the river. The mines that were placed in the river to prevent the Union gunboats from approaching the forts were also under water. Tilghman knew that an enemy with any common sense, in obtaining high water, could control the entire fort, but again he would carry out his orders and

defend the fort. Tilghman's 2,600 poorly-armed men at Fort Henry would have to take on Grant's 16,000 Federal troops.

On February 6, 1862, at 10:15 am, the attack began on Fort Henry. Union Admiral Andrew Foote's gunboats and Union General Ulysses S. Grant's infantry approached. At 12:35am fate again interceded. During the battle, Tilghman's 24-pounder burst, and then he lost his 10-inch Columbiad when it was accidentally spiked. Several of the 32-pounders were lost. Tilghman knew it was time to fall back to Fort Donelson, but after seeing his courageous men working the batteries at Fort Henry, he decided to stay to the end. Tilghman sent all his forces to Fort Donelson except 100 men who endured the fire that was falling into Fort Henry from the gunboats. The gunboats approached within 600 yards of the fort. At 1:10pm his men were exhausted and only four cannons were left at the fort. At 1:30pm Tilghman himself took charge of the one of the 32-pounders.

Tilghman looked around and saw most of the crews were killed or wounded and that the gunboats were breaching the fort. He decided to stop the useless loss of life. After two and a half hours of fighting, he surrendered. Tilghman's plan of saving the Confederate force had worked. He had bought enough time at Fort Henry for the rest of his command to fall back to Fort Donelson. Flag Officer Foote commended Tilghman after the Battle of Fort Henry saying he was "gallant in his defense of the fort." Col. Heiman called Tilghman "heroic."

Unfortunately, Tilghman's work to preserve his army came to an end when the bungling Generals John B. Floyd and Gideon Pillow surrendered Fort Donelson. During the Battle of Fort Donelson, the Confederate army could have escaped capture, because they had broken out of the fort, but Pillow and Floyd decided to fall back to the fort, sealing their fate.

The fall of Forts Henry and Donelson would have detrimental effects on the Confederacy in the Western Theater. The Tennessee and the Cumberland Rivers were now open to invasion from Union forces. The Confederate earthworks and cannons protecting the Mississippi River from Union invasion at Columbus, Kentucky, were abandoned. After the Battle of Fort Henry, Tilghman became a prisoner of war, and was sent to Fort Warren, in Boston, Mass. On August 27, 1862, Tilghman was exchanged for Union General John Reynolds. Also exchanged were 10,000 men who were now under Tilghman's command. Once again, he had to equip, clothe, and arm these men. He also had to form them into artillery, cavalry, and infantry units.

In October 1862, Union General Ulysses Grant began his move toward Vicksburg, Mississippi. Grant was following the Mississippi Central Railroad, a path that would lead him directly to Tilghman's forces at Coffeeville, Mississippi. At 2:30pm on December 5, fighting began in the town of

Coffeeville, where Grant's forces had pushed a mile into town.

General Lovell, commander of the First Corps, had sent a division of Tilghman's men to check the advance. Lovell rode with Tilghman to the front and sent the First Brigade, under Brig. Gen. Baldwin to the right of the main road leading into Water Valley. Col. A.P. Thompson and the Third Kentucky were sent on the road leading out of Coffeeville to the west of the main road, to watch the left flank. Artillery was brought up and soon an artillery duel broke out.

Tilghman's rifled guns soon silenced the Union cannon. Gen. Tilghman asked permission to advance on the enemy. Permission was granted and he ordered the 14th Mississippi, under General Ross, which had been in reserve, to take position on the extreme right of his line. The cavalry under Col. W.H. Jackson was made ready, and moved to the rear of the main line. General Albert Rust, with two brigades on Tilghman's right, was also made ready. Tilghman then ordered the advance. As soon as they got to within 200 yards, the Yankees opened fire on the Confederates. Col. Thompson ordered the 9th Arkansas, and the 8th Kentucky to return fire and press the enemy.

Even though the Yankees made two stands, they were quickly driven off. The Yankees were then pushed to the edge of an open field, where the Federal troops mounted their horses and retreated. When they reached the edge of a wooded area, they dismounted and began to fire at the exposed Confederates who were pursuing them across the open field.

Tilghman feared that General Rust had not moved far enough to cover his right flank and he immediately ordered Lt. J. G. Barbour, commanding his bodyguard, to move to the extreme right. As soon as Lt. Barbour moved into position he was immediately fired upon by the Yankees, who by this time had been pushed almost three miles from

This Model 1850 Foot Officer's sword, sword belt, and a Texas or Mississippi style belt buckle, was worn by Gen. Lloyd Tilghman during the Battle of Fort Henry.
Artifacts courtesy of the Old Bardstown Village and The Civil War Battles of the Western Theater Museum, Bardstown, Kentucky

Coffeeville and commanded the high ground outside of town. The heaviest fire was now directed down upon the 8th Kentucky and 9th Arkansas, but the Confederates pushed on, and soon overran the Yankee position. Their objective of pushing the enemy was complete, and General Tilghman ordered his men to halt and cease fire.

The Confederates killed 34 Union soldiers, including Lt. Col. William McCullough and 2nd Lt. Thomas Woodburn, and captured 17. The Confederates lost seven killed and 43 wounded. The besting of Grant was, in a small measure, General Tilghman's pay-back for the defeat he suffered at Grant's hands at Fort Henry. But this battle did not stop the relentless pursuit of Grant's forces.

Grant came up with several different plans to try and take Vicksburg. He built canals. He tried to maneuver his men and gunboats through the swamps. Each effort failed. During this time Tilghman led a brigade at the Battle of Corinth, Mississippi, and was the rear guard at the Battle of Holly Springs. Grant finally landed his men at Bruinsburg, located below Vicksburg. Confederate General Pemberton, the commander of Confederate forces in Vicksburg, had to abandon Grand Gulf and fall back to the city of Vicksburg. Grant gave up his supply base at Grand Gulf and decided to surround the city of Vicksburg.

On May 16, 1863, at Champion's Hill, Mississippi, Tilghman had a force of only 1,550 men, which was being forced back by 6,000-8,000 men of Grant's army. Tilghman dismounted and took command of a section of field artillery of the 1st Mississippi Light Artillery, and was in the act of sighting a howitzer when he was struck in the hip by a cannonball from the Chicago Mercantile Battery's number two gun. He lived about three hours after he was wounded and was carried to a peach tree where he died in the arms of General Powhattan Ellis.

On July 4, 1863, Vicksburg, Mississippi, fell to Grant's forces after a prolonged siege. The end of the Confederacy was now even closer. The surrender of Vicksburg split the Confederacy in two. The key to the Confederate heartland was now in Lincoln's pocket. Tilghman was survived by his wife Augusta Murray Boyd, and his three sons, Lt. Lloyd Tilghman, Jr., Frederick and Sidell. Unfortunately, two months after Tilghman's death, his son Lt. Lloyd Tilghman, Jr. was thrown from his horse, hit his head on a piece of rail iron and was killed instantly. Another Tilghman gave up his life for the cause.

After the Civil War, General Tilghman's widow brought their children to New York. In 1901, Tilghman's sons had his body removed from his gravesite in Mississippi and moved to Woodlawn Cemetery in New York City, to be buried next to their mother, who died in New York in 1898.

* * *

RAID IN BLUESTONE

By Rowan County Historical Society

Although the most popular writings and movie productions are those that depict the dramas of thousands of soldiers who fought and died in major battles, there were also soldiers who also lost their lives in smaller engagements. During encounters with Home Guards and in small skirmishes, there was gunfire with intent to kill. Raids through Kentucky by Confederates helped to provide much needed supplies and fresh horses. On June 16, 1863, Captain Peter Everett, part of John Hunt Morgan's command, led Company B of the Third Battalion Kentucky Mounted Rifles on a raid into Maysville capturing 50 Union horses, 330 guns and 25 pistols.

While traveling to Rowan County, Everett encountered approximately 170 Home Guards at Mt. Carmel and another company of Home Guards under Major Pennebaker of the Tenth Kentucky Cavalry at Fox Spring. Major Pennebaker, Capts. Evans and Curtis, and one private were killed. When Everett reached an area of Rowan County called Bluestone, his men came upon Colonel John DeCourcy and the Eighth and Ninth Regiments Michigan Cavalry, the Tenth Kentucky Cavalry, and a detachment of the Fourteenth Kentucky Cavalry with sections of the Eighth Michigan and Tenth Kentucky Batteries.

Bluestone, now a quiet community on the top of a hill, drops about 120-140 feet in elevation down to a corn field.

A few miles away is an iron bridge, the Bluestone Bridge, now closed to traffic. The bridge was once made of wood and it is believed that Everett's men came down the steep hill and made haste across the bridge, running from the artillery fire from the opponent that stood on the top of Bluestone Hill. The bridge was the only reasonable access to the road towards the mountains of West Liberty, following the Licking River. There is no record of the burning of the original bridge. However, tales handed down through the generations seem to indicate it might have been burned to slow down the chase. Out of approximately 1,900 men, Everett claimed to have lost only 30 men, killed, wounded or unaccounted for against DeCourcy. Captain Everett raided Maysville again on June 8, 1864.

The raid in 1863 caused unrest among some local Union sympathizers. In particular were the Underwoods of Carter County, Kentucky. The Underwood made robbery raids into Maysville, against citizens that they considered Rebel sympathizers. They later became involved in a feud known as the Underwood feud of Carter County. Shortly after that they became sympathizers of the Tolliver side of the Rowan County war between the Tollivers and the Martins. Many post-war family conflicts The repercussions of even the smallest skirmishes of the Civil War often lasted many years beyond General Lee's surrender.

* * *

ROY S. CLUKE
MORGAN'S BOLD COLONEL

By Dr. James A. Ramage

Filson Historical Society

Morgan's Raid

Confederate Cavalry Colonel Roy S. Cluke, one of General John Hunt Morgan's ablest officers, loved to fight, and you could see it on his countenance. He looked like an alert eagle – a thin, sharp face with eyes intense, wary, and savage. He had sandy hair, a mustache and sideburns. Some said Cluke was more dashing and daring than Morgan, which was quite a compliment. At six feet, two inches in height, he was a bit taller than Morgan's six feet. Like Morgan, he dressed in civilian clothes with no insignia of rank, and like Morgan he often masqueraded as an enemy officer.

Cluke understood Morgan's practice of classic guerrilla warfare and was one of those rare men you could always depend on – not simply to perform his duty, but to go beyond expectations. When Morgan sent Cluke and 750 men into "dead horse camp" in central Kentucky in February 1863, he expected them to forage, rest, strengthen their horses, and simply survive the winter. Instead, Cluke's "war

dogs," as they were called, operated against Union occupying forces so vigorously on such a wide front that Union commanders reported to army headquarters in Washington, D.C., that a large Confederate army was invading the state. Gov. James Robinson said that Generals John Hunt Morgan, Nathan B. Forrest, Humphrey Marshall, and John Pegram were leading the invaders, and demanded "something must be done immediately."

Cluke was born on a farm in Clark County six miles west of Winchester, and when he arrived back home in Kentucky in the winter of 1863, he was very familiar with the roads and could rely on friends for information and support. He had entered Confederate service during Bragg's invasion of Kentucky in September 1862, when Morgan authorized him to recruit the 8th Kentucky Cavalry Regiment. Most of the men were from Clark County and the surrounding area, and they loved Cluke. He was honest, they said, and a vigilant officer who cared for their well being. Like Morgan, he avoided fights that would shed blood without any significant result.

Colonel, later General, Basil Duke, Morgan's second in command, said Cluke and his regiment were exceedingly reliable and "extremely bold and tenacious," and they proved it in their baptism of fire. They had a brief skirmish before they left Kentucky, but their first significant fighting occurred when they participated in Morgan's raid on Hartsville, Tennessee.

Morgan used audacity, darkness, and terrible winter weather to attack the infantry brigade of Colonel Absalom B. Moore, guarding the left flank of the army of General Rosecrans in Nashville. During a snowstorm on Saturday, December 6, 1862, Morgan led 2,140 raiders, infantry and cavalry, on an overnight march of 30 miles from Murfreesboro to Hartsville. Morgan's scouts estimated the enemy at 1,300, and this was an unusual estimate for the Civil War because it was an underestimate – scouts usually exaggerated, reporting enemy strength at twice reality. In this case, the truth was, Moore had about 2,100, about the same as Morgan.

It was cold, and toward Hartsville, they had to cross the icy Cumberland River. The infantry crossed on boats, but Cluke's men and the other cavalry had to plunge into the cold water on horseback and have their horses climb the muddy bank on the other side. It was below freezing, and about half of the cavalry stopped to make fires and dry their uniforms. Cluke's men were among those who ignored the ice on their uniforms and moved on with Morgan.

With 1,200 men, Morgan still hoped to surprise the enemy at daybreak. But as his advance approached the enemy guards, there was gunfire, and a black servant of one of the Union officers ran into the camp shouting, "The Rebels are coming!"

Surprise was lost, and when Cluke and his regiment, under Duke's orders, galloped into the clearing of the camp and dismounted, they saw the Union tents 400 yards away on a slight rise in a wooded area. There seemed to be a great many tents and more men moving around than expected. Between Cluke's men and the enemy there was a large snow-covered meadow, 300 yards across, and on the field there were fresh tracks in the snow made by Federal skirmishers who were standing behind a fence row, pointing their rifles toward Cluke's men, 100 yards away.

As soon as he saw the camp, Duke realized that Morgan's men were outnumbered, nearly two to one, and the enemy had the high ground. Nevertheless, Morgan ordered an assault, with Duke in charge of the cavalry. Duke deployed Colonel D.W. Chenault's 11th Kentucky cavalry regiment on the left, and

Cluke's regiment next to them. Duke yelled, "Charge!" and Cluke's men moved forward at a brisk walk and fired a volley at the skirmishers behind the fence. The Federals withdrew across the field to their camp and joined the defensive line Moore was forming overlooking the meadow.

Cluke's men reloaded, climbed over the fence, and charged across the field on the run in the standard Morgan skirmish line, with two yards between each man so they presented less of a target. The Union infantry fired a volley that went over their heads, and Cluke halted his men within 60 yards of the enemy line and ordered, "Fire!" Then he shouted, "Charge!" and giving the Rebel yell, they ran forward, driving the Union men from their position and forcing them back in confusion. Duke said of Cluke's men, "They had literally made up their minds not to be beaten."

Chenault's regiment advanced on the left, and Morgan's infantry charged on the right – the Federals withdrew, and surrendered. Cluke's men helped round up over 1,800 prisoners. When General Rosecrans was informed, he replied: "Do I understand that they have captured an entire brigade of troops without our knowing it, or [without] a good fight?"

Morgan complimented Cluke's regiment by assigning them to the rear guard on the withdrawal from Hartsville. It was quite an honor, but this was only the first of many times that Morgan placed confidence in Cluke. Another was the time he caused such a stir in Kentucky early in 1863. On that operation, which Cluke turned into one of the most success-ful small cavalry raids in the war, Cluke realized that his detachment of 750 men was not strong enough to attack the strong Union force of General Quincy A. Gillmore in Lexington. But he saw that he could harass Gillmore by capturing the Union outpost at Mount Sterling, about 25 miles to the east. During the extended raid, he captured Mount Sterling three times.

The first time, he and his raiders were so effective with IPB (intelligence preparation of the battlefield) there was no fight. Their rumors of a general invasion frightened the small Federal force occupying the town into evacuating. They were leaving when Cluke's detachment arrived and attacked. The Union men fled toward Lexington, littering the road with rifles, sabers, and other items.

Cluke moved his entire force into Mount Sterling and seized a quantity of supplies that included a new Union overcoat for each man. It was a very cold winter and the warm overcoats were much appreciated. Citizens provided home cooking, and gave plentiful forage for the horses. Cluke gave furloughs to most of the men to visit families in the vicinity. A few days later, when Cluke's scouts reported a brigade of Union infantry advancing from Lexington under Colonel Benjamin P. Runkle, he withdrew without a fight.

He returned and captured the town without firing a shot, with a guerrilla ruse. He sent a squad into town with their blue overcoats, and told them to masquerade as Union army soldiers. They were to hang around Runkle's headquarters, and when nobody was looking, confiscate a few printed blank forms for official orders. They soon returned, with the Federal forms. Cluke took one and wrote a fake order supposedly from Gillmore to Runkle, informing him that a large Confederate army was marching toward Lexington. Runkle was to move immediately to Lexington's relief. Cluke gave the document to his best scout, Clark Lyle, and in his blue overcoat, Clark rode his horse out toward Lexington a few miles, wheeled and raced back into town, all out of breath with his horse winded. At Union headquarters he dismounted and ran in with the order. Runkle left, and Cluke's men moved back into Mount Sterling. Admitting his gullibility, Runkle called the deception "a Morganish trick."

After several days the Union army came in even greater numbers under Colonel Charles J. Walker. Without resistance, Cluke withdrew eastward to Hazel Green and then to a camp near Salyersville. He had not been there long when scouts reported strong enemy forces converging on him from Louisa on his right and Proctor on his left. Walker had left about 200 men in Mount Sterling under Captain William D. Ratcliffe of the 10th Kentucky (Union) Cavalry, and with his main body was attempting to capture Cluke and his raiders. Bets ran high in Mount Sterling that Cluke would be captured.

But Cluke, warned of the trap, moved to capture Mount Sterling a third time. The road toward Mount Sterling was clear of enemy troops, and he surprised the enemy with an extraordinary overnight march of over 60 miles in 24 hours, most of it on difficult muddy roads. Cluke knew this was a fight that could be won, and by capturing the enemy force in Mount Sterling he could create the coup de grace of the raid – a Confederate victory in battle.

With about 300 men – about half had become ill with a fever and were recuperating in the homes of Southern friends – he approached Mount Sterling at daylight on March 22, 1863. A few miles east of town, he divided his men and sent a detachment around the town to charge in from the west, from the direction of Lexington, to prevent their escape. He led the other half on a mounted charge into town from the other direction.

Totally surprised, Captain Ratcliffe retreated to the courthouse and houses in the center of town. Cluke dismounted a squad of 30 men, gave them axes, sledge hammers, and torches, and ordered them to move toward the courthouse. When they were fired upon from a building, they were to set it on fire and break down the doors to get in to seize the enemy. Cluke's squad moved, and when the burning and crashing and yelling approached the courthouse, Ratcliffe surrendered. Confederate and Union alike united in attempting to put out the fires, but several houses burned to the ground. An exaggerated rumor circulated in Lexington that the entire town burned. Before Walker returned, Cluke received orders to reunite with Morgan. He marched south, with his men and horses well fed and rested, and through recruiting, his command was stronger by 18 men than when the raid began. "My command is elegantly mounted and clothed; in fact, in better condition than they ever have been," he reported.

That summer, Cluke led his regiment in the Great Raid into Indiana and Ohio, and after the Battle of Buffington Island, for the last week of the raid, served as brigade commander. In northern Ohio, he was captured and imprisoned with Morgan and other officers in the Ohio state penitentiary in Columbus. Union officials acted on a false report that he had taken an oath of allegiance to the Union before he joined the Confederate army. They tried him on the false charges, and he was acquitted, but rather than send him back to the penitentiary, Union officials sent him to Johnson's Island in Sandusky Bay in Lake Erie. There, he contracted diphtheria, and died at Johnson's Island at the age of 39 on December 31, 1863. He is buried in Lexington Cemetery, Lexington, Kentucky.

* * *

'WHERE HONOR AND DUTY LEAD'
TEBBS BEND: THE DEFENSE OF GREEN RIVER BRIDGE

By Lisa Gaines Matthews

Tebbs Bend Reenactment and Memorial Service

On April 15, 1861, President Abraham Lincoln issued the following proclamation: "Whereas the laws of the United States have been for some time past and are now opposed and the execution thereof obstructed in the States of South Carolina, Alabama, Florida, Mississippi, Louisiana, and Texas by combinations too powerful to be suppressed by the ordinary course of judicial proceedings or by the powers vested in the marshals." Invoking the Constitutional power vested in the executive branch, Lincoln proceeded to "call forth . . . the militia of the several States of the Union to an aggregate number of 75,000, in order to suppress said combinations and to cause the laws to be duly executed."

As a result of the proclamation, the 751,000 citizens of the State of Michigan were asked to provide one fully equipped regiment to the Union cause. On April 16, Michigan governor Austin Blair issued his own proclamation in which the first Michigan Infantry Regiment would be formed from several independent military companies. These units bore the names of their home companies, such as the "Detroit Light Guard," the "Manchester Union Guards," the "Michigan Hussars," and the "Hardee Cadets."

The First Infantry Regiment was fully mustered by April 29, 1861, with an enrollment of 798 men. Initially stationed in Washington, D.C., these men fought bravely at the First Battle of Bull Run (Manassas). They were engaged in the Peninsular Campaign in 1862; the Battles of Antietam, Fredericksburg and Chancellorsville; and on July 2, 1863, the First Michigan defended the base of Little Round Top at Gettysburg.

By the end of 1861, Michigan had mustered 13 infantry regiments, three cavalry regiments, and five batteries of light artillery. On July 2, 1862, the U.S. War Department issued another appeal for troops. Michigan's quota was 11,686 of the 500,000 men needed. On September 22, the 25th Michigan Infantry, led by Col. Orlando Hurley Moore, was formed in Kalamazoo. Prior to leaving camp for Louisville, Kentucky, the regiment was presented with a silk flag, which was inscribed, "This flag is given in faith that it will be carried where honor and duty lead."

The 896 officers and men of the 25th Michigan were initially stationed in Louisville until December 8, 1862. They were then ordered to proceed to Munfordville and skirmished with Confederates on December 27th. By January 8, 1863, the unit was guarding trains and manning picket lines in Bowling Green, Kentucky. By April, the 25th returned to Louisville and was assigned to guard duty within the city.

On June 10, 1863, Col. Moore and five companies ("D," "E," "F," "I," and "K") of the 25th were sent to Lebanon by rail and then moved south to protect the strategically important Lebanon-Campbellsville-Columbia turnpike and the Green River Bridge below Campbellsville. The railroad line and the turnpike were primary transportation routes for the movement of Union troops and supplies into the Confederacy.

The Green River Bridge was a familiar landmark for both sides. In 1862, a portion of Gen. George H. Thomas' troops traveled the turnpike on their way to Mill Springs. John Hunt Morgan and his cavalry used the route during the Christmas Raid of 1862, during which Union supplies were destroyed and a portion of the bridge was burned. Union troops began repairing the bridge in April, 1863, and although the restoration was not completed until December, the position was valued by both sides.

On July 2, 1863, John Hunt Morgan and 2,500 men entered Kentucky again to begin what would become known as The Great Raid. Aware of the federal presence at the Green River Bridge, Morgan decided to engage and defeat that force before heading northward toward Louisville. On July 3, Morgan sent nearly half his men, under the command of Col. Roy S. Cluke, across the Green River to establish a position from which they could attack the bridge from the north and prevent a Union retreat.

Col. O.H. Moore was aware of Morgan's approach. During the day of July 3, his regiment crossed the Green River Bridge to the southern bluffs of Tebbs Bend. He selected a defensive position across the 100-yard wide "narrows entering the bend." During the night of July 3, Confederate Captain Thomas Franks reported "the ringing of axes and the crash of falling timber." It would not be clear until dawn that the 200 men of the 25th had feverishly built an abatis from the felled trees across the narrows. In front of the abatis, a 100-foot rifle pit with earthworks had been dug and was manned with 75 soldiers. Flanked on both sides by the Green River, the position was a defensive masterpiece.

At sunrise on July 4, Union pickets opened fire on approaching Confederate troops. Confederate artillery, located 500 yards to the south, began to fire on Moore's position. At 7am, three Confederate officers approached under a flag of truce and demanded that Moore surrender. His reply, as recorded in his field report was, "the Fourth of July was no day for me to entertain such a proposition."

Morgan's men then unleashed rifle and artillery fire and the 25th "withdrew into the woods." The Confederate guns were soon silenced when Union sharpshooters picked off the gunners. Basil Duke recorded the land approaching the abatis as "the flat summit of a hill, which slopes gently away on both the northern and southern sides." Artillery guns were useless as they were not able to "have borne upon the enemy's position at all." Even with guns properly placed, the gunners had no chance against Union sharpshooters.

Morgan realized that his only recourse was a frontal assault and "the first rush carried men close to the work, but they were stopped by the fallen timber, and dropped fast under the close fire of the enemy." Col. David Chenault, urging on his men of the 11th Kentucky Cavalry, was killed in a charge up the bluff on Moore's right. The 5th Kentucky Cavalry was then sent forward, where "they were stopped as the others had been, and suffered severely."

West of the Tebbs Bend battlefield, the two regiments under Col. Cluke attempted to cross the Green River to take the bridge. The crossing was made impossible by the 40 men of the 8th Michigan Infantry and the 79th New York Highlanders. In this aspect of the Confederate attack, topography won the day as the bluffs along the river proved insurmountable under withering Union fire.

The main battle in the narrows lasted three and a half hours. During that time, 600 Confederates rushed the Union defenses eight times. Moore records that his men "engaged the enemy with a determination not to be defeated. The conflict was fierce and bloody. At times the enemy occupied one side of the fallen timber, while my men held the other, in almost a hand-to-hand fight."

Basil Duke notes that "the rush through a hundred yards of undergrowth, succeeded by a jam and crowding of a regiment into the narrow neck, and confronted by the tangled mass of prostrate timber and the guns of the hidden foe, was more than the men could stand."

Upon hearing of the futility of the battle, Morgan ordered a halt to the engagement with a subsequent withdrawal. Duke notes that "it was his (Morgan's) practice to attack and seek to capture all but the strongest of forces which opposed his advance" and "this was the only instance in which he ever failed of success in this policy."

The Confederates asked for permission to bury their dead which Col. Moore granted, "proposing to deliver them in from of our lines." Moore reported that his casualties were 6 killed and 23 wounded. His estimate of Confederate losses was 50 killed and 200 wounded. Basil Duke records Confederate casualties as 36 killed and 45 or 46 wounded with "enemy" losses at 9 killed and 26 wounded.

There is no question that Morgan's forces lost several valuable officers. Along with Col. Chenault, the battle claimed the lives of Maj. Thomas Y. Brent (5th Kentucky), Capt. Alexander Tribble (11th Kentucky), Capt. Robert H. Cowan (3rd Kentucky), Lt. George Holloway (5th Kentucky), and Lt. James Ferguson (5th Kentucky). Future Kentucky governor, Maj. James McCreary kept a personal diary and wrote of the engagement, "Many of our best men were killed or wounded. The beginning of this raid is ominous." McCreary had assumed command of the 11th Kentucky Cavalry upon the death of Col. Chenault and was promoted to Lieutenant Colonel after the battle.

With the road to the Green River Bridge blocked, Morgan and his men proceeded west and crossed the river at Johnson Ford, then headed north and crossed the Ohio River at Brandenburg. For nearly three weeks, the raiders wreaked havoc in Indiana and Ohio on a raid that represented the deepest penetration into the North by a Confederate force. The raid ended on July 26, 1863, with the capture of Morgan and the remainder of his men near Lisbon, Ohio.

After Tebbs Bend, the 25th Michigan returned to Lebanon where it was joined by the companies that had remained in Louisville. Assigned to the 1st Brigade, 1st Division 23rd Corps of the Army of the Ohio, the 25th marched to Loudon, Tennessee to participate in the defense of Kingston. By January 21, 1864, the 23rd arrived in Knoxville and in

Tebbs Bend – Confederate Cemetery

April, under the command of Gen. John M. Scofield, it moved south to join in the Georgia campaign. The 25th Michigan saw action at Tunnel Hill on May 7, Rocky Face on May 9 and proceeded south to Atlanta where it fought in the Battle of Atlanta on July 22, 1864.

Still attached to the Union Army 23rd Corps, the 25th Michigan marched north to Nashville, which was threatened by Confederate General John Bell Hood. In January, 1865, the men of the 25th boarded steamers bound for Cincinnati and then traveled to Washington, D.C. From the nation's capital, steamers transported Scofield's army to North Carolina where the final pursuit of the Confederate army under General Joseph Johnston began.

The 25th Michigan Infantry Regiment mustered out of the Union army in Salisbury, N.C., on June 24, 1865. The men arrived in Jackson, Michigan, on July 2. In nearly three years of service, the regiment had a casualty rate of 16.9%. Killed in action numbered 22 men, 13 soldiers died from their wounds, and 129 men succumbed to disease. While no photograph of the 25th exists at the State of Michigan Archives, the descendants of these fine soldiers can take pride in the fact that they surmounted great odds and left a permanent record of honor and duty in a little known place in Kentucky called Tebbs Bend.

(Special thanks to Betty Jane Gorin for editorial support.)

* * *

BASIL W. DUKE

A MILITARY GENIUS AND TACTICIAN AHEAD OF HIS TIME

By Dr. James A. Ramage

Confederate General Basil W. Duke was one of the most famous Kentuckians in the Civil War. He was a colonel and second in command of General John Hunt Morgan's raiders, and when Morgan was killed on September 4, 1864, Duke was promoted to brigadier general and served as commander to the end of the war. "He is a military genius of no ordinary kind," declared the New York Times.

Duke was so intelligent it was believed in the North that he was the intellect behind all of Morgan's accomplishments. Union cavalrymen enjoyed the canard, "If you hit Duke on the head, you would knock Morgan's brains out." And it was true that Duke contributed greatly to Morgan's career. In one of his official reports, Morgan wrote that he was "'the right man in the right place.' Wise in counsel, gallant in the field, his services have ever been invaluable to me."

Gen. Basil W. Duke

Morgan did not keep a diary, and therefore Duke's book, *A History of Morgan's Cavalry*, published two years after the war, serves as the most valuable primary source on Morgan and his men. In the book, Duke described how Morgan made the decisions and depended on Duke to execute them. He wrote that when Morgan was killed the chivalry and romance were gone from the war. Certainly, under Duke the men changed from guerrilla raiders to more conventional cavalry.

Born in Scott County, Kentucky, on May 28, 1838, Duke studied at Georgetown College, Centre College, and Transylvania University. He was admitted to the bar in St. Louis and was practicing there when the war began. He returned to Kentucky, married John Hunt Morgan's sister, Henrietta, and in October 1861, enlisted in Morgan's cavalry company. He was elected first lieutenant and began serving as second in command.

From the beginning, Morgan specialized in hit-and-run guerrilla raids behind enemy lines, and by June 1862, he and Duke had developed innovative strategy and tactics for irregular warfare that were ahead of their time and are used by today's special forces. The command was in Knoxville, pausing between raids, and Morgan asked Duke to drill the

men in preparation for the headline-making First Kentucky Raid that would be launched in July. The drilling concentrated on how the men would fight once Morgan's strategy brought them into contact with the enemy. Taking into account the increased accuracy and range of the new rifled musket, Morgan's men threw away their sabers — long knives were as worthless as fence rails against bullets, they said. Most men were armed with short Enfield rifles, handy to carry on horseback.

Duke drilled the men in attacking on horseback, but this was to be used only against a far weaker enemy. Morgan preferred to use the horses to get to the fight, and then dismount the men for the engagement, with one-fourth serving as horse-holders. The tactic of fighting cavalry dismounted was not new; it had been used in the army since the American Revolution. But, the Morgan-Duke system of fighting on the ground was innovative.

He formed the men in an infantry line of single rank, with two yards of space between each man. The left and right flanks were thrown slightly forward, and Duke compared the line to a flexible rope that could be maneuvered depending on where the greatest firepower was needed. Standing on the ground steadied the men, and they were able to make their shots count. "We could maneuver with more certainty, and sustain less and inflict more loss," Duke wrote. The object was to envelop the enemy in enfilading fire, and men could be faced to the left or right and double-quicked to form a mass of strength where required. Taught by Duke, it was Morgan's "jaws of death."

Once this system went into effect, Union cavalry opponents were greatly surprised by its success. Probably no general in the Civil War went into a fight with greater anticipation of success only to meet disaster, as did Union General Richard W. Johnson when he attacked Morgan's men in Gallatin, Tennessee, on August 21, 1862.

General Johnson was a top-notch, brave and efficient commander, selected by General Don Carlos Buell to conduct a search-and-destroy mission against Morgan, who had on August 12 burned the Louisville and Nashville Railroad tunnels north of Gallatin. Morgan's most strategic raid in the war, it closed Buell's supply line for 98 days, stalling his advance on Chattanooga and giving General Braxton Bragg the initiative to invade Kentucky.

Brigadier General Johnson was a fellow Kentuckian, born in Livingston County near Smithland. A graduate of West Point, with service on the western frontier in the infantry and cavalry, he was an intelligent-looking 35-year-old man with a handsome beard and full head of hair. Later in the war he was promoted to major general for gallant and meritorious service, and after the war he was distinguished professor of military science at the University of Missouri and the University of Minnesota.

He had reason to anticipate success because most of the men in his task force of about 700 had given Morgan's men their worst defeat to date. One morning about three months before, under General Ebenezer Dumont, they had surprised and routed the Rebel raiders in Lebanon, Tennessee, running them for miles in what was called "The Lebanon Races."

"I'll catch Morgan and bring him back in a bandbox," Johnson said. Arriving in Hartsville on the night of August 20, he heard that Morgan's men were spending the night in Gallatin, about 12 miles to the west. In the middle of the night, he set out to surprise Morgan the next morning. He expected to win what he hoped would be "The Gallatin Races."

They were only a few miles from the target when the sun came up and the birds began singing in the trees. Beside the Hartsville Road they saw beautiful bluegrass pastures and fields of tall corn. Three miles from Gallatin, the advance guard reported driving in Rebel pickets just outside the town, at the junction of the Hartsville and Scottsville Roads. Johnson ordered the column forward at a gallop. Sure enough, Johnson had found Morgan. But during the night a civilian had warned the Raider, and he and Duke were hurrying the men out of town on the Scottsville Road to avoid a clash with Johnson, who was reported to have at least as many men as Morgan. Both forces were equal, at about 700 men.

Morgan's column was leaving in haste when Johnson's advance opened fire, causing Morgan to halt on the western edge of a large bluegrass pasture at the intersection. Duke had the extremely valuable ability to predict when a fight would succeed, and when he saw Johnson's advance detachment, and looked out across the large meadow before him, he sensed that this was a fight that could be won. He said so, and Morgan replied that he could get plenty of fights, but if these men were lost, it would be difficult getting another command. At that moment, Johnson galloped up with the

main body, took down a section of fence, and formed in battle line on the other end of the meadow. "We will have to whip those fellows, sure enough," Morgan said. "Form your men, and, as soon as you check them, attack."

Johnson's men were armed with carbines, revolvers, and sabers, and following cavalry tactics learned at West Point, he ordered: "Draw sabers!" and "Charge!" Bravely, the Union cavalry thundered across the field, and with their fine horses, blue uniforms and sabers flashing, they were a beautiful sight.

It was as Tennyson described in "The Charge of the Light Brigade:"

> "Boldly they rode and well,
> Into the jaws of Death,
> Into the mouth of Hell
> Rode the six hundred."

Duke ordered the Confederates, on the ground in the skirmish line they had formed countless times in drill, to hold their fire until the Unionists were within 30 yards. Above the sound of the thundering hooves, he shouted "Fire!" and about two-thirds of the riders and horses went down. Riderless horses seemed everywhere – many wounded and rearing and plunging in pain and turning in fear and confusion. The gallant Union men became confused, lost

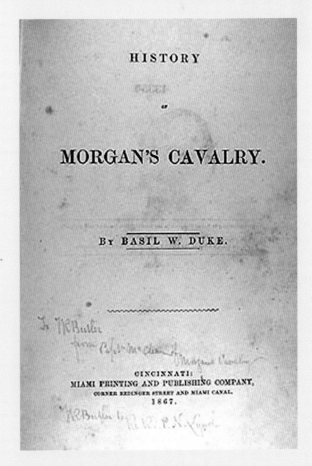

HISTORY

of

MORGAN'S CAVALRY.

By BASIL W. DUKE.

CINCINNATI:
MIAMI PRINTING AND PUBLISHING COMPANY,
CORNER REDINGER STREET AND MIAMI CANAL.
1867.

organization, and went into panic. Those still mounted wheeled and headed back across the field, wildly firing their revolvers in the air. Johnson rallied some of them in the edge of woods beyond the meadow, but Duke's disciplined line attacked, accompanied by the fierce Rebel yell.

At that point, Johnson's men had all they could take; they retreated like "a drove of stampeded buffaloes," according to one of the official Federal reports. Galloping back the way they had come, along the Hartsville Road, they lightened their loads in the hope of escaping. For weeks local civilians found sabers, carbines, pistols, canteens, hats, and other items in the fields along the road. Johnson rallied them one more time, but it was hopeless. He and his staff were captured along with a total of 175 men. He had 21 dead and 47 wounded. Morgan and Duke had 5 killed, 18 wounded, and 2 missing.

Duke's tactics explain the Confederate victory, but these maneuvers were so far ahead of the time, Johnson could not comprehend why he lost. In his official report, he unfairly blamed his defeat on his brave men: "I regret to report that the conduct of the officers and men as a general thing was shameful in the lowest degree, and the greater portion of those who escaped will remember that they did so shamefully abandoning their general on the battle-field." Morgan issued a victory proclamation printed in his regimental newspaper, *The Vidette*, concluding: "Officers and men, your conduct makes me proud to command you. Fight always as you fought yesterday and you are invincible."

Duke was wounded twice – first in the battle of Shiloh, and then in the skirmish at Rolling Fork River north of Elizabethtown on the Christmas Raid. On the Great Raid into Indiana and Ohio he was captured and imprisoned on Johnson's Island and in the Ohio state penitentiary in Columbus. He was exchanged, and at the end of the war commanded the force that escorted Jefferson Davis in his withdrawal from Richmond.

After the war he practiced law in Louisville and worked as chief counsel for the Louisville and Nashville Railroad. He was elected to the Kentucky House of Representatives, and as commonwealth's attorney. He helped establish the Filson Club, today's Filson Historical Society.

Kentuckians respected him for his courteous and humble manner, and he was always friendly and soft-spoken. He befriended young attorney Preston Davie, and Davie told a story in an article in The Filson Club History Quarterly that illustrates Duke's strength of character. One night in his bedroom in Louisville, Duke awakened to discover a burglar at the foot of the bed, pointing his pistol at Duke. Undaunted, the general sat up and launched into a lecture on the criminal penalties of burglary and armed robbery. The man backed out of the room, and Duke jumped up and locked the door, not thinking that he was locking the man in his wife Henrietta's room next door.

Henrietta was not only Morgan's sister, she was a national officer in the United Daughters of the Confederacy. When she sat up and began giving a lecture similar to her husband's, the burglar could take no more – he jumped out of Henrietta's second story window and fled into the night. Duke never revealed what his wife said to him for locking the man in her bedroom, but his friends had many laughs making suggestions among themselves.

Duke died September 16, 1916 and was buried in the Lexington Cemetery, at Lexington, Kentucky.

* * *

Basil W. Duke's grave in Lexington Cemetery

MEADE COUNTY'S PLACE IN THE CIVIL WAR

By Dr. Marshall Myers

The Alice Dean was less than a year old when it was captured by Morgan. It was a 411-ton wooden hull sidewheel packet boat. Her captain was James Pepper.

Few places in the Commonwealth can boast of so much Civil War activity as Meade County, located some 40 miles down-river from Louisville.

Perryville, Mills Springs, Richmond, and Munfordville, among others, are certainly important spots on the Civil War map, but Meade County also distinguishes itself in many ways.

To begin with, President Abraham Lincoln's father, Thomas, helped build what is now Doe Run Inn, a site that became a thriving grain mill on Doe Run Creek.

Prior to the war, the county was the scene of extensive activity for the Underground Railroad. River crossings near Paradise Bottom and the ferry at Brandenburg were places where many flights to freedom began, not only for slaves from Kentucky, but also for many desperate bondsmen from the lower South who filtered secretly into the county in search of escaped slaves, assisted at times by local residents. What made the county especially alluring was that slaves crossing the Ohio River in Meade County had a number of

Confederate General Nathan Bedford Forrest

geographical markers, creeks in Indiana particularly, that led them eventually to the Old Northwest, and on to Canada and freedom.

At the outbreak of the war, the county held 21 percent of its population in slavery. Residents in parts of the county had strong Southern sentiments, especially where land would support large scale farming of tobacco and corn. But those in other areas of the county, where hilly and wooded land prevented extensive farming, generally supported the Union.

In addition, an affidavit in the county records indicates that the organization, Knights of the Golden Circle, a group sympathetic to the Southern cause, met secretly in Meade County.

In the early years of the war, Confederate General Nathan Bedford Forrest, "The Wizard of the Saddle," considered by many military historians as a true military and tactical genius, recruited his first soldiers from Meade and nearby

129

Breckinridge County. These Kentuckians later went on to fame in many daring and successful raids under Forrest's brilliant leadership. In fact, Forrest and his men fought their first battle in Sacramento, Kentucky, where Forrest first displayed his "double envelope" maneuver. Historian Shelby Foote describes Forrest as "standing in the stirrups, swinging his sword and roaring 'Charge!' in a voice that rang like brass." Other soldiers from the county also served the South in Helm's Cavalry, Woodward's 15th Cavalry, and with General John Hunt Morgan's unit.

The county also produced a goodly number of men who joined the Union cause, with many enlisting in the 12th Kentucky Cavalry and the 27th Regiment. In all, Meade County sent over 220 soldiers to fight in the war.

Early in the war, in the northern portion of the county, Union General William Tecumseh Sherman trained his ragged band of volunteers on Muldraugh's Hill, a long chain of high hills that stretches over several counties, in part on Meade County soil. Sherman later went on to break the back of the Confederacy with his massive and destructive sweep through Georgia, South Carolina, and into North Carolina, slashing, destroying, and burning anything that might have been used to support the Confederacy.

Meade County, too, was the location of extensive guerrilla activity, when bands of Confederate partisans, mostly in the person of Thomas DuPoyster, wreaked havoc on those sympathetic to the Union cause. Fortunately, for the record, Lizzie Schreiber, a Meade County resident during the war, kept a journal in which she recorded how frequently guerrillas from outside and from within the county visited Brandenburg. According to her quite accurate notes, there was, indeed, extensive activity. The most famous incident involved a Union supporter and prominent farmer, David Henry, who was murdered by a Captain Bryant and his men, another band of guerrillas active in the county. In retaliation, on orders of Union General Stephen G. Burbridge, four Confederate prisoners of war were taken from their Louisville stockades, transported to the Henry property, near Brandenburg, and summarily shot. Still, this retaliation did not quench the thirst of the guerrillas for mayhem and mischief, as guerrilla activity continued throughout the war.

One of the most notorious guerrillas, "Sue Mundy," was captured in a barn in Meade County near Guston. Mundy, celebrated and berated by those for or against the Confederate cause, was thought to be a woman with long, flowing locks, who gained fame for famous raids into various parts of the state for the glory of the Confederacy. Actually, Mundy was young Jerome Clarke, a former Morgan man. At daylight on March 12, 1865, Mundy was taken into custody and quickly transported by steamboat to Louisville, where, after a brief trial, he was hanged.

Perhaps the biggest day in the life of Meade County during the war was July 8, 1863, when General John Hunt Morgan and his troops of gray-clad soldiers used Brandenburg as a launching point for the so-called "Great Raid" through parts of Indiana and Ohio, a raid that struck fear in the hearts of many Union supporters and frightened residents in nearby Louisville, as well. Morgan used two steamboats, the *Alice Dean* and the *John B. McCombs*, to ferry his men into Union territory. He burned the *Alice Dean* when his men were safely across the Ohio River, but spared the *John B. McCombs*, since the captain was a friend of Basil Duke, Morgan's second in command.

As noted earlier, the extensive pool of African American slaves provided many potential soldiers from Meade County, especially when Lincoln attached freedom for the volunteer and his family in exchange for service to the Union cause. Yet after the war, bands of ex-Confederate soldiers from the county, vowing to rid the county of blacks, continued the mayhem by driving the now-freed slaves out of Meade County into other parts of the country.

As the years since the war have gone by, Meade County has gradually reconciled itself and become acclimated to an integrated society, putting away the deep divisions that divided the county during this irrepressible conflict.

* * *

FIND HISTORY AND MORE IN MEADE COUNTY

THE PATH OF HISTORY

Follow the route taken by General John Hunt Morgan and his men in 1863 as they dashed across Meade County on their way to Indiana and Ohio. Visit the site where the troops rested before completing their march to Brandenburg. See where two steamboats ferried more than 2,200 men and their horses across the Ohio River for 16 hours while being fired on by the home guard in Indiana.

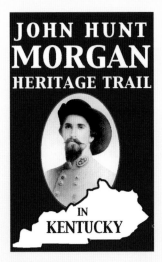

THE OHIO RIVER

Meade County has more miles of bank along the Ohio River than any other county in Kentucky. Visit this recreational and economic powerhouse at 3,600-acre Otter Creek Park in eastern Meade County or at downtown Brandenburg's Riverfront Park, where sternwheelers are known to stop. Consider taking the Four Seasons Scenic Drive, where you can get river views from both sides as you drive inside The Bend, where the river makes a turn of nearly 360 degrees.

FESTIVALS & EVENTS

- Farm Toy Show—First weekend in March.
- Farmers' Market—Saturdays (and some weekdays) from May through September.
- River Heritage Bluegrass Festival—First Friday and Saturday in July.
- Threshing Days—Weekend after Independence Day.
- Christmas by the River—Thanksgiving week through New Year's Day.

MEADE COUNTY FAIR

The Meade County Fair prides itself on being a family affair at affordable prices. That means gate admission gets fairgoers into every event and on every ride. The fair, which takes place the last full week of July, draws visitors from across the South. And, because of its quality, it is recognized as an All-Kentucky County Fair. Carnival rides, beauty pageants, exhibits, horse shows, and good fun—it's everything you want at the county fair!

Kentucky
UNBRIDLED SPIRIT

BATTLE OF CORYDON

ONE OF THE FEW CIVIL WAR BATTLES FOUGHT ON NORTHERN SOIL

By Nicole Twigg

The Battle of Corydon was the only Civil War battle fought on Indiana soil. It occurred on July 9, 1863, when 450 members of the Harrison County Home Guard attempted to delay General John Hunt Morgan's 2,400 Confederate soldiers, in hopes that Union reinforcements would arrive and stop Morgan's march through southern Indiana.

Morgan's Raid began at New Sparta in eastern Tennessee on June 11, 1863. It was intended to divert the attention of the Union Army of Ohio from Confederate forces in Tennessee. Morgan was ordered to confine his raid to Kentucky only and not to cross the Ohio River. For some unexplained reason, Morgan defied General Braxton Bragg's command and led his cavalrymen on a 46-day, 1,000-mile raid. It ended with his capture near New Lisbon, Ohio, on July 26, 1863.

Morgan and most of the division were from Kentucky and they were welcomed with open arms throughout much of that state. However, they were forced into skirmishes with federal troops and home guards at several points. On the morning of July 8, they arrived at the small Kentucky river town of Brandenburg. Two steamers were seized, the *Alice Dean* and the *J.T. McCombs*, to transport the troops across the Ohio River to the Indiana shore east of Mauckport.

The crossing was interrupted by some artillery fire from a small company of the Harrison County Legion, and the riverboat, the *Lady Pike*. When Morgan's artillery returned fire, the *Lady Pike* retreated and the six-pounder on the Indiana shore was silenced. The crossing was completed without further incident and the *Alice Dean* could be seen at low water resting on a sand bar near the Indiana shore. The gun which had fired on Morgan was captured, along with several prisoners.

Indiana Governor Oliver P. Morton, on receiving the information of the invasion of Indiana soil, issued a proclamation ordering all able-bodied male citizens in the counties south of the National Road to form into companies and to arm themselves with such arms as they could procure.

On the morning of July 9 the advance guard, led by Morgan's brother Colonel Richard Morgan, moved north on the Mauckport Road. One mile south of Corydon, the county seat of Harrison County, the scouts encountered the Harrison County Home Guard (officially the Sixth Regiment of the Indiana Legion).

The Home Guard, under Colonel Lewis Jordan, had drawn a battle line behind a hastily thrown up barricade of logs. In a short but spirited battle lasting less than an hour, Morgan met his first and only resistance in the Hoosier State. By outflanking both wings at the same time, Morgan's men completely routed the militia. Four of the guards were killed, several were wounded, 355 were captured, and the remainder escaped. The victory was not without cost to the Raiders. Eleven Raiders were killed and 40 wounded.

Morgan paroled the prisoners upon entering the town of Corydon. The Raiders began collecting the spoils of victory. Most of the afternoon was spent plundering the stores and collecting ransom money. The Harrison County treasurer was relieved of $690; two leading stores were relieved of $600 each, and contributions of $700 to $1,000 were demanded from the three mills to save them from being burned.

Later that day, the rebels left Corydon and marched northward. The main column took New Salisbury. Several companies made sorties over the countryside to other villages, collecting fresh horses and plundering. They camped along the road south of Palmyra for a few hours that evening. On the morning of July 10, 1863, the troops reunited in Salem and the raid continued east.

* * *

Sue Mundy:
Kentucky's Most Infamous Guerrilla

By Richard Taylor

Few names excited more fear in Kentucky during the closing months of the Civil War than Sue Mundy, the nom de guerre of Marcellus Jerome Clarke. Though Confederate troops had not posed a major threat since Braxton Bragg's ill-fated invasion in 1862, newspapers in Kentucky contained almost daily accounts in 1864 of killings and robberies performed by guerrilla bands not controlled by any military authority.

When the state was placed under martial law to maintain civil order, the harsh policies of General Stephen Burbridge, who vowed to annihilate the guerrilla bands, added to Kentucky's growing disenchantment with the Union presence within its borders. One of the chief lords of misrule in the state during this time was a 20-year old from south-central Kentucky.

Marcellus Jerome Clarke

Marcellus Jerome Clarke (1845-1865) was born near Franklin, Simpson County, located on the border between Kentucky and Tennessee, the son of Brigadier General Hector M. Clarke and Mary Hail Clarke.

Jerome's grandfather, Chester M. Clarke, was a seven-year veteran of the American Revolution and had immigrated to Kentucky from Virginia in 1815. His son Hector married and settled on a 300-acre farm, later serving as the postmaster of Franklin, Kentucky, and eventually rising to the rank of Brigadier General in the Kentucky Militia.

Before he entered his teens, Jerome had lost both of his parents and lived with his aunt, Nancy Clarke Bradshaw, who saw that he was educated in the public schools of Simpson County. When his two brothers married two sisters named Lashbrook in 1859 and moved to McLean County, Jerome went along and came under the influence of a relation of the Lashbrooks, Mrs. Mary Tibbs, who has been described as an "estimable lady of that section." Her nephew, John L. Patterson, 10 years older than Jerome, was one of a series of males who exerted a strong influence over him. Before the war, Patterson served as an assistant engineer on a steamboat along the Mississippi and Ohio Rivers. On August 15, 1861, he and Jerome enlisted together in the

Fourth Kentucky Infantry, part of the First Kentucky Brigade, at Henderson, Kentucky.

They were ordered to rendezvous at Camp Burnett on August 25, 1861, Clarke's 16th birthday. He was assigned to an artillery battery under Major Rice E. Graves, and Patterson became a part of the infantry delegated to guard the battery. When General U.S. Grant moved his army against Fort Henry and Fort Donelson in western Tennessee, Graves' battery was sent to their defense. At Donelson, Clarke won his first commendation for "serving with distinction," having volunteered to lead a company of soldiers, lost on the battlefield, back to the Confederate lines.

When the fort was surrendered on February 16, 1862, Clarke and Patterson were among the 12,000 prisoners. Placed on the steamer *Dr. Kane*, they were taken upriver and then overland to Camp Morton near Indianapolis. After a short imprisonment, they managed to escape in May or June of 1862. Evading Home Guards and Union scouts, they reached Evansville where they stole a skiff and crossed the Ohio River into Kentucky. At Henderson they were among the first recruits of Captain (later General) Adam R. Johnson, who was recruiting troops behind enemy lines under the Partisan Ranger Act of the Confederacy. They participated in Johnson's bold capture of arms that were stored across the river from Henderson in Newburgh, Indiana.

Using some logs, stovepipes, and a wagon chassis, Johnson set up what appeared from Newburgh to be an artillery battery, threatening to shell the town if his demands were not met. Before the dazed Unionists realized that they had been duped, Johnson succeeded in rowing the arms across the river, his "invasion" at the time marking the farthest northern penetration of Union-held territory.

When the Federal garrison crossed the river in pursuit, Clarke, Patterson, and others continued to make their way south. There followed what may have been a chief turning point in Clarke's life. Near a town called Slaughtersville in Union County, Patterson, who was riding ahead of his

"Your money or your life." Guerrilla tactics

comrades, approached a small troop of cavalry whom he thought to be Confederates.

When he realized they were not, he tried to shoot his way through but was captured. Surrendering, he was shot by a Union scout and blinded in both eyes. When Jerome later pieced together what had happened to his friend, he is said to have vowed that he would never take another Union prisoner.

After rejoining Graves' battery, he was captured again, exchanged, and sent to Vicksburg but switched units and returned to Kentucky where he was reassigned to Kirkpatrick's Second Kentucky Battalion under General John Hunt Morgan. To disrupt communications and destroy rail lines, Morgan began a series of raids from Tennessee into Kentucky and beyond. Clarke accompanied the Second Cavalry on the Christmas Raid in 1862, the so-called Great Raid into Ohio and Indiana in 1863, and the last Kentucky Raid in June of 1864. This last raid ended at Cynthiana where Morgan's men were scattered and Clarke was wounded in the hand. Managing to rejoin Morgan's command after the battle, he was serving in an artillery battery on September 4, 1864, when Morgan was surprised and killed in Greeneville, Tennessee.

Eight days after Morgan's death, Clarke was in Nelson County, Kentucky, acting as a scout and courier. The political climate in Kentucky had changed, largely due to the harshness of the military rule under Gen. Stephen Burbridge, who took reprisals for Union men killed by guerrillas. Since many of the victims were ordinary Confederate prisoners of war (many of them Kentuckians), sentiment against the Union presence in Kentucky mounted. In part, Burbridge's policies toward guerrillas created the circumstances out of which Clarke became a guerrilla.

Sometime during the closing months of 1864, Jerome Clarke, C.S.A., became Sue Mundy, Kentucky's most notorious guerrilla. This reputation came largely through the publicity generated by George D. Prentice, editor of the *Louisville Daily Journal*. Prentice used the persona of a female guerrilla in his stories to embarrass the Union authorities. Over the next few months the papers contained accounts of Mundy and his band's activities in Shelby, Nelson, Jefferson, Spencer, Bullitt, Hardin, Washington, and other counties in the south-central region of Kentucky. On October 7, 1864, Sue Mundy, Samuel O. "One-Armed" Berry, and three others, robbed a stagecoach near Harrodsburg. They proceeded to Harrodsburg where they skirmished with local home guardsmen. In the weeks that followed, there were numerous accounts of shootings and robberies, some of them committed by Sue Mundy and his band, others falsely attributed to them.

Prentice exploited the persona of Sue Mundy and referred to him as a "she-devil in pantaloons." Henry C. Magruder, another ex-Confederate soldier, became active in the band, later penning an account of his activities from his prison cell. (He was executed in 1865.) Accompanied by Clarke, Magruder led a party that robbed a train in Nelson County on September 12, 1864.

In January of 1865, Mundy and Bill Marion's band joined forces with the infamous William C. Quantrill, burning the railway depot at Midway and raiding Woodburn Farm where they stole some of the most valuable thoroughbreds in Kentucky. On January 26, Clarke was with a party of guerrillas that attacked a government cattle train outside Simpsonville, killing about 35 of the black soldiers guarding the herd, some of them after they had surrendered.

On March 3, Clarke, Magruder, and two others, riding south in Hancock County on their way to rejoin the regular army in Paris, Tennessee, were ambushed by local Home Guards. With Magruder seriously wounded and one other companion dead, the survivors took refuge in a tobacco barn in Meade County so Magruder's wound could heal. When General Palmer, the military commander of Kentucky who succeeded Burbridge, received word, he sent a detachment from Louisville to Brandenburg by steamboat. After surrounding the barn and having four of his troops wounded, Major Cyrus Wilson negotiated a surrender with Clarke, and the three guerrillas were conducted in chains to Louisville where Clarke was tried in a military court, found guilty, and sentenced to die.

When he was informed that he was to be executed the next day (March 15), he wrote four letters, enclosing a lock of his hair in each. One was to his sweetheart, probably a young woman named Mary Thomas:

"My Dear ----: I have to inform you of the sad fate which awaits your true friend. I am to suffer death this afternoon at four o'clock. I send you from my chains a message of true love, and as I stand on the brink of the grave I tell you I do truly, fondly and forever love you. I am truly yours.
M. Jerome Clarke"

He was conducted from the Military Prison at Tenth and Broadway to the state fairgrounds at 18th and Broadway where 10,000 to 12,000 onlookers were assembled to witness his execution. The charges and death order were read, and he made the following statement: "I am a regular Confederate soldier and have served in the Confederate army four years. I fought under General Buckner at Fort Donelson, and I belonged to General Morgan's command when I entered Kentucky. I have assisted and taken many prisoners, and have always treated them kindly. I was wounded at Cynthiana and cut off from my command. I have been in Kentucky ever since. I could prove that I am a regular Confederate soldier, and I hope in and die for the Confederate cause."

A white hood was drawn over his head and the order given to trip the mechanism, thus ending the life of Kentucky's most infamous guerrilla, dead before his 20th birthday. He was buried at the cemetery near his birthplace at Franklin, Kentucky.

* * *

Guerrillas seizing horses

Kentucky Historical Society

GUERRILLAS OF THE CIVIL WAR

By William E. Matthews

Official statistics indicate that the Civil War, from 1861 to 1865, was the costliest war in American history in terms of lives lost and men wounded. In fact, more Americans were killed or wounded in that conflict than in all the other American wars combined.

But even these statistics do not count the thousands of men, women, and children killed during the lawlessness that swept through Western Missouri and Eastern Kansas from the mid-1850s to the end of the war. And these numbers do not include the human toll exacted by the dozens of guerrilla gangs operating on both sides in Shelby, Nelson, Spencer, Meade, Breckinridge, and many other counties in the Bluegrass and in Western Kentucky prior to and during the war.

William Clarke Quantrill

One of the most infamous guerrillas, William Clarke Quantrill, came to Kentucky in the spring of 1865 because the Federal government had dispatched thousands of troops to hunt him down following the Lawrence (Kansas) Massacre on August 21, 1863. Quantrill and his men killed more than 200 unarmed, non-resisting men and teenage boys, leaving 85 widows, and orphaned 250 boys and girls. Nearly 200 homes and stores were torched. Even after Lawrence, Quantrill seemed to be living a charmed life, evading capture following still more incidents of violence against Jayhawkers and unsuspecting communities.

It was in 1860, according to Edward H. Leslie's book, *The True Story of William Clarke Quantrill*, that Quantrill joined the fight as a Confederate raider. He proved a paradox to newspaper editors in Washington during the war because this once quiet Ohio schoolteacher became known as the "gray ghost" for his ability to vanish from his pursuers after successful attacks. An outstanding horseman who commanded a fierce loyalty, Quantrill enjoyed the companionship of such men as Frank and Jesse James and the Younger brothers, who would become legendary outlaws after the conflict.

Few people are aware that, while Quantrill was the Union army's "most wanted" man because of his nefarious deeds in Missouri and Kansas, he actually met his end at the hands of the Shelby County Home Guard, and their murderous renegade leader, Edwin Terrell. The word "renegade" is used advisedly

because Terrell originally swore an allegiance to the Confederacy, but "switched horses" after being court-martialed for killing a Confederate officer.

It is said that more than half of Terrell's 26 years were spent in violence. Born in Harrisonville in Shelby County, Terrell had his first encounter with the law, according to *The Shelby Sentinel*, at the age of 14 while performing as a bareback rider for a circus in Baltimore. Terrell got into an argument with a saloon keeper over the quality of the whiskey being served, and after the saloon keeper took a shot at him, Terrell grabbed the man's own gun and shot him. He was acquitted on grounds of self-defense.

Terrell returned to Kentucky and joined the Dixie Home Guards which were mustered into the 1st Confederate Kentucky Regiment. He was then sent to arrest two Union soldiers who were hiding in a barn in Shelby County. After one of the soldiers fired at him, Terrell rushed into the barn and killed both soldiers at point blank range. A few weeks later, Terrell was cursed by a Confederate officer, whereupon he drew his revolver and killed the man instantly.

Edwin Terrell was court-martialed out of Confederate service and escaped imprisonment by tunneling out from under the jail. He then promptly offered his services to the Union army and was enrolled in Company D, 37th Kentucky Union Volunteer Mountain Infantry. Seven weeks later he was arrested on unspecified charges and was held in the Bowling Green Stockade until March 1864, when he was returned to duty. According to army records, he was mustered out on Oct. 19, 1864.

Little is known about Terrell's activities from October 1864 until April 1, 1865, when Gen. John Palmer, Military Commander of Kentucky, put him on the Secret Service payroll at $50 per month. Palmer apparently believed that only Terrell could track down Quantrill because Terrell was familiar with local geography and did not fear the legendary guerrilla. Seeing Quantrill captured or killed would be another personal triumph for Palmer who had overseen the execution of another well-known guerrilla, Marcellus Jerome Clarke, alias "Sue Mundy," on March 15, 1865.

Quantrill had come to Kentucky because he had friends in the Bluegrass, and because it had simply become too hot for him in Kansas and Missouri following the massacre of Lawrence, Kansas in August 1863.

In May 1865, Quantrill and his gang of 21 men took up residence at a farm owned by James H. Wakefield in Spencer County, just a few miles from Taylorsville, and 25 miles from Louisville. On May 11, Quantrill was asleep in the loft and many of the men were playing cards when the alarm was sounded, "Here they come."

Taken by surprise, Quantrill was shot down as he tried to mount his horse. After killing or chasing off all of Quantrill's men, Terrell's scout returned to where Quantrill lay wounded. They pulled off his boots, stole his pistols, and searched his clothing. He was then placed on a cot, carried into Wakefield's house and laid on a lounge.

Interrogated by Terrell, Quantrill insisted that he was a Captain Clarke of the 4th Missouri Confederate Cavalry. He asked to be allowed to remain on the farm to die. But, he did not die immediately, and the next morning, May 12, he was placed in an old Conestoga wagon drawn by two mules, and began the trek to Louisville.

Kentucky Historical Society

Edwin Terrell

Quantrill was incarcerated in the infirmary at the military prison, and given last rites by a Catholic priest, Michael Power, who converted him to Catholicism. According to Leslie's book, Quantrill is said to have remained quite cheerful to the end. He maintained his old silence toward his family, making no effort to his mother in Dover, Ohio, to tell her he was dying or to ask her to come to his side.

Quantrill died at 4pm on June 6, 1865, 27 days after he had been wounded and captured. He was 27 years old.

And what happened to Edwin Terrell. Having brought Quantrill to justice, he became something of a hero in Shelbyville and surrounding towns. He and several associates stayed at The Armstrong Hotel, the town's finest, on several occasions.

But townspeople quickly tired of his bullying and violent tactics, and in just a short time he was charged with murdering four different men in four different counties.

On Sunday, August 27, 1865, a young man pulled the body of William R. Johnson out of Clear Creek, a mile and a half south of Shelbyville. Johnson had been shot in the back of the head and robbed of $1,600. Since he had last been seen with Terrell and his one-time lieutenant, John H. Thompson, both men were arrested and charged with murder.

A 10-day trial resulted in a hung jury, and the two men were transferred to a Louisville jail, and then to a "brand new" facility in Taylorsville. Unfortunately, on April 13, 1866, seven men terrorized the jailer into opening Terrell's cell, along with that of another man, John L. Wethers.

Now free, Terrell returned to Shelbyville, accompanied by his uncle, John Baker. *The Louisville Journal* reported that all three men, Terrell, Baker, and Wethers, were "armed to the teeth. They dashed into town and began abusing and threatening the citizens, drinking and carousing and disputing the power of any man or set of men to arrest them. For a while, they had complete charge of the town, and the intimidation of the people appeared to favor their devilish intentions and warrant the impunity of their hectoring, defiant conduct."

However a judge ordered their arrest, and the marshal, taking no chances, formed a posse of 35 men. Wethers eluded capture and got away. But Terrell and Baker were cornered, and tried to escape. The posse fired upon the two men and Baker fell immediately and died. Terrell was struck in the back, near the spinal column. He was mortally wounded.

But Terrell rallied for a time, and he was pronounced fit enough to stand trial. Then, just as suddenly, his health declined, and he received permission to go live with his brother-in-law in Mount Eden.

The sack of Lawrence, Kansas

His health further deteriorated and he returned to Louisville on Nov. 4, 1868. He died there on Dec. 13 at the age of 26. He was buried in a pauper's grave in the cemetery of the workhouse. Later, a so-called "brother" arrived at the jailhouse, and asked for the body. It was then exhumed, and given to the man. To this day, no one knows what happened to either the "brother" or the corpse.

Captain Ed Terrell was only one of many guerrillas who threatened Shelbyville. Even before the war, in 1858, town citizens erected a 12x18-foot log blockhouse in the intersection of Main Street and 5th Street to defend against and act as a deterrent to gangs of marauders operating within the region. Holes for guns were placed on all sides. Apparently the blockhouse was successful because the town withstood several attacks.

In August, 1864, Captain David "Black Dave" Martin attempted to capture guns stored in the Shelby County courthouse which stood about 50 feet north of the blockhouse. Thomas C. McGrath, a merchant, and J. H. Masonheimer, tailor, and several other townspeople used the blockhouse as part of their defense. Three guerrillas were killed and McGrath was wounded. The attack failed. Martin died in 1896, and is buried in Shelbyville's Grove Hill Cemetery.

There are historic markers for both Quantrill and Terrell in Kentucky, the former near the tiny community of Wakefield where he was finally shot and captured, and the other in downtown Shelbyville telling the story of Terrell's failed mission. These men, and hundreds like them, may not have been a decisive factor in determining the outcome of the Civil War, but the damage they caused, and the lives they took provide a dark chapter in this bitterly fought war.

* * *

THE 'REIGN OF TERROR'
IN GRAVES COUNTY

By Lon Carter Barton

On July 19, 1864, perhaps the most terrifying single period in the history of Graves County began. Known since simply as the "Reign of Terror," its advent was marked by the assumption of command by Gen. Eleazar Arthur Paine of the Union Headquarters of Western Kentucky at Paducah. Its close was to come only after 51 days of dictatorial rule in Graves County, and to result, finally, in disgrace to the commander himself.

In 1861, Graves County's representative in the Kentucky State Legislature, the Honorable A.R. Boone, was expelled from that body because of his suspected Confederate leanings, and his alleged assistance to the "rebel" cause.

In September of that year, a large Confederate base, Camp Beauregard, was established in Southwest Graves County. Two months later, the County sent five delegates to the "sovereignty convention" at Russellville where a short-lived Confederate Provisional Government for Kentucky was adopted. Even during Kentucky's early neutrality period, secession sentiment in the Jackson Purchase was shown when representatives from those counties met in Mayfield to discuss separation from the Commonwealth and the Union to form a confederate state in that region.

Before the war had entered its second year, approximately 900 men from Graves County had been mustered into Confederate service, as compared with an estimated 150 who entered the Union ranks. Nine full companies left Graves County as attachments to Confederate regiments, all of them composed of infantry troops, except one, which was made part of the 12th Kentucky Cavalry.

Despite their pro-southern sentiments, the residents of Graves County could not ignore the fact that the star of Yankee fortune was just rising over a stronghold of Kentucky's Confederacy. When General U.S. Grant's forces arrived in Paducah on September 5, 1861, the Union occupation of west Kentucky began. Before leaving the following day, Grant issued an amnesty proclamation to the city's populace, noticed the presence of a few "secesh flags," and left instructions for his successor, Gen E.A. Paine, to follow, which, among other things, specifically forbade the plundering of private property by troops. Just three days earlier, Paine had been a colonel in the 9th Illinois Volunteer Infantry. Paine's command, however, did not last long. Having transcended his authority, Paine was removed and replaced in Paducah by Gen. C. F. Smith.

Gen. Eleazar Arthur Paine

The fall and winter in Graves County during 1861 and 1862 saw the establishment of Camp Beauregard to which hundreds of Confederate soldiers were sent, as well as the first Union expedition in the county. When Forts Henry and Donelson fell to advancing Federal forces in February, 1862, Graves Countians realized the consequences. Motivated by these surrenders, Gen. Leonidas Polk evacuated his position at Columbus to escape a flanking movement from the victorious army of Grant at his rear. Following this, the Confederate command at Camp Beauregard was also withdrawn south. By the middle of March, a county of almost overwhelming Confederate sympathy was left with no organized Confederate defenses whatever.

With the Confederate presence gone, Union rule began in earnest. Fortunately, from mid-1862 until 1864, Union administration was not unreasonable. Post commanders at Paducah administered affairs with tact, tempered usually with justice. Graves Countians were far more troubled by local guerrilla bands than by the orders of Federal commanders of the District. Many residents of the county were experiencing little difficulty in evading edicts of the military rules, particularly those pertaining to trade.

Early in the war, Secretary Salmon Chase had strictly prohibited trade between the west-of-the-Cumberland region of Kentucky and the Union states. Soon after occupying Paducah, Grant issued another order stopping all trade and commerce between southwestern Kentucky and Illinois. But the enforcement machinery was lax, and during a great part of the war, Graves County sent vast stores of salt, sugar and leather to the Confederacy on its southern border. As these supplies were not produced in the county, it was apparent that illicit trade was being conducted and materials from the North were entering the South via Graves and other southern Kentucky counties.

Men loyal to the Union despaired over this flagrant flaunting of the rules by Southern sympathizers and on July 11, 1864, the Paducah branch of the Union League of America wrote to the Federal commander of West Tennessee that "the Rebels are doing all of the business and are reaping all of the advances of trade." The letter concluded, however, with the hopeful note: "We have heard with pleasure the probability of our old and tried friend Gen. Paine being assigned to command here, and from him we hope and expect to obtain relief, believing as we do that he will be able to protect Union men and give traitors and secret Southern sympathizers their just dues." Eight days later the desires of the Western Kentucky Unionists were fulfilled when Gen. E.A. Paine assumed command at Paducah.

The General had entered the army from Mercer County, Illinois, early in 1861. Born in Parkman, Geauga County, Ohio, in 1815, Paine had graduated from West Point in the class of 1839 and, upon receiving his commission as a lieutenant in the United States Army, was sent almost immediately to Florida, for service there against the Seminole Indians.

He resigned his commission the following year, and turned to the legal profession, becoming a counselor-at-law in Painesville, Ohio, in the 1840s, and, retained that vocation after moving to Monmouth, Illinois, in 1848. In the mid-1850s Paine was elected to the Lower House of the Illinois Legislature, and, after the war's outbreak in 1861 organized his own regiment, the 9th Illinois Volunteers, and became its colonel.

Two months later, he was promoted to the rank of brigadier-general in the United States Volunteers, and sent to Paducah for three moths. After this period he was given a division in the Army of the Mississippi, and successfully commanded its operations against New Madrid, Missouri, and Island No. 10. The general then participated in the advance upon and the siege of Corinth, Mississippi, and was entered in combat at Farmington, Mississippi, in May 1862. He then was given a month's leave of absence, placed in command of the District of West Tennessee for a short period following his return, and in November 1862 he assumed command of the Gallatin, Tennessee, post, accepting the responsibility of guarding the railroad from Mitchellsville to Nashville, Tennessee.

Upon his arrival in West Kentucky, Paine immediately began a 51-day reign of violence, terror, theft, summary executions, and military murder. To inaugurate his main policy, Paine, from his Paducah headquarters, levied a tax of $100,000 on the people of the First District, nominally for the benefit of families of Union soldiers of that area. This was followed by a $95,000 tax placed on McCracken County residences because he considered them Confederate sympathizers. He then exiled several prominent West Kentuckians to Canada, and passed onerous trade laws which affected Graves County adversely, as they did the rest of region.

Chief among the restrictions were orders placing a tax of $10 on every hogshead of tobacco exported, as well as a 25% ad valorem duty on all cotton which had ever been property "in part of in whole" of any save unconditional Union men. Since Paine was generally sole judge himself of the degree of the citizen's attachment to the Union, several were heavily taxed, not because of their war sympathies, but on account of their opposition to the ruthless command. In fact, later investigation revealed that many of the most loyal were assessed in large sums, and that critical Unionists suffered as did the Secessionists.

To obtain an even firmer grip on inhabitants of the Purchase, Paine seized several storehouses, along with their goods, and arrested the owners and clerks of the establishments. Although theoretically this was a punitive measure directed against Confederate sympathizers, the dictatorial Paine did not hesitate to confiscate Unionists' property when they opposed his administration. The general at one time even went to the extreme of levying a tax of from 10 to 50 cents on most of his own soldiers' mail leaving Paducah.

Not all of Paine's relations were entirely unfriendly to West Kentuckians, however. A few who assisted him during his regime were richly rewarded in various ways. One, a prominent Graves Countian who collaborated with the general for personal gain, was a wealthy tobacco and cotton planter of the section. In the fall of 1864 he found that the commander had generously provided him with a government steamer (the *Convoy*), on which to load his market-bound cotton and tobacco, plus the services of a group of soldiers whom he detailed to do the loading.

Gen. Paine was not averse to using violence to maintain order in the district. Persons with relatives in the Southern Army, of whose Southern leanings were too well known, were shot by firing squads on "Rebel spy" charges. Frequently, no trial at all was held, as was the case with at least five Graves Countians executed by order of Paine's subordinate in Mayfield, Co. W. W. McChesney of the 134th Illinois Infantry. An estimated total of 43 victims in the entire District were shot by order of Paine in 51 days.

But the worst, and most widely-felt edict of Paine to affect Graves County was his "fort building" decree of early August 1864. More to punish suspected "Rebels" than for military protection, the General ordered the erection of a fort on the public square of Mayfield, to be built by conscript labor. Hundreds of law-abiding residents of Graves (as well as a goodly number from McCracken and Hickman Counties) were impressed into "labor battalions" and placed under the rigid guard of black soldiers and forced to do construction work on the fort which was totally unnecessary from a strategic standpoint. In the "draft" of civilians for this purpose, few exemptions were accepted, since later data provided that "cripples, sick, and infirm old men" were made to do hard manual work on the fortifications. In one such case an elderly man suffering from a large carbuncle on his neck was not excused from the labor, and died before reaching home.

Although age or physical condition were not considered when a detachment of Paine's force marked a local pro-Confederate for enforced labor, many well-to-do persons purchased immunity by paying various amounts to Paine himself. This practice, which approached bribery in many respects, continued throughout the building program, and increased the personal wealth of Paine and his followers.

Such an administration could not last indefinitely, however, and when conditions continued to grow worse, Gov. Bramlette requested of President Abraham Lincoln an investigation of affairs in Paine's district. The request was made on September 2, 1864, and shortly afterwards Maj. Gen. Stephen Burbridge, the state commander for Kentucky, appointed a commission to go to West Kentucky and report on the conduct of Paine and his subordinates. This committee, composed of Brig. Gen. Speed Fry and Col. John Mason Brown, arrived in Paducah, and soon amassed enough evidence to charge Paine with extreme misconduct. Upon learning of the investigation, the central figure fled to Illinois along with his principal subordinates. In the face of this report, with its outspoken criticism and exposures of the Paine rule, little was left for Burbridge to do except request Paine's removal from command.

After the findings of the commission, Gen. Paine was ordered to appear before a military court martial for formal trial and sentence. The long-awaited and much-talked about trial of the general finally got underway in the early weeks of March. West Kentuckians who, despite the fact that they hadn't seen Paine in almost six months, had not forgotten his autocratic administration, wished to see a severe punishment meted out to their former ruler. The military commission before which the General's case was tried apparently lent its sympathy to his plight. For, when the hearings were begun, the court – presumably by order of Joseph Holt, Advocate-General of the United States – omitted the most startling, terrible and easily proved outrages, and ordered trial on those charges which were least material and most plausibly explained. The total omission of these more serous charges not only thoroughly disappointed those who had hoped to see justice performed, but also caused even more intense anger and ill will to be directed toward Paine himself.

Not until early November 1865 did interested West Kentuckians and Illinoisans learn the sentence given Gen. Paine. The General, who had been found guilty on only part of the charges, was sentenced to be merely reprimanded for the certain offenses in general orders. This shamefully inadequate sentence was made more ridiculous somewhat later when even the "reprimand order" was altogether remitted. Despite this absurd "punishment," by the War Department, Paine's actions and reputation were remembered for many years by Graves Countians who had once felt the hardships of his yoke.

(Editor's Note: Gen. E. A. Paine resigned from the army on April 5, 1865, long before his sentence was pronounced by the court which had been convened to try him. He died at the age of 67 in Jersey City, New Jersey on December 16, 1882.)

* * *

142

MAYFIELD, KENTUCKY
CIVIL WAR SITES

Bayou de Chine Church

Beauregard Tomb

Mayfield Courthouse

Mayfield, KY 42066
270.247.6101
tourism@mayfieldchamber.com

*Printed in cooperation with the
Kentucky Department of Travel*

GEORGETOWN GENERALS
PROMINENT FIGURES IN THE CIVIL WAR

As the nation moved toward civil war, county politics took a back seat to state and national issues. The attitudes of local citizens are perhaps best characterized by the attitudes of the two most prominent citizens of Scott County – Confederate Governor George W. Johnson and Union Governor James F. Robinson. Both were Scott Countians, landowners, neighbors and acquaintances, but from different political persuasions.

Scott County had not only two governors, but six generals, who were either born in the county or lived and worked here. They were:

Jacob Ammen

Jacob Ammen graduated from the U.S. Military Academy in 1831 and taught at Georgetown College from 1848 to 1855. He was promoted to brigadier general of volunteers on July 16, 1862, having mainly administrative duties in garrison commands and courts-marshal. He went on to be a member of the board of visitors of the Military Academy, and accompanied the Isthmus of Panama commission to examine canal routes.

General Basil W. Duke

Confederate General Basil W. Duke, born in Scott County in 1828, assumed command of Gen. John Hunt Morgan's cavalry after Morgan's death. After the war, Duke was a successful attorney and wrote *The History of Morgan's Cavalry.*

Bushrod Rust Johnson

Bushrod Rust Johnson, a graduate from West Point, taught from 1848 to 1850 at the Western Military Institute in Georgetown, Kentucky. He attained the rank of Major General on May 21, 1864. Fighting with the Army of Northern Virginia, his division was devastated at Sayler's Creek. Thereafter ineffectual in the war, he went on to become chancellor of the University of Nashville.

Confederate General Joseph H. Lewis became commander of the Kentucky "Orphan Brigade" in 1863 and fought Sherman across Georgia and the Carolinas during the March

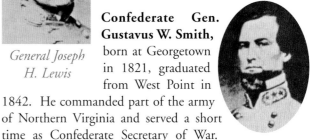

General Joseph H. Lewis

to the Sea. After the war, he served in the Kentucky Legislature, U.S. Congress, and as Chief Justice of the Kentucky Court of Appeals. Lewis died at Duvall Station in Scott County in 1904.

Gen. Gustavus W. Smith

Confederate Gen. Gustavus W. Smith, born at Georgetown in 1821, graduated from West Point in 1842. He commanded part of the army of Northern Virginia and served a short time as Confederate Secretary of War. From 1870 to 1876 he was the Insurance Commissioner of Kentucky.

General Richard M. Gano

Confederate General Richard M. Gano took part in the 1862 capture of Georgetown as an officer in Morgan's Command. After the war, as a minister of the Christian Church (Disciples of Christ), he preached to Scott County congregations on many occasions.

General Stephen Gano Burbridge

Union General Stephen Gano Burbridge was born near Stamping Ground in 1831. His policies while U.S. Military Commander of Kentucky, including the executions of Confederate prisoners of war, made him so hated in his native state that he was forced to leave Kentucky after the war. "My services to my country have caused me to be excluded from my home," he wrote before his death in New York City in 1897.

Union General John M. Palmer, born in Scott County in 1817, became the U.S. Military Commander of Kentucky after Gen. Burbridge's dismissal from command. After the war, Gen. Palmer served the state of Illinois as governor and as U.S. Senator.

General John M. Palmer

GEORGETOWN-SCOTT COUNTY MUSEUM • 229 E. MAIN STREET. GEORGETOWN, KY • (502) 863-6201
www.georgetownky.com

UNION GENERAL STEPHEN GANO BURBRIDGE
THE MOST HATED MAN IN KENTUCKY

Dr. Marshall Myers

Stephen Gano Burbridge was born on August 19, 1831, to a prominent Scott County, Kentucky family. His father served in the War of 1812 and his grandfather fought in the Revolutionary War. Young Burbridge attended Georgetown College and Frankfort Military Institute. Although he studied law, he never practiced.

At the outbreak of the Civil War, Burbridge was a prominent farmer in Logan County. He assisted in organizing the Union 26th Kentucky Regiment. He mustered in at the rank of colonel on August 27, 1862, and was brevetted a major general on July 4, 1864, after defeating Confederate general and fellow Kentuckian, John Hunt Morgan at Cynthiana on June 12, 1864. He and the 26th fought gallantly at Shiloh, Vicksburg and Arkansas Posts. He earned the admiration of Gen. William T. Sherman, who saw leadership potential in Burbridge. Sherman would later defend Burbridge from many virulent attacks. Gen. Burbridge, with Governor Bramlette's recommendation, was appointed the commander of the Military District of Kentucky on August 7, 1864. The major problem he faced was guerrilla warfare, the almost daily attacks on homes and businesses by roving bands of marauders. These bands fell into two categories: men who were legitimate Confederate soldiers who had broken from their units, and groups of criminals who used the war as an excuse for raping, burning, murdering and robbing innocent Kentuckians.

Prior to Burbridge's taking his post, President Abraham Lincoln had suspended the Writ of Habeus Corpus and declared martial law, on July 5, 1864. Unfortunately for many Kentuckians, this edict emboldened Burbridge. On August 14, 1864, he issued an order in which Confederate sympathizers within five miles of a guerrilla attack could be deported. Many Kentuckians were. Order 59 also stated that the property of Confederate sympathizers could be seized and used to pay for damages inflicted by guerrillas. "Whenever an unarmed Union citizen is murdered," Burbridge continued, "four guerrillas will be selected from the prisoners in the hands of the military authority, and publicly shot to death in the most convenient place near the scene of the outrage."

The executions soon began. Captured guerrillas and even legitimate Confederate prisoners were summarily shot in Louisville, Eminence, Williamstown, Midway, Maysville, Jeffersontown, Morganfield, Munfordville and Pleasureville. In Meade County, four prisoners were executed in retaliation for the murder of prominent farmer and Union supporter, David Henry. There were fifty total executions.

Burbridge also dallied with censorship with Order Number 39, which ordered confiscation of books like *The Life of Stonewall*

Stephen Gano Burbridge

Jackson. Booksellers were threatened with confiscation of their entire stock if they sold books that met with Burbridge's disapproval.

Critics of the Lincoln administration, including the Chief Justice of the Kentucky Supreme Court and Lieutenant Governor Richard Taylor Jacob, were arrested. And according to one historian, Burbridge interfered with an election in Kenton County, when a candidate for sheriff was struck from the ballot because he did not meet Burbridge's test for loyalty.

The ancient Greeks speak of hubris, that is, excessive pride so powerful that it blinds a man from seeing the consequences of his actions. It was the so-called "Great Hog Swindle," which brought an end to Stephen Burbridge's tenure. The brainchild of Burbridge's subordinate, Maj. Henry Clay Symonds, it was decided that the U.S. Army, under Symonds direction, would buy surplus hogs from Kentucky farmers for "fair market value." Pork would be processed by a group of meat packers, who, as it turned out, were friendly to the proposition and loyal to the Union.

It soon became apparent that "fair market value" was costing Kentucky farmers close to $300,000 in lost profits. They were prevented from shipping their hogs across the Ohio River and began to refuse to sell to Symonds' buyers. By November 14, Gov. Bramlette wrote to President Lincoln, imploring him to remove Burbridge. By November 27, Burbridge realized that the furor had become a firestorm and he rescinded the order that allowed the Federal government to buy hogs from the farmers. The backlash, however, was too great. A Kentucky delegation met with Lincoln on February 22, 1985, and on that day the Administration announced, tersely, that "General Palmer (John A.) relieves Brevet Major General Stephen G. Burbridge from command of the district of Kentucky." After all the controversy, Stephen Burbridge could not remain in Kentucky. He resigned from the Army in December, 1865. In 1867 he wrote "My services to my country have caused me to be exiled from my home, and made my wife and children wanderers." He lived the remainder of his life in Brooklyn, New York, and died on November 30, 1894.

There is a well-worn cliché in the Commonwealth that says that Kentucky joined the Confederacy after the Civil War, noting that the state turned decidedly Southern in her sympathies. Many would argue that one man, Stephen Gano Burbridge, was largely responsible for this attitude. For in his time, he was indeed, the most hated man in Kentucky.

* * *

KENTUCKY CONFEDERATE CEMETERY IN PEWEE VALLEY

By Victoria Rose

In the quaint town of Pewee Valley, Kentucky, home of the pewee bird, is the resting place for 313 Civil War veterans. The Kentucky Confederate Cemetery is located approximately 18 miles east of Louisville off Highway 146 on Maple Avenue. Henry Smith and other prominent citizens of Pewee Valley established the 15-acre cemetery on a ridge of land called Villa Ridge in May 1871.

The gate to the cemetery is a metal arch with the words "Kentucky Confederate Home" framed by pewee birds. The archway was the entry to what was once a healthcare facility for Confederate soldiers and veterans. The original Confederate home, an impressive three-story structure that boasted the majestic architecture of the period, was originally a turn-of-the-century luxury summer resort called the Villa Ridge Inn.

Bennett H. Young, a native Kentuckian, along with a former Confederate soldier and a businessman, had noticed a need for a refuge for aging Civil War veterans who often suffered from war-related injuries and were unable to find adequate care. Young, who is credited with conceiving the idea of a home, formed a group that began to raise funds. A bill giving the project state support passed unanimously in both houses of the legislature and a 15-member board was appointed to oversee the project. The Villa Ridge Inn of Pewee Valley was purchased, and open its doors to the first occupant in 1902.

The Daughters of the American Revolution purchased Villa Ridge and operated it as a healthcare resource as well as a nursing facility for former Confederate soldiers, which included John Hunt Morgan's Raiders.

In 1904, the adjacent cemetery site was divided into three sections: one section was for the white populations of Pewee Valley and surrounding areas, one section was for the blacks, and one was for the veterans from the Confederate Veterans Home. The black section, Section B, is located on the north side of Maple Avenue. The white, Section A, and Confederate sections are located on the south side of Maple.

On March 25, 1920, a fire destroyed a large section of Kentucky Confederate Home, but fortunately, no lives were lost. Over time, 700 veterans had been housed there, but as the years went on, the number of veterans dwindled until the Home was closed in 1934. At its closing, only five residents remained, and they were transferred to the Pewee Valley Hospital/Sanatorium, which was near the existing Friendship Manor nursing facility.

A visit today finds the Kentucky Confederate Cemetery resting peacefully among trees, the craggy headstones marking the grave sites of soldiers lined up in traditional military fashion. A monument inscribed "In Memory of Our Dead Confederates" is one of two-dozen Civil War obelisks that were erected in Kentucky. This one obelisk, cast in zinc, stands tall and proud, undisturbed, sheltered in trust and honored by its caretakers.

The ornate gate is the only remnant of the Kentucky Confederate Veterans Home and is listed in the National Register of Historic Places.

* * *

WILD WOLF
THE 'EYES AND EARS OF THE UNION'

By Ron Wolford Blair

Colonel Frank Lane Wolford

Even though many people today know little about Colonel Frank Lane Wolford, during the Civil War he was considered one of the war's most colorful Kentucky figures. Commander of the oldest Union cavalry regiment, the First Kentucky Cavalry, Wolford was considered by many Confederate officers, such as Longstreet, Mosgrove, Morgan, and others, as the most feared and the most dreaded leader to meet on the field of battle. His regiment was sometimes referred to as Wolford's Cavalry or, as Sgt. Eastham Tarrant preferred to call them "The Wild Riders of the First Kentucky Cavalry."

They fought successfully in over 300 battles and skirmishes and were instrumental in protecting General George Thomas's movement toward Chattanooga after the battle of Chickamauga. Thus Wolford was granted another distinction: "Thomas's Secret."

An icon of battle worshiped by many, Wolford, wearing his non-military red floppy hat and brown farmers jacket, commanded the "Wild Riders" at the battles of Wildcat Mountain, Mill Springs, Perryville, and the little-recognized but most strategically significant Battle of Knoxville, to name a few. Though most often at the center of action in battle, he was also known as the "eyes and ears of the Union" in the "central campaign" as well as the wise commander of scout cavalry fighters unsurpassed in the annals of warfare.

Colonel Wolford was highly respected for his generosity and deeply loved by his men even though other military leaders, Tarrant called "the red tape men," considered his style unorthodox and somewhat humorous. For commands he used a series of nonmilitary terms such as "huddle up," "scatter out," and "git up and git." When he wanted enfilade he ordered, "Scatter and shoot across 'em." For a flanking movement he shouted, "Scatter and scrooch up behind 'em." The Wild Riders, many of them wild mountain men themselves, understood and obeyed him. Wolford was admired for his belief that "a soldier's effectiveness was more in his fighting qualities than in his capacity to perform fancy evolutions."

A veteran of the Mexican War, Wolford had fought alongside John Hunt Morgan and Jefferson Davis at the Battle of Buena Vista where he led a daring charge to save the body of Henry Clay Jr. His rivalry over principle with John Hunt Morgan was known as one of the greatest rivalries in Civil War history.

Wolford successfully surprised Morgan at the Battle of Lebanon, Tennessee, only to be severely wounded, captured and ultimately rescued. Morgan lost almost all of his men and had to escape across the Cumberland leaving his famous steed "Black Bess" behind. A year later, Wolford, still bleeding from his wounds, casting a reddish-brown stain to his saddle, rode over 1,000 miles from the Kentucky-Tennessee border to near the Great Lakes in northeastern Ohio to capture John Hunt Morgan.

President Lincoln offered Col. Frank Wolford the rank of brigadier general for his role in capturing his nemesis and Kentucky rival General John Hunt Morgan in New Lisbon, Ohio. Wolford declined the honor stating, "One regiment was trouble enough without having a whole brigade to manage." Lincoln ignored Wolford's refusal by giving him a brigade to command under the modest rank of Colonel and telegraphed the message "You should be a brigadier whether you take the brigade or not."

Col. Wolford went on to successfully command a division through the strategically important East Tennessee campaign. However, Wolford's political activity as a Peace Democrat and state president elector for McClellan during the presidential election of 1864 placed him at odds with Lincoln and the military rule under Gen. Stephen Burbridge.

On March 10, at the Melodeon Hall in Lexington, Wolford was presented with a jeweled sword, sash, pistols and spurs by distinguished Kentuckians, including Governor Bramlette, for his patriotic war effort, many accomplishments, and especially for his role in capturing Morgan. In his acceptance speech Wolford took the opportunity to make a long oration on the subject that entered most every Kentuckian's mind at the time. He charged Lincoln with wantonly trampling upon the Constitution and crushing the rights of the people under the "iron heel of military power." Wolford deemed the enrollment of slaves into the Union army as unconstitutional and usurpation of power against states' rights.

Many Kentuckians feared arming the freed slaves and moved for a more gradual emancipation. They also felt that the federal government was treating them as a Confederate state both in commerce and politically. Wolford was quoted as saying during the speech, "The government of the United States is being crucified between two thieves - the authorities at Richmond and at Washington City." His speech was received with the most rapturous applause, but this is where Wolford's political strife began.

Two days later, General U.S. Grant dispatched an order directing him to Maj. Gen. J.M. Schofield at Knoxville, under arrest. Schofield was directed to court-martial Wolford but, for whatever reason, he did not immediately proceed with the hearing.

Finally, on March 24, 1864, despite being a Union hero and having been wounded eight times, Colonel Wolford was dishonorably dismissed from the service by direct order from President Lincoln.

News traveled throughout the country about Wolford's arrest. Some called him "a hero gone bad" while others called him "the Morgan of the North." Many Kentuckians called him a brave and bold spokesman for the Constitution and people's rights. Evidence suggests that Wolford was brought to Washington before Lincoln to plead his case. A highly respected criminal lawyer before the war, Wolford pleaded guilty for his comments about the country being "crucified between two thieves" and said that he was ready for trial. But Lincoln had eliminated the writ of habeas corpus and Wolford was never granted a trial.

It has been estimated that during the course of the war as many as 30,000 individuals had been arrested due to Lincoln's policy. Many among them were Kentuckians, many were loyal Unionists, and many were arrested merely because they were Democrats. Some were reportedly hanged. While in captivity, Wolford later wrote the famous "Letter to the President" in which he identifies Lincoln's decision to change the Constitution as a precedent that the country would pay dearly for in the future regarding liberty for the people.

Before the presidential election of 1864, reports scattered that politicians and Democrats were being detained and restricted from voting and that black Union soldiers were intimidating voters with bayonets at the polls. Wolford, outraged by the reports, climbed a stump and announced in a public speech, "The man who stands between me and the polls on the day of the ensuing presidential election will die." On November 8 Wolford proudly cast his vote for McClellan and no one dared to prevent

Col. Wolford during his Congressional years

him. McClellan won with an overwhelming majority in the state of Kentucky, making a bold statement to the re-elected Lincoln about the conditions in his birthplace state.

After the War, Wolford was elected to the state legislature where he was instrumental in granting amnesty for Confederate Kentuckians, thus healing the many wounds of war. In late 1865, Wolford was appointed Adjutant General of Kentucky to stop the "regulators" from committing atrocities against the newly freed blacks and to control the guerrillas that were still plaguing Kentucky. Wolford was later elected as Congressman for two terms (1883-1887), and was appointed to a powerful position as the head of the pension committee.

Wolford was an advocate in granting pensions to women war victims as well as getting war veterans out of poor houses and into a much more dignified system of care. He also was successful in granting pensions to the widows of fallen black soldiers. This was not an easy feat since laws did not recognize previous slave marriages as legal.

A transformation of the man coincided with the transformation of a country. Due to complications from his old war wounds, Col. Frank Lane Wolford died on August 2, 1895, at the age of 77. High on a hill overlooking the little town of Columbia, Kentucky, people gathered from counties far and wide: men, women, and children, white and black alike, around Wolford's grave. The Governor of Kentucky and Wolford's previous second in command, Col. Silas Adams, spoke at Wolford's funeral. The once young Silas Adams showed his emotions during his talk about his famed leader. His watery eyes demonstrated sincerity in proclaiming Col. Frank Lane Wolford, "The bravest man that ever lived." A few months later the grief stricken Silas Adams died.

* * *

PATRIOTS WITHOUT POLITICS

THE LIVES OF TWO KENTUCKY WOMEN DURING THE CIVIL WAR

By Lisa Gaines Matthews

When attempting to study the role of women during the Civil War, it must be acknowledged that only a small percentage of 19th century women left any record of their lives. The Civil War diary of Mary Boykin Chestnut of Charleston, South Carolina, quickly comes to mind but it hardly reveals the life of a typical Southern woman. Mary Chestnut was raised within and married into the aristocratic planter class of the Old South and her diary reflects thoughts and opinions from a very narrow point of view. Literacy among Southern women was low and the sporadic preservation of original letters and diaries makes generalization about the experience of women nearly impossible.

Generalizations have been avoided here and yet it can be said that the ideas entertained by the two young women who are the topic of this article are representative of their age and class. Undoubtedly, their political views were a direct result of their family patriarchy and yet they perpetuated the views with definite purpose. Their political allegiances were strong despite the fact that they could not directly influence the political world.

Elizabeth (Lizzie) Pendleton Hardin and Frances Dallam Peter were both literate, knowledgeable women who represented the higher echelon of their society. They were both white, were born and raised in central Kentucky and they were both direct descendants of some of Kentucky's finest families. At the outbreak of the Civil War, Elizabeth Hardin was 22, while the younger Frances Peter had just turned 18. Neither woman ever married. Educated, articulate, and capable of astute observation and opinion, both women kept a diary. These documents are dramatically different in style and content. Furthermore, the diaries reveal opposite political allegiances. Elizabeth Pendleton Hardin was passionate in her identity as a Southern woman in support of the Confederacy, whereas Frances Dallam Peter's entries establish her firmly in the Union camp.

Elizabeth Hardin (1839-1895) was born in Harrodsburg on February 5, 1839. Her grandfather, Ben Hardin, had been a respected lawyer, state legislator and U.S. Congressman. Her

Elizabeth Pendleton Hardin

father, James Hardin, attended the U.S. Military Academy, served in the Black Hawk War and went on to complete a degree in medicine in Pennsylvania. He then pursued a legal career until his premature death in 1842 at the age of 32. Elizabeth's mother, Jane Chinn Hardin, was the daughter of Mercer County Judge Christopher Chinn.

Men from the Hardin and Chinn families fought for both the Union and Confederate causes even though most were slaveholders. Lizzie's cousin Christopher (Kit) Chinn was barely 16 when he joined Gen. John Hunt Morgan's troops in Knoxville, Tennessee, and her first cousin, Confederate General Benjamin Hardin Helm was married to Mary Todd Lincoln's half sister, Emilie Todd.

Elizabeth Hardin was educated at Mrs. Tevis's School in Shelbyville, Kentucky, and toured through Europe prior to the outbreak of the war. She kept a journal during the war, which she then rewrote as the "Diary kept during the War." Using a leather bound accounts ledger, which she decorated with portraits of Confederate generals, she transposed her journal entries verbatim. Her narrative style is more prose than journalistic. Dates are rarely indicated so that the chronology of her diary must be pieced together through references to events.

The diary is divided into chapters with headings such as "At Last I Saw John Morgan," and the attention grabbing "Over the Lines." The latter refers to the fact that in August 1862, Elizabeth Hardin, her sister Jamesetta (Jimmie), and her mother were all put on trial by the Provost Marshall in Harrodsburg for disloyalty to the United States. The three women were given a chance to sign an Oath of Loyalty, which they refused. This refusal resulted in a brief confinement in a federal prison in Louisville and then they were summarily sent south behind the Confederate lines, where they remained until April, 1865. On hearing about the evacuation of Richmond, Elizabeth Hardin wrote, "It is too horrible to think of Richmond being given up. I have often felt the deepest gloom for our defeats but Richmond is the first place for which I have shed tears. I did believe four years of horror and bloodshed had taught me more fortitude."

Lizzie Hardin declares early on to be a "true believer" in the motto of the state of Kentucky, "United We Stand, Divided We Fall." For her, the Civil War was a "war of independence." Initially she understood that her "...love for the Union arose only from an idea that it was beneficial to the South." As war approached, she came to believe in "the will and the power of the North to injure us. Yankees politically and personally were an abomination in my sight." Hardin refers to Abraham Lincoln as the "Black Republican President" and gleefully reports on the response of the Arkansas Governor to Lincoln's call for 75,000 troops in April 1861, that "he had no troops" for him, and earnestly urged the immediate trip to a "nameless locality smelling of sulphur."

She was ecstatic when John Hunt Morgan and his "eleven hundred Southern horsemen" rode into Harrodsburg. He was "exactly my idea of a dashing cavalryman. Tall and well formed with a very handsome face... His whole dress was scrupulously clean and neat..."

Thirty-eight miles away in Lexington the third child of Robert Peter, M.D., Frances Dallam Peter (1843-1864) was born. Dr. Peter (1805-1894), who had been born in Cornwall, England, immigrated to America in 1817. Educated at Transylvania University, he became one of the most respected physicians and scientists in the country. He did not serve in the military during the war. As a medical doctor his services were invaluable in the hospitals of Lexington, where Union and Confederate soldiers were treated. His wife, Frances, a Lexington native, was descended from the Henry, Preston and Breckinridge families in Virginia and Kentucky.

Frances, their daughter, suffered from epilepsy and this little understood condition kept her confined to her home for most of her short life. She was educated at Sayre Female Institute in Lexington and she amused herself at home by writing poetry and short stories, drawing, and keeping a diary.

Her diary, which was recorded in eight hand-made booklets crafted from scrap paper, begins abruptly on January 19, 1862 (the date of the Battle of Mill Springs), just prior to her 19th birthday and ends on April 4, 1864, four months prior to her death. They are remarkable booklets. Peter's writing style is clear, observant, and revealing about daily life in Lexington. The prose has a journalistic quality, as if her intent was to report on the activities she saw, read about in newspapers when they were available, or heard about through the "grapevine." In many cases, articles about military or political events were copied verbatim from newspapers, a silent acknowledgment that these spheres belong to men and yet certainly had an effect on the daily life of women.

For a girl of 18, Miss Peter's opinions and biases are well-established. She was a staunch believer in the U.S. Constitution, the founding fathers, and always records George Washington's birthday on February 22. She refers to Confederates as "secesh" or "rebels" and some of her most scathing remarks are reserved for Gen. John Hunt Morgan, whose mother, Henrietta, lived around the corner from her. According to Frances Peter, the flamboyant Confederate raider was a "rascal and notorious rebel." She refers to his men as "guerrillas" and during the brief occupation of Lexington by Confederate troops in September and October 1862, she describes Morgan's men as "a nasty, dirty looking set."

Frances Peter was leery of the presidency of Abraham Lincoln, although it was better to support a "weak administration" than to follow the path espoused by the Peace Democrats, a party that tried to broker an early peace between the Lincoln administration and the Confederacy. The Civil War would end, she wrote, when "the rebels laid down their arms and returned to their allegiance to the Union."

Both Elizabeth Hardin and Frances Peter were patriotic to their respective causes. Patriotism, however, did not have a political meaning for either woman. They lived in a time in which women lacked political representation and if either woman had heard of the Seneca Falls Convention of 1848 they make no mention of it and, given their distrust of "Yankees," it is more than a bit likely that they would have dismissed the idea of suffrage as irrelevant.

The fact that politics was beyond the sphere of women is only fleetingly addressed by both women. Frances Peter, in narrating a remark of Mrs. Sarah Jane Miller of Trimble County, records that Mrs. Miller "left politics to men." Lizzie Hardin makes a more direct reference to herself when she says, "having only the boy's privilege of 'hollering' for my candidate, and being denied even that, except in very secluded situations, I determined to leave the country in the hands of the men..." There is no rancor nor wistfulness in either account.

Lacking political status did not keep them from tackling hot, political issues. Neither woman favored an end to slavery. Both diaries help illustrate the unusual position Kentuckians found themselves in during the Civil War. Pro-Union Kentuckians believed that if the state remained loyal, the federal government would not tamper with the "necessary evil" within their borders. The Emancipation Proclamation of January 1, 1863 only applied to slaves within the

Confederacy yet Kentuckians found themselves in a quandary when many slaves eagerly ran away to enroll in the Union army. Violence often resulted when an owner followed his slave to a training site such as Camp Nelson, near Nicholasville, and demanded that the slave return to his property.

In February, 1863, the Kentucky States Rights party changed its name to the Democratic Party and tried to hold a convention in an unsuccessful attempt to nullify the potential effect of the Emancipation Proclamation within the state. In March 1863, Union Democrats met in Louisville as part of a national movement (Peace Democrats) to end the war while preserving their property. When the Federal Conscription Act was announced in the summer of 1863, Kentucky legislators denounced the drafting of local slaves and free blacks as U.S. troops.

Frances Peter referred to abolitionists as "mean men" and that "it is very right" when Gen. Quincy Adams Gillmore issued an order in February, 1863 that "...no negroes are to be allowed to enter the camps and that any negro found in the United States uniform shall be arrested and punished." In 1864, she denounces the entire concept of black conscription as a "course fraught with evil" leaving Kentuckians with "no hope of compensation."

Elizabeth Hardin viewed abolitionism as a "Yankee" idea and implied through anecdotal stories that the slaves whom she knew supported the Southern cause. By 1865 she conceded that there was little anyone in the South could do to stem the momentum created by the Emancipation Proclamation and the "time we fear is not so distant when even our Negroes will go to the Provost Marshall and blossom into freedom." She believed that freeing the slaves "is unfair to them as they have no place to go" and at least two of the Hardin slaves remained within that household after receiving their papers. On August 9, 1865 she records the fact that Kentucky did not ratify the 13th amendment to the U.S. Constitution which ended slavery in America. To this day the states of Kentucky and Mississippi are on record as never having ratified the amendment.

Individual interpretations of the Constitution are also discussed. Hardin squarely aligns herself with the Confederate States of America and describes Confederate troops as men who left their homes to "strike in the far South a blow for Liberty and old Kentucky." This strict construction of the Constitution is countered by Frances Peter who believed that liberty resided in the preservation of the Union and in the "constitution of our fathers."

The issue then arises as to what role did these two women regard for themselves, and for women in general, in view of the fact that they did not have political status. The diaries record dutifully traditional roles for women, such as Ladies Aid Societies which provided clothing and supplies for the men on the battlefield. According to Elizabeth Hardin, sewing was "a woman's part in peace or war." Frances Peter often reported how the women of Lexington went to the hospitals to maintain sanitation and provide food and drinking water. Nursing as a profession for women did have its genesis during the Civil War, but it was mainly a northern phenomenon. The women of Lexington investigated building a Soldiers Home on the Cincinnati model, were noted for maintaining the graves of soldiers and, after the war, were instrumental in raising money for the placement of war memorials.

These roles have stong connections with hearth and home and few would argue that this particular sphere was ruled by a woman. The home represented a powerful influence on men and women. It was the center of the family and within its walls children were born and raised. Children represented the foundation of the future and, since childbearing has always been the sole province of women, it can be surmised that they operated from a position of strength within their domain.

During the Civil War, women were often called upon to defend their homes and property. Such acts of bravery and displays of personal fortitude ultimately served to provide inspiration and moral support to the men at home and on the battlefield. Political allegiances dictated courses of action even without the ballot box. One woman was reported to have said to her son as he prepared to leave for his post in the Confederate army, "I want you to fight like a tiger, and if you die, die game!" It was the role of women to make the men "ready for the fight" and then they bravely maintained the home while the war raged elsewhere. It was also acceptable to demonstrate loyalty to a cause and pay the penalty for such loyalty. Perhaps no higher tribute to contemporary women as a whole could have been paid than the parting words of the command of Gen. John Hunt Morgan when they left Harrodsburg in July, 1862. "Hurrah! for the noble women of Kentucky!" Hurrah, indeed, for without the women of Kentucky, their strength, courage and endurance, hope of the future would not have been possible.

* * *

PICKET DUTY
THE KENTUCKY HERITAGE COUNCIL &
THE PRESERVATION OF KENTUCKY CIVIL WAR SITES

By Thomas W. Fugate

Since its inception in 1966, the Kentucky Heritage Council has strived to assist federal, state and local preservation groups with the identification, registration, preservation and interpretation of those surviving cultural and historic features that make living in, working in, and visiting Kentucky a unique experience.

As an agency of state government, it is the Council's responsibility to ensure for future generations of Kentuckians that the surviving vestiges of their cultural heritage are not arbitrarily lost in America's rush to abandon the family farm and our historic downtowns. New subdivisions and ever expanding transportation routes are among many twentieth, and now twenty-first, century improvements that have greatly enhanced the quality and convenience of our daily lives. We should, however, strive to remember the past and to protect those things that make our individual communities unique. If we loose our individuality, what will separate us from the masses of unidentifiable cluttered concrete landscapes where mindless drones move to and from a profusion of indistinguishable fast food restaurants and strip malls that are surrounded by a sea of asphalt?

Thus, for the past decade, preserving Kentucky's Civil War sites has been a key component of what the Kentucky Heritage Council does and what we deem vital to the preservation of the Commonwealth's rich martial heritage.

The preservation and interpretation of Kentucky's role in this watershed moment in America's history, for generations, had focused solely on the Perryville Battlefield Historic Sites and the Columbus-Belmont State Park. However, during the fall of 1990, the Kentucky Heritage Council joined ranks with the newly-established American Battlefield Protection Program of the National Park Service to conduct a survey of the Commonwealth's Civil War battlefields. From this survey, 11 principal sites were identified as having a high level of significance and deemed worthy of preservation. These are: the Battle of Barbourville, which occurred in Knox County on September 19, 1861; the Battle of Camp Wildcat, which took place in Laurel County on October 21, 1861; the Battle

of Ivy Mountain, which took place in Floyd County on November 8-9, 1861; the Battle of Rowlett's Station, which occurred in Hart County on December 17, 1861; the Battle of Middle Creek, which occurred, again in Floyd County, on January 10, 1862; the Battle of Mill Springs, which took place in both Pulaski and Wayne counties on January 19, 1862; the Battle of Richmond in Madison County, which took place on August 29 and 30, 1862; the Battle of Munfordville, which finds us back in Hart County on September 14 to 17, 1862; and, the Battle of Perryville, which took place in Boyle County on October 8, 1862. The next engagement listed took place on March 25, 1864, and became known as the Battle of Paducah. The last to be listed is the Battle of Cynthiana in Harrison County, which occurred on June 11 and 12, 1864.

With identification of the surviving battlefields completed, the Heritage Council launched the Kentucky Civil War Sites Preservation Program. This program initiated the process of identifying local preservation-minded leaders to foster and build positive community support for the protection of these battlefields and the hundreds of other Civil War sites located across the Commonwealth. Our goal has been to tie together, in a systematic fashion, the story of Kentucky's role in the war.

Today, Perryville is still recognized as the commonwealth's premier Civil War site. However, it no longer tells that story in a vacuum. The effort to enhance Perryville has led to the expansion of state and national efforts to build partnerships in Kentucky that reach out to and include local preservationists, the Kentucky Transportation Cabinet, the Tourism Cabinet, and other sate and local government agencies to ensure that sites like Mill Springs, Camp Wildcat, Munfordville, Middle Creek, and Richmond have been provided with the funds necessary to guarantee their success as well. These sites have also been augmented by wonderfully successful programs like the one at Sacramento in McLean County that has become Kentucky's best attended Civil War reenactment for the past several years, and Fort Duffield

Battle of Sacramento Reenactment

at West Point, where the hard work of local volunteers has ensured the protection of Kentucky's largest and best preserved earthen fortification. At the Battle of Tebbs Bend, the determination of a single driven preservationist has produced one of the state's best-interpreted driving tours. The Camp Nelson Heritage park, operated by Jessamine County government, currently includes more than 500 acres of the original 4,000 which served as the state's largest Union Army Supply Depot and training center for African American soldiers. Here and at other battlefields across the commonwealth, educational programs are conducted each year where hundreds of area school children learn about the lives of the soldiers and refugees

Camp Nelson National Cemetery

who lived there. We are also working hard in Cynthiana, Winchester, Frankfort, Calhoun, Fort Wright, New Haven, and in Calloway County where plans are underway to expand the Fort Donelson National Military Park and make the site of Fort Heiman an extension of that facility.

In preparation for the 200th Birthday Commemoration celebrations, Lincoln's Birthplace National Park has acquired the site of Lincoln's Boyhood Home at Knob Creek and is expanding its facilities. Other efforts are underway to revive the earlier preservation efforts at Fort Sands in Hardin County and the Northern Kentucky Fortifications.

The Kentucky Heartlands Driving Tour is now complete and The Kentucky Ohio River Civil War Heritage Corridor is moving forward and is scheduled to be completed in 2005. We have initiated the Central Kentucky Civil War Heritage Trail, which brought together six central Kentucky battlefields in a first of its kind, weeklong tourism program that brought more than 1,200 visitors from 10 different states to Kentucky. This program was so successful that it has now been expanded to include 10 sites and will become an annual event. We have also completed the design and construction of monuments at the Battle of Ivy Mountain and at the Vicksburg National Military Park in Vicksburg, Mississippi.

We are currently working with sixty-two separate Civil War battlefields and associated historic sites located across the commonwealth and every day we strive to encourage local citizens and historical organizations to join our effort. The community of Russellville is just one of these. On November 18-20, 1861, a formal convention met in the Clark Building, now a law office, to form the provisional Confederate government of Kentucky. In 2005 this historic structure will be opened for public tours.

At the outbreak of the Civil War, President Abraham Lincoln stated, "To lose Kentucky would be nearly the same as to lose the whole game." As we enter the twenty-first century, we also feel that for Kentucky to fail to preserve her cultural and heritage sites would be again "the same as to lose the whole game." We encourage you to ensure that this does not occur by getting involved in local preservation efforts or by taking a few moments of your busy time to visit each of these wonderful sites, where you will certainly learn about Kentucky's rich and active role in American military history.

* * *

KENTUCKY CIVIL WAR QUIZ

By Dr. Marshall Myers

All right, all you Civil War buffs, here's a quiz for you. Most of the questions are directly or indirectly related to the Civil War in Kentucky, so here's your chance to show what you know about the "War Between the States" in the Bluegrass State.

1. Name the Presidents of the United States and the Confederate States of America during the Civil War?

2. Where in Kentucky was each born?

3. Who was the Kentucky-born commander who surrendered Fort Sumter to begin the war?

4. During the war, what was the name of the fiery editor of the *Louisville Journal* whose wife was a Southern sympathizer?

5. At what town in Kentucky did John Hunt Morgan and his men cross the Ohio River into Southern Indiana as part of the Great Raid?

6. Where did Union commander John Wilder ask Confederate General Simon B. Buckner if Wilder should surrender?

7. Who were the two principal commanders at the Battle of Perryville?

8. What future President of the United States was a Union commander at the Battle of Middle Creek?

9. What Confederate general, who lost an arm and a leg in battle for the Southern cause, grew up near Mount Sterling?

10. During the war, what religious community in central Kentucky fed thousands of soldiers on both sides?

11. Who was the near-sighted Confederate general who mistakenly rode into the Yankee line and was killed at the Battle of Mill Springs?

12. Who was the governor of Kentucky at the time of the outbreak of the Civil War who refused Lincoln's call for Union soldiers?

13. What is the name of the devoted abolitionist Kentuckian who was Ambassador to Russia during the Civil War and who grew up near Richmond at White Hall?

14. Who was the Kentucky-born Confederate general from Elizabethtown who was killed at the Battle of Chickamauga?

15. Who was the Union general murdered at the Galt House in Louisville by Union General Jefferson C. Davis?

16. What Confederate general was commander at the Yankee rout at the Battle of Richmond?

17. What was the name of the famous Union recruiting station in Garrard County?

18. What Louisville newspaper was an outspoken advocate of the Confederate cause?

19. What well-known Union general, who would later make a devastating sweep through the South, was commander of a ragtag number of troops early in the war at Muldraugh's Hill?

20. Who was the 300-pound Confederate general from Kentucky who was commander at the Battle of Middle Creek?

21. What was the designated Confederate capital of Kentucky?

22. What was the nickname of the famous First Kentucky Brigade?

23. What famous Kentucky Confederate general was known as "The Thunderbolt of the Confederacy"?

24. Early in the war, what well-known Union general quickly occupied Paducah when Confederate General Gideon Pillow occupied Columbus on September 4, 1861?

25. What is the name of the first Confederate governor of Kentucky who was killed at the Battle of Shiloh?

26. What were the 5,000 guns called that were shipped to Kentucky and distributed by Kentuckian William "Bull" Nelson early in the war?

27. What famous Confederate Missouri guerrilla was killed near Bloomfield on May 10, 1865?

28. What Kentucky agricultural economic scandal of 1864 was associated with Major Henry C. Symonds?

29. What was the real name of the well-known Kentucky guerrilla called "Sue Mundy"?

30. What was the name of the colorful Englishman and soldier of fortune who rode with Morgan's Raiders for awhile?

31. What was the name of the Union spy and actress who began her career in espionage in Louisville?

32. At Tebb's Bend, what Union colonel told CSA General John Hunt Morgan that July 4th was "a bad day to surrender"?

33. What is another name for the Battle of Wildcat Mountain?

34. What was the name of the colorful Confederate cavalry general who commanded his troops at the Battle of Paducah on March 25, 1864?

35. In commenting on the possibility of Kentucky's seceding from the Union who said, "I think to lose Kentucky is nearly the same as to lose the whole game"?

36. On December 18, 1860, what Kentucky United States senator tried to offer a compromise to prevent the Civil War?

37. At the end of the war, how much a month were privates in the army of the Confederate States of America and the Union army paid?

38. Who was Richard Hawes and what does he have to do with the Civil War?

39. Who was the Shelby County African-American soldier who joined the 12th U.S. Colored Artillery, fought in Kentucky, wrote letters for fellow Black soldiers at Camp Nelson, and later helped found Simmons Bible College in Louisville?

40. What is the name of the island in the Ohio River where Basil Duke surrendered 700 of his men as they tried to move into southern Ohio?

41. What is the name of the former Vice President of the United States and native Kentuckian who served as a general and fought for the South?

42. What is the more colorful name of General Adam Johnson whose ruse led to the surrender of a federal arsenal at Newburgh, Indiana, on July 18, 1862?

43. What famous Kentucky senator and presidential nominee was Abraham Lincoln's political idol?

44. Of what Kentucky general and veteran of three wars was President Jefferson Davis speaking when he said, "If _____ is not a general...we have no generals"? Hint: He was killed at the Battle of Shiloh.

45. What is the name of the place where General John Hunt Morgan and his men were incarcerated after being captured at the end of the Great Raid?

46. What is the name of the daring Kentuckian who organized the ill-fated "Northwest Conspiracy," an attempt to lure the states of the Old Northwest into the Confederacy?

47. What was the name of Abraham Lincoln's best friend who lived near Louisville at Farmington and who advised the President against issuing the Emancipation Proclamation?

48. Who was the commander of the military district of Kentucky from Logan County who managed to enrage thousands of Kentuckians with his draconian tactics?

49. What is the name of the largest Civil War battle fought in Kentucky?

50. What is the name given to the group of local soldiers commissioned to defend their home towns and largely guard against marauding guerrillas?

ANSWERS:
1. President Abraham Lincoln of the United States of America and President Jefferson Davis of the Confederate States of America.
2. Lincoln was born near Hodgenville; Davis was born near Fairview.
3. Major Robert Anderson
4. George Prentice
5. Brandenburg, Kentucky
6. The Battle of Munfordville
7. General Don Carlos Buell for the Union and General Braxton Bragg for the Confederacy.
8. President James Garfield
9. General John Bell Hood
10. Pleasant Hill, Kentucky, known as Shakertown

11. General Felix Zollicoffer
12. Governor Beriah Magoffin
13. Cassius M. Clay
14. General Benjamin Hardin Helm
15. General William "Bull" Nelson
16. General Edmond Kirby Smith
17. Camp Dick Robinson
18. *The Courier*
19. General William Tecumseh Sherman
20. General Humphrey Marshall
21. Bowling Green
22. "The Orphan Brigade"
23. General John Hunt Morgan
24. General U.S. Grant
25. George W. Johnson
26. "Lincoln Guns"
27. William Clarke Quantrill
28. "The Great Hog Swindle"
29. Jerome Clarke
30. George St. Leger Grenfell
31. Pauline Cushman
32. Colonel Orlando Moore
33. The Battle of Rockcastle Hills or The Battle of Camp Wildcat
34. General Nathan Bedford Forrest
35. President Abraham Lincoln
36. Senator John J. Crittenden
37. The C.S.A. paid $18 per month, the Union $16.
38. Richard Hawes was installed as Governor of Kentucky on October 4, 1862 when the Confederates captured the capital for a day.
39. Elijah P. Marrs
40. Buffington Island
41. John C. Breckinridge
42. "Stovepipe" Johnson
43. Henry Clay
44. General Albert Sidney Johnston
45. Ohio State Penitentiary
46. Thomas H. Hines
47. Joshua Speed
48. Stephen Gano Burbridge
49. The Battle of Perryville
50. Home Guard

So how did you do? If you got 47 or above correct, you know your Kentucky Civil War history (maybe you should be writing this quiz). If you got 42-46 answers correct, you're better than most at your Kentucky Civil War history. If you had 38-41 correct, you're getting there; keep digging. Below 37 means you can look forward to learning a much more about Kentucky Civil War history.

* * *

BIOGRAPHIES

Tim Asher is a graduate of Western Kentucky University (MA) and financial advisor for World Financial Group. He is chairman of the Hardin County History Musuem.

Lon Carter Barton, a native of Mayfield, is a graduate of Murray State College (now University), and taught history 30 years at Mayfield High School. He served eight years in the Kentucky House of Representatives (1956-64), and is a U.S. Army veteran of the Korean War.

Ron Wolford Blair is a Civil War historian and author of a biography *Wild Wolf* the first book-length study on the life of Col. Frank Lane Wolford, Union Commander of the First Kentucky Cavalry. Blair is the namesake and great-great nephew of Col. Wolford.

Charles H. Bogart, Frankfort, has a BA in History from Thomas More College. He is the author of numerous articles concerning railroad, naval, and military history. He is a volunteer engineer and conductor at the Bluegrass Railroad Museum in Versailles, and gives railroad history walking tours of Frankfort. He is a member of the Kentucky Civil War Round Table and the L&N Historical Society.

Bryan A. Bush is the author of four books on the Civil War in the Western Theater: *The Civil War Battles of the Western Theater* (Paducah: Turner Publishing, Inc., 2001), *The 8th Texas Cavalry: Terry's Texas Rangers* (Paducah: Turner Publishing, Inc. 2003), *Confederate General Lloyd Tilghman and the Western Theater* (Paducah: Turner Publishing, Inc., 2004), *My Dearest Mollie: The Civil War Letters of Brig. General Daniel F. Griffin, 38th Indiana Volunteer Infantry* (Bedford: JoNa Books, 2003).

Tom Fugate is former curator of the Kentucky Military History Museum and current Site Identification Program Administrator and Military Heritage Sites Preservation Coordinator for the Kentucky Heritage Council. He is a 1983 graduate of Lincoln Memorial University, Harrogate, TN., with a degree in Museum Studies.

Dr. Lowell H. Harrison, a Russell Springs native, is Professor Emeritus of History at Western Kentucky University. He is the author of 11 books and 115 articles. He received his BA from what is now Western Kentucky University (1946); and his MA (1947) and PhD (1951) degrees in history from New York University, then did post-doctoral work at the London School of Economics as a Fulbright scholar. He is a veteran of WW II.

Mary Jo Harrod is a graduate of Indiana University and an award-winning freelance writer for several magazines and newspapers. Though she is a native Hoosier, she has a great love for Kentucky people, places, and history. Mary Jo also speaks to groups about writing and little-known women in history.

Dixie P. Hibbs, a longtime council member and now Mayor of Bardstown, Ms. Hibbs has written several books, including *Nelson County: A Portrait of the Civil War.*

Sam Hood, of Huntington, W.V., is a collateral descendent of General John Bell Hood. He is a graduate of Kentucky Military Institute (1970) and Marshall University (1976). A veteran of the U.S. Marine Corps, he is president of the John Bell Hood Historical Society and serves on the Board of Directors of Confederate Memorial Hall Museum of New Orleans and the Blue and Gray Education Society of Danville, VA.

Nicky Hughes is the Curator of Historic Sites for the City of Frankfort, and is the former Curator of the Kentucky Military History Museum.

Steve Kickert is an employee of the U.S. Department of Agriculture Forest Service on the Daniel Boone National Forest in Kentucky.

Dr. James C. Klotter, a native Kentuckian, is the author or editor of over a dozen books. He is the State Historian of Kentucky and a Professor of History at Georgetown College. His most recent book is *Kentucky Justice, Southern Honor, and American Manhood, Understanding the Life and Death of Richard Reid.*

Charles Lemons is curator of the Patton Museum of Cavalry and Armor, Fort Knox, as well as the captain of Company A, 7th Kentucky Volunteer Infantry (US) and president of the Rolling Fork Historical Preservation Association, Inc.

Lisa Gaines Matthews has a Master of Arts degree in history from the University of Tennessee. She is the editor and marketing manager for *Kentucky Festivals & Events.*

William E. Matthews, a native of Shelby County, Kentucky, is co-owner of Back Home In Kentucky, Inc., and the publisher of Volumes I, II, and III of *Kentucky's Civil War 1861-1865*. He is a past president of the Kentucky Press Association.

Dr. W. Stephen McBride is Director of Interpretation and Archaeology at Camp Nelson Civil War Heritage Park. He has a B.A. in Anthropology from Beloit College, and M.A. and Ph.D. in Anthropology from Michigan State University. He has conducted extensive historical research and archaeological excavations at Camp Nelson, Kentucky, a Union Civil War Depot and the 3rd largest recruiting and training center for U.S. Colored Troops in the United States. Dr. McBride works with varied governmental agencies and preservation groups to aid in the protection of important historic sites around Kentucky and the Ohio Valley.

Charles Reed Mitchell has served as editor of *The Knox Countain*, the journal of the Knox Historical Museum, since 1994, and as a museum officer since 1989. He edited and co-authored *Knox County, Kentucky: History and Families* (1799-1994), has published widely on local history and motion picture history, and contributed to The Kentucky Encyclopedia. He was a member of the English Department at Union College and operated movie theatres in Barbourville for several years.

Robert C. Moody is a retired attorney. He has a Bachelor of Arts in Anthropology from the University of Kentucky, and J.D. Law, UK. He operated the family farm in Richmond and is one of the principals in the Richmond Battlefield Preservation movement. He is a member of the Battle of Richmond Association, Madison County Historical Society and Civil War Preservation Trust.

Dr. Marshall Myers grew up in rural Meade County, near Brandenburg, where General John Hunt Morgan and his men crossed the Ohio River into the North to begin "The Great Raid." He earned his BA at Kentucky Wesleyan College, his MA at EKU, and PhD from the University of Louisville. He is Professor of Rhetoric and Composition at Eastern Kentucky University. He is President of the Madison County Civil War Roundtable, and recently authored a history of the war in Meade County.

William A. Penn has a B.A. in Commerce from the University of Kentucky and is a CPA. He is author of *Rattling Spurs and Broad-Brimmed Hats: The Civil War in Cynthiana and Harrison County, Kentucky*, is co-editor of *Cromwell's Comments* (Cynthiana history articles), and editor of *Harrison Heritage News*, an historical society publication.

Dr. James A Ramage, a Paducah native, is Regents Professor of History at Northern Kentucky University. He is the author of *Rebel Raider: the Life of General John Hunt Morgan* (Lexington: University Press of Kentucky, 1986) which won the Douglas Southall Freeman Award and was co-winner of the Kentucky Governor's Award. He won the 2003 Acorn Award for teaching excellence from the Kentucky Advocates for Higher Education.

Joseph R. Reinhart, a native of Louisville, is author of *A History of the 6th Kentucky Volunteer Infantry U.S.: The Boys Who Feared No Noise*, and editor and translator of *Two Germans in the Civil War: The Diary of John Daeuble and the Letters of Gottfried Rentschler, 6th Kentucky Volunteer Infantry.*

Dr. Charles P. Roland, Emeritus Alumni Professor of History at the University of Kentucky, received his M.A. from Vanderbilt University, and his Ph.D. from Louisiana State University. One of the nation's foremost Civil War scholars, Dr. Roland has written eight books including *An American Iliad: A History of the Civil War.*

Victoria Rose, of Crestwood, Kentucky, is a member of several poetry and writing organizations, and former secretary for the Kentucky Writers Coalition. She is currently working on a journal entitled, "Loose Things."

Stuart W. Sanders is Director of Interpretation for the Perryville Battlefield Preservation Association.

Dr. Richard Taylor is a professor of English at Kentucky State University. A former Kentucky Poetry Laureate (l999-2001), he is the author of five books of poetry, a novel, and several histories relating to Kentucky. He is currently finishing a novel on Sue Mundy and Kentucky guerrillas.

Larry D. Thacker, a native of Middlesborough, is Dean of Students for Lincoln Memorial University at Harrogate, TN, at Cumberland Gap. He earned his BA in History and MA in Education and Guidance from LMU. He is a columnist ("Mountain Meditations") for the *Daily News of Harrogate.*

Dr. L. Michael Trapasso is a professor of physical geography and climatology in the Department of Geography and Geology at Western Kentucky University in Bowling Green. Through his 25 years of residence in Bowling Green he has extensively studied Civil War History as an avocation. He is a Civil War reenactor with the 7th Tennessee Cavalry, and a staunch Civil War Site preservationist. In the realm of Civil War history he has been on the Civil War Round Table speaker circuit, and has written several articles, a book chapter, and a book review concerning the Civil War in Kentucky.

Nicole Twigg is the Marketing Manager for the Harrison Convention & Visitors Bureau in Corydon, Indiana.

INDEX